The publication of this volume has been made possible through the generosity of the late

ABRAHAM ERLANGER

who died October 1, 1929, and who left a bequest to The Jewish Publication Society of America.

Jewish Pioneers and Patriots

OTHER BOOKS BY LEE M. FRIEDMAN

EARLY AMERICAN JEWS
Harvard University Press

ROBERT GROSSETESTE AND THE JEWS
Harvard University Press
(*Printed at the Merrymount Press*)

ZOLA AND THE DREYFUS CASE
The Beacon Press, Inc.

RABBI HAIM ISAAC CARIGAL
HIS NEWPORT SERMON AND HIS YALE PORTRAIT
(*Privately printed at the Merrymount Press*)

The Gideon Family Coat of Arms

Jewish
Pioneers and Patriots

LEE M. FRIEDMAN

with a Preface by
A. S. W. ROSENBACH

PHILADELPHIA
THE JEWISH PUBLICATION SOCIETY OF AMERICA
5704–1943

Copyright, 1942, by

THE JEWISH PUBLICATION SOCIETY OF AMERICA

———————

———————

Second Impression, 1943

PRINTED IN THE UNITED STATES OF AMERICA
PRESS OF THE JEWISH PUBLICATION SOCIETY
PHILADELPHIA, PENNA.

"The American people need no reminder of the service which those of Jewish faith have rendered our nation. It has been a service with honor and distinction. History reveals that your people have played a great and commendable part in the defense of Americanism during the World War and prior wars, and have contributed much in time of peace toward the development and preservation of the glory and romance of our country and our democratic form of government."

FRANKLIN D. ROOSEVELT
Address to the Jewish War Veterans, August 26, 1938

To

ELSIE T. FRIEDMAN
SOPHIE M. FRIEDMAN

SISTERS AND COMPANIONS ON OUR
HAPPY LIFE'S JOURNEY

TABLE OF CONTENTS

LIST OF ILLUSTRATIONS

PREFACE

It is particularly fitting that at the present time Lee M. Friedman should publish *Jewish Pioneers and Patriots*. The second world war has created a need for such a book. Mr. Friedman knows his subject as few others, and he has been a student, not only of American affairs, but particularly of American Jewish History. He, more than any other scholar, has popularized this subject and made it especially attractive to the layman. Although in this volume Mr. Friedman has discussed some subjects that were known to historians of the past, he brings to his work a freshness and exuberance found in no other volume. But in addition to this he has made discoveries of the utmost importance to the history, not only of the Jews of the United States, but of national interests as well. These are revealed for the first time in this book.

In this year was celebrated the 450th Anniversary of the discovery of America by Christopher Columbus, who many scholars have thought was a Jew. This interesting question has been ably discussed by Mr. Friedman in one of the chapters, but I think we will have to know far more than we do at present before this can be definitely determined. The time has not arrived for a definitive history of the Jews on this continent. If we only had more students like Mr. Friedman the work would be accomplished sooner.

I think that this book would never have been written if, in addition to his scholarship, Mr. Friedman had not been a collector of books. From his youth he was interested in gathering everything relating to the life of the Jews of the Americas. He scoured two continents for books bearing on the history of the Jews and, in the last thirty-five years, he has secured some remarkable treasures. Not only did he go in for the printed word but for manuscripts, documents and autograph letters. Many of the illustrations in this volume are from his own collection.

Of course, as a leading citizen of Massachusetts, he has been especially interested in Israelites who lived and worked in New England. This will be particularly noticed in his *Early American Jews*, issued by the Harvard University Press, and *Rabbi Haim Isaac Carigal, His Newport Sermon and His Yale Portrait*, privately printed at the Merrymount Press. Although the whole of New England had not so many Jews in the early days as either Pennsylvania or New York, it had more students of the Hebrew language and its literature than there were in any other part of the original Colonies. Mr. Friedman has made an exhaustive treatment of this subject. He, strangely enough, deals also with those converted to the Jewish faith.

What should place this book in every public library in this country (Oh, would that it could be placed in the libraries of Germany!) is the section dealing with the Presidents of the United States and some Jewish problems. Nowhere is better shown the breadth of feeling, the greatness and the humanity of George Washington, Thomas Jefferson, Abraham Lincoln and Theodore Roosevelt, than in the chapters devoted to their Jewish associates. It is particularly important that at the present time these facts should be known to every member of our faith and particularly to the larger world.

As to the student interested in the part played by Jews in American society and the economic life of America, I refer them to what many will consider the most delightful chapters in an altogether delightful volume.

I cannot let the appearance of this work pass without mentioning the indebtedness of all scholars, including Mr. Friedman, to the American Jewish Historical Society. Mr. Friedman has contributed many papers to the publications of this Society and in his notes he mentions the help received from the Society, which was founded fifty years ago in the city of New York in answer to a call issued by the late, beloved Dr. Cyrus Adler. The American Jewish Historical Society has done a truly noble work in placing before the American people statements of what the Jews have done in building up this country. Our records show that in all our wars there have been American Jews willing to suffer and die for the common good. This war will be no exception.

A. S. W. ROSENBACH

Jewish Pioneers and Patriots

FOUR HUNDRED AND FIFTY YEARS

(BY WAY OF INTRODUCTION)

WHEN, as never before, events in Europe are drawing the Jew to the attention of America, may it not clarify consideration of some of the problems involved to explain something of the long Jewish participation in American history?

Lincoln once said, "We cannot escape history." Past, present, and future are never distinct and unrelated. The roots of the past, the developments of our times and the flower of tomorrow are inextricably one. A knowledge of the past gives a vision of the future. Today we realize that conditions in the United States have so many different aspects that there is no easy solution to many problems which cut deep into our national life. We only know that any solution must rest in a real understanding of our American people. More than ever we are re-examining our past that its more careful study may yield a truer knowledge of ourselves and lead to the discovery of roads of sure progress.

The old order of historians was content to confine itself to a narration of events with explanations of cause and a picture of effect. We now have come to believe that history must present, not only a sequence of events, but an exposition of attendant sociological, intellectual, industrial, political and economic conditions, with such philosophical and scientific analyses as will enable the student to arrive at conclusions comparable to those of a post-mortem inquest

3

at the hands of medical scientists. There must be available for the scholar, to create such history, collections of data and archives of exact and scientifically catalogued information, as well as annals collected from isolated incidents from day to day.

America is the fusion of many peoples and of many cultures. Every nation, race and creed of the earth has contributed to build our country. The settlers on our shore have brought, not only the work of their hands, but ideas and traditions as well for a contribution to our civilization.

To obtain additional knowledge of our American history we are now throwing the searchlight of investigation upon the story of racial and religious groups, the raw material in our American melting pot which, from the days of its discovery, has been ceaselessly boiling the stock out of which is brewed the American.

Madame Derby, who was an early eighteenth century worthy of Plymouth County, Massachusetts, wrote:

> History must of necessity be a collection of tradition, and of isolated incidents gathered here and there, until a sufficient mass is collected to be welded by learned and philosophic scholars into a connected and understandable whole.

As yet the history of the Jew in America is in the stage of gathering these isolated historical incidents. From the beginning, more than four and a half centuries ago, Jews have been, and are, part of the development of this western world. Theirs is the common story of the "founders" as well as that of our later immigrants who sought in a new land of freedom the liberty and opportunities denied them at home.

Generally speaking, our early settlers were rarely brought

here by any planned scheme of colonization. Often, European religious, social, political or economic conditions shaped the destinies which operated to force minority groups to our shores. In times of stress, unrest or depression, minorities are the victims of oppression which too often forces them to seek asylum abroad. This is particularly true of the Jew.

The Jew's very existence has been dependent on his self-reliance, initiative, daring and perspicacity, qualities which peculiarly fitted him for American adventure.

In a way the role of the Jew in the modern world has been that of pioneering. He could be no competitor to entrenched privilege in fields which the gentile had already staked out as his own. Christian aristocrats and capitalists in possession of the soil and opportunities of their native land were immune to Jewish rivalry.

Not as a result of innate characteristics, but by force of economic and social discriminations and persecutions, the Jew, not given parity in community life and opportunities, is restricted to participation in a limited inventory of occupations. His aptitudes, character and achievements are the products, therefore, of regional historical forces and circumstances.

The economic history of the Jew in Europe has been that of the outsider filling the interstitial places in the local economy, forced into the marginal jobs, never quite secure, no matter the length of his residence, no matter how great or successful his accomplishment, nor, even, how beneficial to the people.

It is only the underprivileged, those without political, religious or economic security, who are compelled to take the risks and the uncertain speculations of migrating and of pioneering. As new countries: America, the West Indies,

South Africa;* new sciences: chemistry, electricity, modern medicine; new industries: sugar, oil, clothing, the cinema; open new frontiers of opportunity, you find the Jew bringing fresh energies to make a place for himself. He ever chases the vision of new horizons where politically, socially and economically, he hopes to find a Utopia. Truly he is the wandering Jew, restlessly exploring the outposts of civilization, not only the outermost boundaries of the earth, but those of trade, of science and of ethics.

It is possible, in a very general way, to divide the coming of Jews to America into three periods, each with its background of European upheaval, each a period when Jews had been a dissenting or liberal minority in their country and victims of reactionary zeal which for the time gained control. Religious liberty, political freedom and economic freedom were each in turn the magnetic attraction which drew these Jews to America.

In the earliest period it was religious intolerance which drove Jewish emigration to America when, towards the close of the fifteenth century, an Universal Catholic Church, by its inquisition, struggled to maintain a totalitarian control over religious thinking.

The second period was when, after the defeat of Napoleon, the old European rulers, particularly those of Germany, regained control and restored autocratic government crushing out the political liberty which had been won in the wake

*Even in ancient days, we note this same movement of Jews. They followed the conquests of Alexander into Egypt, and spread into Syria, into the Crimea, and into Russia. Again, following after the victorious arms of Rome, Jews settled in its outposts of the conquered Rhineland, in Worms, Köln and Trier. When William the Conqueror overcame the Saxons of Britain, Jews crossed the Channel to settle in England.

of the French Revolution. The restoration of these reactionary authorities reimposed ancient restrictions on Jews, many of which had been previously abolished. German Jews, thus faced with the loss of all the social and political gains of the Napoleonic era in Germany, had the choice of submitting to a return to mediaeval conditions, joining the liberals in a rebellion, or leaving the fatherland where they had dwelt for centuries. First rebellion was tried and, when the Revolution of '48 failed, there was a widespread exodus of Jewish youth from Germany to the United States to obtain political freedom.

The third was the period of Jewish emigration from Eastern Europe, largely Russian, begun when Tsarist Russia imposed restrictions so limiting Jews to a residence within a prescribed pale that it threatened the very existence of millions of them. Like water squeezed from a dripping sponge, Jews fled from Russia to the four corners of the earth in such numbers that the civilized world stood aghast. It was a new diaspora. During the last decade of the nineteenth century every incoming steamer to our shores brought Jewish refugees, in unprecedented numbers, seeking asylum where they might find economic opportunities to survive.

In the very early days Jewish immigration had, to a great extent, come from Spain and Portugal, often through Holland or England. Daring merchants, adventurous shipowners, and ubiquitous traders, they joined whichever of the struggling settlements chance drew them to. Thus they settled in Spanish, Portuguese, Dutch, French and English colonies as pioneers sharing in their foundings and up-buildings.

While the number of Jews coming to America tapered off during the Revolutionary period, as the immigration of Spanish and Portuguese Jews lessened, immigration of Jews from other European lands gradually increased. The liberal uprisings having ended in the defeats of '48, German Jews felt compelled to seek a more congenial haven than their fatherland. They turned to America, swelling the tiny trickle to which Jewish immigration had shrunk into a rising, vigorous, youthful tide of another generation of enterprising immigrants. Many of them settled in the cities and towns of the north and south; others were caught in the great American rush westward, which was then creating for our country a new empire stretching to the Pacific. Swept by the passions of the day in their newly found home, some of these became soldiers in our Civil War in the Union Army, others with the Confederates. In the post-war period these immigrants and their children were of the generation which built industrial America.

This second Jewish immigration had, by 1870, decreased to insignificant proportions. Upon the enactment in Russia of the infamous "May Laws" in 1882 and their cruel enforcement, so many millions of oppressed Russian Jews came to the United States that this third epoch of Jewish immigration may fairly be characterized as predominately Russian, or, at least, as East European.

This immigration rushed to the Atlantic seaports, bringing new ghettos to our great eastern cities. The struggle for existence of vast numbers of these Russian Jews, sturdy, intelligent and ambitious, soon made itself felt in our industrial life. The East Side of New York City, where so many of them lived, furnished new social and economic problems, only too soon to be duplicated in many other cities as they spread out into every section of the country.

This story is still too new to be presented with justice to its many complicated angles and wide sweeps. Already it has its literature in America: biographies, learned economic, social, statistical and industrial studies, religious dissertations, tales of romance and adventure and volumes of humor and anecdotes. In the less than sixty years of their American life, these Jews have made varied and abundant contributions, not only to art, drama, music, science, literature and philosophy, but also to social and economic thinking in America; and it is all so recent, that it may be said to be history still in the making.

Today the five million Jews in the United States are made up of descendants of the founders who arrived in the western hemisphere even before the Pilgrims landed at Plymouth, of second, third, fourth, or fifth generations of later stock who have been born and educated here, and of immigrants themselves—a fairly representative cross-section of the population of the country at large.

The early Jew was singularly inarticulate in leaving records of his American experience. Only here and there, often accidentally, diligent research is uncovering fragments of this history. The expanding America of the nineteenth century, with its mad gold-rush, its quickening industrial development, its growing cities and mushroom towns, with the economic struggle of a civil war and of the following reconstruction, with enlarging horizons, swept the next body of Jewish arrivals into a vortex of fevered activities; they had no time to write their history as they went along.

Slowly and laboriously, from fragments gathered here and there and from neglected miscellaneous material, the future historian will weave an inspiring and surprising epic of Jewish adventure and achievement spreading into every corner of the United States. It may not be wholly a story of great events or of important names. Much of it, of necessity, must be the drab annals of poor immigrants and the chronicle of many humble and inconspicuous lives, the homely everyday details of lowly folk which is the American saga.

The following chapters try to tell incidents in this American Jewish history. Hardly one of them of prime importance in itself, each is illustrative of Jewish adventure in America. Together they show how, from the beginning, Jews have had their part in the building of America. In part, also, they tell of the reaction of the Jew on the American mind. After all, American Jewish history must be both the effect of the Jew on America as well as the effect of America on the Jew. In becoming American, the Jew has modified America.

I realize that, while some of these chapters present new material, others but retell old tales and well known incidents. American Jewish history has so many ramifications that perhaps no single historian can tell the whole story. Events and personalities worthy of being included here have been omitted consciously. In *Early American Jews*, I have already presented some of this material, such as the careers of Haym Salomon and of Judah Monis. Practical considerations demand that the presentation of other material be deferred to the future.

I acknowledge that I have gathered much and freely from many sources.

> When 'Omer smote 'is blooming lyre
> He'd 'eard man sing by land and sea;
> An' what he thought 'e might require.
> 'E went an' took — the same as me!

The trivial and the serious are here presented, again offering "neglected bits of color" of Jewish adventure in America. Both have a place in reconstructing the American Jewish past. If this book is only a newsreel recording kaleidoscopic views from many facets of American Jewish life, it will at least help to make the place of the Jews in the development and history of America more understandable.

PRESIDENTS AND SOME JEWISH PROBLEMS

1

GEORGE WASHINGTON AND JEWS OF HIS DAY

WHILE for many years Washington's diaries and letters have been public property, and while much was
written about him by his contemporaries, historians still
disagree about his personality. In the most elaborate
of his biographies, Rupert Hughes presents him as an
aristocrat with very little interest in common people and
claims that Washington regarded the "common run with a
profound contempt."[1] On the other hand, John Corbin
presents him as having had more contacts with people of all
sorts and conditions than any other American statesman
and as having been animated by a broad and deep regard
for all manner of men, towards whom he was impartial in
his judgments, considering only merit and ability.[2]

Whichever view you adopt, it was only natural that
Washington, as a wealthy Virginian landowner and aristocrat, would not have had many contacts with Jews. By
and large, the Virginian Jews of his day were of the humbler
middle class: merchants, artisans, shopkeepers, small manufacturers and traders. The Virginia colony, dominated by
its great landowners who lived the life of English gentlemen
cultivating their estates by slave labor, had so few centers
of commercial importance that it afforded but a limited
opportunity to Jews and never attracted any large number
of them in the colonial days. Although Jews had settled in
Virginia as early as 1621,[3] they had played no conspicuous

15

part in the colony's life, and it was not until 1790 that Virginia's first Jewish congregation was established in Richmond, the sixth of our American Jewish congregations.[4]

Up to the time when Washington became the outstanding military and political figure in America his career had been that of the usual large landowning agriculturist. Although Hezekiah Levy was one of the early members of the Fredericksburg Lodge of Masons No. 4, to which Washington belonged,[5] there is no evidence that he had any Jewish contacts earlier than 1754, when Lieutenant-Governor Dinwiddie commissioned him as Colonel to lead a Virginia regiment against the French. With this expedition were two young Jewish soldiers, Michael Franks of Captain Van Braam's company and Jacob Myer who served under Captain Mercer.[6] In so small and informal an army it was inevitable that officers and privates should have had more or less personal knowledge of one another, but there is no record to indicate any personal relations between them and Washington.

Late in 1758, when Washington reorganized the provincial troops after Braddock's defeat, a Jew, David Franks of Philadelphia, was the purveyor of supplies for the Virginian companies and as such carried on active dealings with him during the campaign to capture Fort Duquesne.[7] The following letter from Washington to David Franks shows the importance of this relationship:[8]

May 1, 1758.

Sir: I shall be much obliged, if you would provide for me, and send immediately to this place, by the Bearers waggon, the following articles: vizt.

As much green half-thick's, as will make indian-leggings for 1,000 men: if *green* can not be had, get white; if there is not enough of that, then get any other *colour*.

Two proper English pack-saddles, for carrying field-baggage on; and four wanteys (*sic*) suited to ditto. Three leading-halters. A travelling letter-case, with stands for ink, wafers, &c. A pair of light shoe-boots, round toes, without linings, and jockey-tops made of thin, english calf-skin, by the enclosed measure. A hair-cloth, (trunk) to go under a field-bed. Half a dozen *china* cups and saucers.

Unless those articles come to hand speedily, they will be useless to me. Mr. White, I believe, can furnish the *Leggings*, if you have them not by you; and may be usefully employed in providing the other Things (*Boots* and *china* excepted.) I sent a few weeks ago for 4 Pack-saddles; and the *dutchman* who undertook to procure them, brought common *saddles*, such as indian traders generally use, that were of little service to me.

Please to send your accompt with these things, and the money shall be paid to your order, or lodged with any person in this place, whom you shall think proper to direct.

I must beg to know how our paper money passes with you; for I suppose I shall be under the necessity of paying in that currency, having little of another kind with us. I hope you will excuse the liberty I have here taken, without *first* knowing whether it would be agreeable to you. I am Sir, etc."

During the Revolution, when General Washington was commander-in-chief, two Jewish officers served on his staff: Major Benjamin Nones[9] and Colonel Isaac Franks.[10] Even before the Declaration of Independence, after Washington had taken command of the Continental Army, it became necessary for Congress to supply him with funds in order to maintain the seige of Boston. March 21, 1776, the President of Congress, John Hancock, arranged to send him two hundred and fifty thousand dollars. To undertake the important task of the safe transportation of this large sum from Philadelphia to Cambridge, Hancock selected three men whom he sent to Washington, recommending them in the letter of transmission as "gentlemen of character whom I am confident will meet your notice." Moses Franks of Philadelphia was one of the three.

Philip Moses Russel was with Washington as surgeon at Valley Forge in 1777–1778. When he retired in 1780, he received "a letter of commendation from General Washington for his assiduous and faithful attention to the sick and wounded."[11]

This presents, on the whole, but a meager list of attenuated Jewish contacts, quite modest in contrast with claims advanced by other religious and racial groups concerning their influence and relations with the Father of our Country. Expansive Germans have claimed that Washington's bodyguard was made up exclusively of German-speaking Germans. "Washington couldn't trust anyone else. Seventy-five per cent of the soldiers at Valley Forge were German-speaking Germans." They go on to boast that "we Germans" did as much towards creating America as any group, until this recalls the story of the Irish lad who listened to similar boasting from an ardent Irish patriotic historian. He turned to his father and asked, "We Irish licked the British and won the War for the Yankees, didn't we?"

It is often repeated that, at Washington's inauguration as President, the Reverend Gershom Mendes Seixas, rabbi of the Shearith Israel Congregation of New York, was one of fourteen clergymen who took part in the ceremonies;[12] but this has not been substantiated.

In 1793, when, during an epidemic of yellow fever, the seat of government was temporarily removed from Philadelphia to Germantown, President Washington rented and occupied the house of Colonel Isaac Franks.[13]

The Congregation Mikveh Israel of Philadelphia dates from 1740 and, at the time Washington was in that city, conducted public worship in a house located in Sterling Alley.[14] Although, when Washington was in Philadelphia in 1774, he attended services at the Episcopal, Congregational, Presbyterian, Quaker and "Romish" (Roman Catholic) churches of the city and remarked that this was the first opportunity he had had of observing some of these modes of worship, he fails to record any visit to the synagogue.

While Washington was a constant attendant at church services, especially those of the Episcopal church of which he was a formal member, little is known of his personal religious viewpoint. In accordance with the style of the day, his public and private writings are replete with references to the Deity, religious sentiments and biblical allusions. They convey the impression of being abstract and impersonal. In contrast with Jefferson, if Washington ever found time to reason on the finer points and problems of religious thinking, nothing of that sort has been found in his writings — not a thing about the Jews or Judaism, ancient or modern.

On his assuming the presidency, in 1790, the several Jewish congregations of New York, Newport, Philadelphia, Savannah, Richmond and Charleston presented three congratulatory addresses to Washington. The synagogues of

New York, Philadelphia, Richmond and Charleston joined together, while Newport and Savannah each sent separate addresses. Washington acknowledged these in three replies.

These three Washington letters are the sole record of his attitude towards the Jews which has come down to us. Couched in the stately, if somewhat stilted phraseology of a more formal age, they embody an abstract expression of principles of general broad toleration towards all people. Religious liberty, as is well known, was a cardinal principle of Washington's political philosophy. He had fought for it in the Virginia Constitutional Convention. In writing to the Quakers of Pennsylvania he had expressed his views:

> The liberty enjoyed by the people of these states of worshipping Almighty God, agreeably to their consciences, is not only among the choicest of their *blessings* but also of their *rights*. While men perform their social duties faithfully, they do all that society or the state can with propriety demand or expect and remain responsible to their Maker for the religion or modes of faith which they may prefer or profess.[15]

Rather impersonal in his attitude towards the Jewish congregations, and with a certain consciousness of "liberality and philanthropy," he points out in these letters that "the children of the stock of Abraham" are included under the protecting aegis of the political philosophy of the "New Deal" of his day. As a good Federalist interpreting the Constitution broadly, he expounds the conception of the new American principles of religious freedom so that within its sweep are included Jews as well as other "inhabitants of every denomination." He takes pride that in his country for the first time, "unparalleled in the history of nations," not tolerance but fundamental political principles secure "inherent natural rights" of religious freedom.

These three letters of Washington deserve to rank with the Constitutional interpretations of Chief Justice Marshall and of Alexander Hamilton's *Federalist*. As if issuing an Emancipation Proclamation, Washington rose to the opportunity which the addresses from these Jewish congregations afforded. He gave point to the theory of American democracy which, finally and expressly embodied in 1791 in the Bill of Rights, struck from the Jews of the United States the shackles of disabilities, survivals of the past in other lands, handicapping them politically and restricting them in the enjoyment of their religion. Too little known to the general public, these letters stand enshrined in a place of honor in American Jewish history.[16]

THE ADDRESS FROM THE HEBREW CONGREGATION OF THE CITY OF SAVANNAH, GEORGIA, WHICH WAS PRESENTED TO WASHINGTON, THE FIRST PRESIDENT OF THE UNITED STATES, BY MR. JACKSON, ONE OF THE REPRESENTATIVES FROM GEORGIA.

SIR: We have long been anxious of congratulating you on your appointment, by unanimous approbation, to the presidential dignity of this country, and of testifying our unbounded confidence in your integrity and unblemished virtue. Yet however exalted the station you now fill, it is still not equal to the merit of your heroic services through an arduous and dangerous conflict, which has embosomed you in the hearts of her citizens.

Our eccentric situation, added to a diffidence founded on the most profound respect, has thus long prevented our address, yet the delay has realized anticipation, given us an opportunity of presenting our grateful acknowledgments for the benediction of heaven through the magnanimity of federal influence and the equity of your administration.

Your unexampled liberality and extensive philanthropy have dispelled that cloud of bigotry and superstition which has long as a vail shaded religion — unrivetted the fetters of enthusiasm — enfranchised us with all the privileges and immunities of free citizens, and initiated us into the grand mass of legislative mechanism. By example you have taught us to endure the ravages of war with manly fortitude, and to enjoy the blessings of peace with reverence to the Deity and benignity and love to our fellow-creatures.

May the Great Author of the world grant you all happiness — an uninterrupted series of health — addition of years to the number of your days, and a continuance of guardianship to that freedom which under auspices of heaven your magnanimity and wisdom have given these states.

LEVI SHEFTAL, President.

In behalf of the Hebrew Congregations.

To which the President was pleased to return the following:

TO THE HEBREW CONGREGATION OF THE CITY OF SAVANNAH, GEORGIA.

GENTLEMEN: I thank you with great sincerity for your congratulations on my appointment to the office which I have the honor to hold by the unanimous choice of my fellow-citizens, and especially the expressions you are pleased to use in testifying the confidence that is reposed in me by your congregations.

As the delay which has naturally intervened between my election and your address has afforded me an opportunity for appreciating the merits of the Federal Government and for communicating your sentiments of its administration, I have rather to express my satisfaction rather than regret at circumstance which demonstrates (upon experiment) your attachment to the former as well as approbation of the latter.

I rejoice that a spirit of liberality and philanthropy is much more prevalent than it formerly was among the enlightened nations of the earth, and that your brethren will benefit thereby in proportion as it shall become still more extensive; happily the people of the United States have in many instances exhibited examples worthy of imitation, the salutary influence of which will doubtless extend much farther if gratefully enjoying those blessings of peace which (under the favor of heaven) have been attained by fortitude in war, they shall conduct themselves with reverence to the Deity and charity toward their fellow-creatures.

May the same wonder-working Deity, who long since delivered the Hebrews from their Egyptian oppressors, planted them in a promised land, WHOSE PROVIDENTIAL AGENCY HAS LATELY BEEN CONSPICUOUS IN ESTABLISHING THESE UNITED STATES AS AN INDEPENDENT NATION, still continue to water them with the dews of heaven and make the inhabitants of every denomination participate in the temporal and spiritual blessings of that people whose God is Jehovah.

G. WASHINGTON.

ADDRESS OF THE NEWPORT CONGREGATION TO THE PRESIDENT OF THE UNITED STATES OF AMERICA.

SIR: Permit the children of the stock of Abraham to approach you with the most cordial affection and esteem for your person and merit, and to join with our fellow-citizens in welcoming you to Newport.

With pleasure we reflect on those days of difficulty and danger when the God of Israel, who delivered David from the peril of the sword, shielded your head in the day of battle; and we rejoice to think that the same spirit which rested in the bosom of the greatly beloved Daniel, enabling him to preside over the provinces of the Babylonian Empire, rests and ever will rest upon you, enabling you to discharge the arduous duties of the Chief Magistrate of these States.

Deprived as we hitherto have been of the invaluable rights of free citizens, we now — with a deep sense of gratitude to the Almighty Disposer of all events — behold a government erected by the majesty of the people — a government which to bigotry gives no sanction, to persecution no assistance, but generously affording to all liberty of conscience and immunities of citizenship, deeming every one of whatever nation, tongue or language, equal parts of the great governmental machine.

This so ample and extensive Federal union, whose base is philanthropy, mutual confidence and public virtue, we cannot but acknowledge to be the work of the great God who rules in the armies of the heavens and among the inhabitants of the earth, doing whatever seemeth to Him good.

For all the blessings of civil and religious liberty which we enjoy under an equal and benign administration, we desire to send up our thanks to the Ancient of days, the great Preserver of men, beseeching Him that the angels who conducted our forefathers through the wilderness into the promised land may graciously conduct you through all the difficulties and dangers of this mortal life; and when, like Joshua, full of days and full of honors, you are gathered to your fathers, may you be admitted into the heavenly paradise to partake of the water of life and the tree of immortality.

Done and signed by order of the Hebrew Congregation in Newport, Rhode Island.

Moses Seixas, Warden.

Newport, August 17, 1790.

WASHINGTON'S REPLY TO THE HEBREW CONGRE-
GATION IN NEWPORT, RHODE ISLAND.

GENTLEMEN: While I received with much satisfaction your address replete with expressions of esteem, I rejoice in the opportunity of assuring you that I shall always retain grateful remembrance of the cordial welcome I experienced on my visit to Newport from all classes of citizens.

The reflection on the days of difficulty and danger which are past is rendered the more sweet from a consciousness that they are succeeded by days of uncommon prosperity and security.

If we have wisdom to make the best use of the advantages with which we are now favored, we cannot fail, under the just administration of a good government, to become a great and happy people.

The citizens of the United States of America have a right to applaud themselves for having given to mankind examples of an enlarged and liberal policy — a policy worthy of imitation. All possess alike liberty of conscience and immunities of citizenship.

It is now no more that toleration is spoken of, as if it were by the indulgence of one class of people, that another enjoyed the exercise of their inherent natural rights. For happily the Government of the United States, which gives to bigotry no sanction, to persecution no assistance, requires only that they who live under its protection should demean themselves as good citizens, in giving it on all occasions their effectual support.

It would be inconsistent with the frankness of my character not to avow that I am pleased with your favorable opinion of my administration and fervent wishes for my felicity.

May the children of the Stock of Abraham, who dwell in this land, continue to merit and enjoy the good will of the other inhabitants, while every one shall sit in safety under his own vine and fig-tree and there shall be none to make him afraid.

May the Father of all mercies scatter light, and not darkness, upon our paths, and make us all in our several vocations useful here, and in His own due time and way everlastingly happy.

G. Washington.

"Charleston, S. C., July 15th, 1790.

TO THE PRESIDENT OF THE UNITED STATES:

Sir: We presume to divert your attention for a few moments from the more important matters which require it, in order to express the sincere desire and lively gratitude we experience, in common with our fellow citizens, in your election to and acceptance of the exalted office of President of the United States. As soon as the Federal Government was instituted, the eyes of your fellow-citizens throughout the States were drawn towards you; their unanimous voices at once proclaimed you the most worthy to preside over it, and their anxious wishes awaited your consent to assume your proper station. The spontaneous effusions of heartfelt satisfaction which burst forth, the unstudied plaudits which universally and publicly resounded on the occasion, seemed to us to obviate the necessity of any particular address. But as these have been presented to you from different classes and sects of our fellow-citizens, as additional attestations of your eminent deserts, and their well assured prospects of increasing happiness from your wise and virtuous administration, we are desirous even thus late not to appear deficient in this respect, especially as every day which has intervened has tended to realize what we so fondly anticipated. Various, extensive and invaluable are the benefits which your fellow-citizens have derived from the glorious revolution which, under Providence, you have been the principal instrument in effecting. To them it has secured the natural and inalienable rights of human nature — all the requisite privileges and immunities of freedom, and has placed within their reach peace, plenty and the other blessings of good government. To the equal participation and enjoyment of all these, it has raised us from the state of political degradation and grievous oppression to which partial, narrow, and illiberal policy and intolerant bigotry has reduced us in almost every other part of the world. Peculiar and extraordinary reason have we, therefore, to be attached to the free and generous Constitution of our respective States, and to be indebted to you, whose heroic deeds have contributed so much to their preservation and establishment. In a degree commensurate to its wise and enlarged plan, does the general government attract our regard, framed on principles consentaneous to those of the Constitution of the different States, and calculated by its energy to embrace and harmonize their various interests, combine their scattered powers, cement their union, and prolong their duration. They have already felt their salutary effects. The great exploits you performed while you commanded in chief the armies of the United States, during the arduous and perilous conflicts which purchased their freedom; the toils, fatigues and dangers you surmounted during that glorious warfare, entitled you to honorable exemption from public services, and to spend the remainder of your valuable life under the shade of your well earned laurels in sage retirement and dignified repose to which your truly magnanimous disposition invited, and for the pure and rational enjoyment of which your conscious virtue fitted you. But the infancy of the Federal Government particularly required your fostering care, and invoked the aid of your virtues to animate its friends and reconcile its adversaries. The genuine authority which you alone possessed, which has its source in virtue, and is built on the sure basis of merited esteem and implicit veneration, and which once recognized, has more irresistible sway than arbitrary power itself, was requisite to launch the Federal Government on its new and untried voyage into the ocean, clear of rocks and quick sands, and with favorable gales.

Your consummate prudence and firmness were necessary to trace out to your successors the courses they should steer, your example to enlighten, excite and strengthen them. When laudable ambition had nothing more to tempt you with, when fame had wearied itself in trumpeting your renown; yielding to the disinterested impulses of uniform protestations, and the urgent invocations of your fellow-citizens, you quitted your peaceful and pleasurable mansion to involve yourself in the cares and fatigues which now throng on you; and you have shown yourself as eminently qualified to preside at the helm of government, as at the head of armies. While historians of this and every age shall vie with each other in doing justice to your character, and in adorning their pages with the splendor of your endowments, and of your patriotic and noble achievements; and while they cull and combine the various good and shining qualities of the Pagan and modern heroes, to display your character, we, and our posterity, will not cease to chronicle and commemorate you, with Moses, Joshua, Othniel, Gideon, Samuel, David, Maccabeus and other holy men of old, who were raised up by God, for the deliverance of our nation, His people, from their oppression. May the Great Being, our Universal Lord, continue propitious to you and to the United States; perfect and give increase and duration of prosperity to the great empire which He has made you so instrumental in producing. May He grant you health to preside over the same, until He shall after length of days, call you to eternal felicity, which will be the reward of your virtues in the next, as lasting glory must be in this world. I have the honor to be,

Very respectfully, your obedient servant,

JACOB COHEN,

President Congregation

'Beth Elohim.'

THE ADDRESS OF THE HEBREW CONGREGATIONS
IN THE CITIES OF PHILADELPHIA, NEW YORK,
RICHMOND AND CHARLESTON TO THE PRESIDENT
OF THE UNITED STATES

SIR: It is reserved for you to unite in affection for your character and person every political and religious denomination of men; and in this will the Hebrew congregations aforesaid yield to no class of their fellow citizens.

We have been hitherto prevented by various circumstances peculiar to our situation from adding our congratulations to those which the rest of America have offered on your elevation to the chair of the Federal Government. Deign, then, illustrious Sir, to accept this our homage.

The wonders which the Lord of Hosts hath worked in the days of our forefathers have taught us to observe the greatness of His wisdom and His might throughout the events of the late glorious revolution; and while we humble ourselves at His footstool in thanksgiving and praise for the blessing of His deliverance, we acknowledge you, the leader of American armies, as His chosen and beloved servant. But not to your sword alone is present happiness to be ascribed; that, indeed, opened the way to the reign of freedom; but never was it perfectly secure till your hand gave birth to the Federal Constitution and you renounced the joys of retirement to seal by your administration in peace what you had achieved in war.

To the eternal God, who is thy refuge, we commit in our prayers the care of thy precious life; and when, full of years, thou shalt be gathered unto thy people, thy righteousness shall go before thee, and we shall remember, amidst our regret, "that the Lord hath set apart the Godly for himself", whilst thy name and thy virtues will remain an indelible memorial of our minds.

MANUEL JOSEPHSON,

For and in behalf and under the authority of the
several congregations aforesaid.

To which the President was pleased to return the following reply:

TO THE HEBREW CONGREGATIONS IN THE CITIES OF PHILADELPHIA, NEW YORK, CHARLESTON AND RICHMOND.

GENTLEMEN: The liberality of sentiment toward each other, which marks every political and religious denomination of men in this country, stands unparalleled in the history of nations.

The affection of such a people is a treasure beyond the reach of calculation; and the repeated proofs which my fellow citizens have given of their attachment to me and approbation of my doings form the purest source of my temporal felicity.

' The affectionate expressions of your address again excite my gratitude and receive my warmest acknowledgment.

The power and goodness of the Almighty were strongly manifested in the events of our late glorious revolution, and His kind interposition in our behalf has been no less visible in the establishment of our present equal government. In war He directed the sword, and in peace He has ruled in our councils. My agency in both has been guided by the best intentions and a sense of the duty which I owe my country. And as my exertions have hitherto been amply rewarded by the approbation of my fellow citizens, I shall endeavor to deserve a continuance of it by my future conduct.

May the same temporal and eternal blessings which you implore for me, rest upon your congregations.

G. WASHINGTON.[17]

2

THOMAS JEFFERSON AND RELIGIOUS LIBERTY

AS IS well known, the Puritans, seeking a new land where unmolested they might worship according to their own faith, did not propose that each man there should be free to follow his own religious ideas. "They had come to incarnate in institutions certain definite, rigid convictions and to prevent any opposing institutions from finding a foothold beside them. They had come to escape a tyranny which they had found hateful and to establish a tyranny which they believed beneficent and essential." Although at that time advanced thinkers were already speculating on liberty of conscience, as yet there was nowhere a separation of church and state. It was recognized as the duty of rulers and magistrates to uphold an official church and enforce religious regularity as well as defend the state itself.

The spirit of the times is well exemplified by an enactment of a law, in 1631, by the Great and General Court of Massachusetts Bay:

> It is ordered that henceforth no man shall be admitted to the freedom of this commonwealth but such as are members of the churches within the limits of this jurisdiction.

Within five years, in 1636, Roger Williams, in conflict with the authorities in Salem, was forced to flee from that town. Roger Williams had been an outspoken challenger of the

right of civil magistrates to exercise jurisdiction over conscience. He declared that "forcing of conscience is a soul
rape." Settled finally on the shores of Narragansett Bay,
he initiated, for the first time, the experiment of putting into
practical operation the practice of religious liberty. He
founded a community where "all men may walk as their
conscience persuade them, every one in the name of his
God."

Although the Rhode Island experiment apparently worked
no great evil, it was a shock and a scandal to conservative
neighbors where as yet ideals of religious liberty were making
but slow progress. Other colonies, too often dominated by
some religious sect, were fearful that any weakening of
church ties and dominance would be dangerous to their
moral and spiritual safety. Prejudice and fear die slowly.

By 1776, while the Declaration of Independence proclaimed to the world that the colonies accepted as a cardinal
principle that "We hold these truths to be self-evident, that
all men are created equal, that they are endowed by their
Creator with certain unalienable Rights, that among these
are Life, Liberty and the pursuit of Happiness," the idea
of religious liberty was still a subject of contentious debate.

It was not until 1789 that radical political philosophy had
become sufficiently accepted to transfer theories of religious
liberty into workable democratic practice and safeguard
such newly won freedom by a direct constitutional limitation
on the newly established government that it "shall make no
law respecting an establishment of religion, or prohibiting
the free exercise thereof."

No understanding of this accomplishment of educating the
public conscience is complete without recognizing to what

a great extent, in the United States, this was the work and triumph of a single man.

As the eighteenth century was approaching its seventh decade, the swing of the radical political philosophy of the day was evolving the idea that the state was not the over-lord of its subjects but rather only an instrumentality to serve the individual to attain a more abundant life. Feudalism, with its rigidly stratified society and dominance of the privileged, was facing a direct challenge for a new order in the philosophy of John Locke and in the writings of the great French radicals. These leaders were sowing ideas which eventually germinated into a whirlwind of European upheavals and an American Revolution.

Thomas Jefferson, imbued with the viewpoint of John Locke and of this French political philosophy, saw government as a convenant of free and equal men to safeguard the elemental rights of individual liberty. Political equality, religious liberty and social and economic opportunity for all alike were primary elements of his faith. That all men are free and equal was a new and radical idea, for the first time put to a practical test here in America. So far as he could, Jefferson aimed to make the experiment a living reality and success.

Although no churchman, Jefferson was a deeply religious man,[1] believing that as the government had been freed from the dead hand of the past so, too, religion should be liberated from the bonds of tradition and prejudice and become the free conviction of reasoning and enlightened thought. He was a serious student of religion. Oblivious to his unconscious predilections, his restless mind attempted to acquaint itself with all religious systems and sects.

Obviously taking his ideas on Judaism from his own interpretation of the Old Testament, Jefferson knew little of post-biblical Judaism. He confessed that he was "little acquainted with the liturgy of the Jews or their mode of worship."[2]

In his day historical and critical interpretation of the Bible was unknown. He had no first-hand knowledge of Jewish scholarship and philosophy. Consequently, Jefferson had but a mean opinion of Judaism:

> I think you give a just outline of the theism of the three religions when you say that the principle of the Hebrew was the fear, of the gentile, the honor, and of the Christian, the love of God.[3]
> Jews. 1. Their system was Deism; that is, the belief of one only God. But their ideas of him & of his attributes were degrading & injurious. 2. Their ethics were not only imperfect, but often irreconcilable with the sound dictates of reason & morality, as they respect intercourse with those around us; & repulsive & anti-social, as respecting other nations. They needed reformation, therefore, in an eminent degree.[4]

Yet thirteen years after writing this, Jefferson wrote the following in a letter to John Adams, describing his impressions of David Levi's *Letters to Dr. Priestley in answer to those addressed to the Jews inviting them to an amicable discussion of the evidences of Christianity*:[5]

> I have lately been amusing myself with Levi's book in answer to Dr. Priestley. It is a curious and tough work. His style is inelegant and incorrect, harsh and petulant to his adversary, and some of his reasoning flimsy enough. Some of his doctrines were new to me ... he avails himself of his advantage over his

adversaries by his superior knowledge of Hebrew, speaking in the very language of the divine communication while they can only fumble on with conflicting and disputed translations. Such is the war of giants. And how can such pigmies as you and I decide between them? For myself I confess that my head is not formed *tantas componere lites*.[6]

In spite of whatever views he entertained regarding their religion, towards the Jews themselves he ever expressed sentiments of regard, sympathy and indignation against the bigotry which imposed social and economic barriers against them. Realistically he saw that in spite of the enactment of laws, popular prejudices and discriminations still limited the opportunity of Jews to take their place in social life as American citizens. He felt that only popular education could enlighten public opinion to the theoretical standards embodied in laws. Thus to Mordecai M. Noah he wrote:

Monticello, May 28, 1818.

Sir:— I thank you for the Discourse on the consecration of the Synagogue in your city, with which you have been pleased to favor me. I have read it with pleasure and instruction, having learnt from it some valuable facts in Jewish history which I did not know before. Your sect by its sufferings has furnished a remarkable proof of the universal spirit of religious intolerance, inherent in every sect, disclaimed by all while feeble, and practiced by all when in power. Our laws have applied the only antidote to this vice, protecting our religious, as they do our civil rights, by putting all on an equal footing. But more remains to be done. For altho' we are free by the law, we are not so in practice. Public opinion erects itself into an Inquisition, and exercises its office with as much fanaticism as fans the flames of an Auto da fé.

The prejudice still scowling on your section of our religion, altho' the elder one, cannot be unfelt by yourselves. It is to be hoped that individual dispositions will at length mould themselves to the model of the law, and consider the moral basis on which all our religions rest, as the rallying point which unites them in a common interest; while the peculiar dogmas branching from it are the exclusive concern of the respective sects embracing them, and no rightful subject of notice to any other. Public opinion needs reformation on this point, which would have the further happy effect of doing away the hypocritical maxim of 'intus ut lubet, foris ut moris.' Nothing I think would be so likely to effect this as to your sect particularly as the more careful attention to education, which you recommend, and which placing its members on the equal and commanding benches of science, will exhibit them as equal objects of respect and favor. . . I salute you with great respect and esteem.'

A letter to Dr. De La Motta, written by him in the third person two years later, expresses the same sentiments:

Th. Jefferson returns his thanks to Dr. De La Motta for the eloquent discourse on the Consecration of the Synagogue of Savannah, which he has been so kind as to send him. It excites in him the gratifying reflection that his country has been the first to prove to the world two truths, the most salutary to human society, that man can govern himself, and that religious freedom is the most effectual anodyne against religious dissension; the maxim of civil government being reversed in that of religion, where its true form is "divided we stand, united, we fall." He is happy in the restoration of the Jews, particularly, to their social rights, and hopes they will be seen

Sir   Monticello May 28. 18.

I thank you for the Discourse on the consecration of the Synagogue
in your city; with which you have been pleased to favor me. I have
read it with pleasure and instruction, having learnt from it some
valuable facts in Jewish history which I did not know before. your
sect by it's sufferings has furnished a remarkable proof of the universal spirit of religious intole-
-rance, inherent in every sect, disclaimed by all while feeble, and
practised by all when in power. our laws have applied the only anti-
-dote to this vice, protecting our religious, as they do our civil rights
by putting all on an equal footing. but more remains to be done.
for altho' we are free by the law, we are not so in practice. public opi-
-nion erects itself into an Inquisition, and exercises it's office with
as much fanaticism as fans the flames of an Auto da fé. the prejudice
still scowling on your section of our religion, altho' the elder one, cannot
be unfelt by yourselves. it is to be hoped that individual dispositions will
at length mould themselves to the model of the law, and consider the moral
basis on which all our religions rest, as the rallying point which unites
them in a common interest; while the peculiar dogmas branching from it
are the exclusive concern of the respective sects embracing them, and no
rightful subject of notice to any other. public opinion needs reformation on
this point, which would have the further happy effect of doing away the
hypocritical maxim of 'intus ut libet, foris ut moris.' nothing I think
would be so likely to effect this as to your sect particularly as the more
careful attention to education, which you recommend, and which pla-
-cing it's members on the equal and commanding benches of science,
will exhibit them as equal objects of respect and favor. — I should not
do full justice to the merits of your discourse, were I not, in addition to that
just matter, to express my consideration of it as a fine specimen of style &
composition. I salute you with great respect and esteem.

Mr. Mordecai M. Noah.   Th: Jefferson

Jefferson to M. M. Noah

taking their seats on the benches of science as preparatory to their doing the same at the board of government.[8]

He exhibited a spirit of liberality in his relations to individual Jews. In 1782, Jefferson, as one of the commissioners for making a treaty of peace with England, had made all preparations to go abroad when the trip was abandoned upon learning that the treaty had been consummated without waiting his arrival. Among the party he had selected to accompany him was Colonel David S. Franks, the well-known Jewish Revolutionary soldier.[9] As president, he considered for a time appointing a Mr. Levy, a Jewish lawyer of Philadelphia, as his attorney general.[10]

Of all Jefferson's services to his country and to mankind perhaps none is more outstanding than that of which the Jews were amongst the beneficiaries — the successful fight which he waged in the cause of religious liberty. Although, in 1652, the Rhode Island and Providence plantations had enacted into law that "all men of whatever nation soever they may be, that shall be received inhabitants of any towns shall have the same privileges as Englishmen, any law to the contrary notwithstanding," that state had long stood alone in granting absolute religious liberty. Its charters had guaranteed that "no person within the said Colony at any time hereafter shall be in anywise molested, punished or disquieted or called in question for any difference in opinion in matters of religion who do not actually disturb the civil peace of our said Colony." Although the charters of Maryland and Pennsylvania contained safeguards for liberty of conscience, even there there were but varying degrees of real toleration for minority religious sects.

It was Jefferson, more than any other, who made religious freedom a cardinal American principle. In one of his early memorandums dealing with religion, probably prepared as material for speeches in the House of Delegates on the disestablishment of the Episcopal Church in Virginia, Jefferson attempts to formulate his views in answer to the query how far a duty of religious toleration extends. This is a sort of road map to his democratic ideas of individual freedom and minority rights.

We have no right to prejudice another in his CIVIL enjoinments because he is of another Church. If any man err from the right way, it is his own misfortune, no injury to thee; nor therefore art thou to punish him in the things of this life because thou supposeth he will be miserable in that which is to come — on the contrary accdg to the spirit of the gospel, charity, bounty, liberality is due to him.

Each church being free, no one can have jurisdn over another one, not even when the civil magistrate joins it. It neither acquires the right of the sword by the magistrate's coming to it, nor does it lose the rights of instructions or excommunion by his going from it. It cannot by the accession of any new member acquire jurisdn over those who do not accede. He brings only himself, having no power to bring others. Suppose for instance two churches, one of Arminians, another of Calvinists in Constantinople, has either any right over the other? Will it be said the orthodox one has? Every church is to itself orthodox; to OTHERS erroneous or heretical.

No man complains of his neighbor for ill management of his affairs, for an error in sowing his land, or marrying his daughter, for consuming his substance in taverns, pulling down building &c. in all these he has his liberty; but if he do not frequent the church, or there conform to ceremonies, there is an immediate uproar.

The care of every man's soul belongs to himself. But what if he neglect the care of it? Well what if he neglect the care of his health or estate, which more nearly relate to the state. Will the magistrate make a law that he shall not be poor or sick? Laws provide against injury from others; but not from ourselves. God himself will not save men against their wills.

If I be marching on with my utmost vigour in that way which according to the sacred geography leads to Jerusalem straight, why am I beaten & ill used by others because my hair is not of the right cut; because I have not been dresst right, bec. I eat flesh on the road, bec. I avoid certain by-ways which seem to lead into briars, bec. among several paths I take that which seems shortest & cleanest, bec. I avoid travellers less grave and keep company with others who are more sour and austere, or bec. I follow a guide crowned with a mitre & cloathed in white, yet these are the frivolous things which keep X^{ns} at war.

If the magistrate command me to bring my commodity to a publick store house I bring it because he can indemnify me if he erred & I thereby lose it; but what indemnification can he give one for the kdom of heaven?

I cannot give up my guidance to the magistrates, bec. he knows no more of the way to heaven than I do, & is less concerned to direct me right than I am to go right. If the Jews had followed their Kings, among so many, what number would have led them to idolatry? Consider the vicissitudes among the Emperors, Arians, Athana &c. or among our princes, H. 8, E. 6, Mary, Elisabeth, LOCKE'S WORKS 2d Vol.

The magistrate has no power but w^t ye people gave. The people h^{ve} n^t giv^n h^m the care of souls bec. y^e

c^d not, ye c^d not, because no man h^s RIGHT to abandon ye care of his salvation to another.

No man has POWER to let another prescribe his faith. Faith is not faith with^t believing. No man can conform his faith to the dictates of another. The life & essence of religion consists in the internal persuasion or belief of the mind. External forms of worship, when against our belief are hypocrisy & impiety. Rom. 14.23. "he that doubteth is damned, if he eat, because he eateth not of faith: for whatsoever is not of faith, is sin?"

Compulsion in religion is distinguished peculiarly from compulsion in every other thing. I may grow rich by art I am compelled to follow, I may recover health by medicines I am compelled to take ag^t my own judgment, but I cannot be saved by a worship I disbelieve & abhor.

He (Locke) said "neither Pagan nor Mahomedan nor Jew ought to be excluded from the civil rights of the Commonwealth because of his religion." Shall we suffer a Pagan to deal with us and not suffer him to pray to his god? Why have X^{ns} been distinguished above all people who have ever lived, for persecutions? Is it because it is the genius of their religion? No, it's genius is the reverse. It is the refusing TOLERATION to those of a different opn which has produced all the bustles and wars on account of religion. It was the misfortune of mankind that during the darker centuries the X^n priests following their ambition and avarice combining with the magistrate to divide the spoils of the people, could establish the notion that schismatics might be ousted to their possession & destroyed. This notion we have not yet cleared ourselves from. In this case no wonder the oppressed should rebel, & they will continue to rebel & raise

disturbance until their civil rights are fully restored
to them & all partial distinctions, exclusions & in-
capacitations removed.[11]

Throughout his thoughts and writings Jefferson constantly
reiterated this broadminded attitude of absolute religious
liberty. His view was "your own reason is the only oracle
given you by heaven; and you are answerable not for the
rightness but for the uprightness of the decision." This idea
is well summarized in one of his letters:

> Our particular principles of religion are a subject
> of accountability to our God alone. I inquire after no
> man's, and trouble none with mine; nor is it given to
> us in this life to know whether yours or mine, our
> friends or our foes, are exactly the right . . . .
> Let us not be uneasy then about the different roads
> we may pursue, as believing them the shortest, to
> that of our last abode; but following the guidance of
> a good conscience, let us be happy in the hope that
> by these different paths we shall meet in the end.[12]

He considered the passing of the Virginia Act of Toleration
in 1785 an achievement ranking with the Declaration of
Independence. Indeed, so proud was Jefferson of his services
in this cause that he wrote as the epitaph to be placed on his
tombstone that he was the "Author of the Declaration of
Independence and of the Statute of Virginia for Religious
Liberty."

In his autobiography Jefferson has described his first great
legislative victory in Virginia in his untiring fight to establish
not religious toleration but religious liberty:

> The bill for establishing religious freedom, the
> principles of which had, to a certain degree, been
> enacted before, I had drawn in all the latitude of

reason and right. It still met with oppositions; but, with some mutilations in the preamble, it was finally passed; and a singular proposition proved that its protection of opinion was meant to be universal. Where the preamble declares that coercion is a departure from the plan of the holy author of our religion, an amendment was proposed, by inserting the words "Jesus Christ," so that it should read, "a departure from the plan of Jesus Christ, the holy author of our religion;" the insertion was rejected by a great majority, in proof that they meant to comprehend, within the mantle of its protection, the Jew and the Gentile, the Christian and Mahometan, the Hindoo, and Infidel of every denomination.[13]

Even when, years later, victory had placed in the United States Constitution, as the first article of the Bill of Rights, that "Congress shall make no law respecting an establishment of religion, or prohibiting the free exercise thereof," and many of the states followed with similar provisions in their constitutions or in their statutes, Jefferson did not rest content. He realized that the letter of the law was not enough. The fight must still go on against prejudice and intolerance.

But more remains to be done. For altho' we are free by the law, we are not so in practice. Public opinion erects itself into an Inquisition, and exercises its office with as much fanaticism as fans the flames of an Auto da fé.

3

ABRAHAM LINCOLN AND JEWISH ARMY CHAPLAINS

FROM the time when warrior-priests led in arousing their followers on battlefields to fanatic feats of heroic sacrifice in holy causes to the modern day, when the army chaplain is still regarded as an instrument to "add greater efficiency to those engaged in the military defense of the country," the post of religious leader in an army has been an important and highly honored one.

The origin of the office is lost in tradition. It is said:

> Naturally chaplains were not endowed with military status or rank in the early days because ecclesiastical offices were at that time everywhere regarded as superior to other professions. In the days of the later Byzantine emperors chaplains were given a semimilitary office and were attached to the immediate personal retinue of those sovereigns to care for their spiritual welfare. With the later Crusades came a further development; the chaplains often were officers of the military orders, such as the Knights Templar and the Knights of Malta or Hospitallers, and were granted the high military rank befitting their knighthood or assignments. The chaplain was frequently not only the ecclesiastic of a princely retinue but also the active holder of one of the most exalted military commands. The idea that the chaplain was a necessary part of the staff of a military commander had in a short time extended

throughout the entire western empire, and chaplains
were present not only with the larger forces of the
kings but every petty feudal baron and knight
placed such an ecclesiastic among his necessary re-
tainers ... It is not surprising to find careful
provisions made for chaplains in the military regulations of Great Britain, and there is available
some accurate information of those associated with
the expeditions that came at an early date to colonize
America.[1]

In its latest official manual the War Department of the
United States, in an outline of suggestions to army chaplains
for the proper discharge of their duties, calls attention to
the Jewish holidays and advises:

If possible get a rabbi to conduct services on
special Jewish feast days, if no Jewish chaplain is
available.

Here is a recognition that in the army there is a large
body of Jewish soldiers whose religious needs must be
looked after and that the rabbis have held, and do hold,
the office of chaplain in the federal military service. There
is a story behind the implications of this paragraph.

While Jews served in the war of the Revolution, in the
War of 1812 and in the Mexican War, their numbers were not
so large, nor were they so grouped together as to have
necessitated any official attention to their special religious
needs. Indeed, while in the war of the Revolution, General
Washington called ministers of the gospel to the colors and
they were paid an allowance equal to the pay of a major,
they held no actual official rank. It was not until 1791
that Congress first enacted legislation which recognized the
office of chaplain as part of the country's military establish-

ment. From that time on successive acts alternately abolished and recreated that office. It was not until 1838 that the office of army chaplain was finally and permanently established as part of the national military organization with a permanent military rank. Since that year there has never been any question of their official standing. During the Mexican War the number of army chaplains was increased so that for the first time, under authority of Congress, a chaplain was provided for each regiment.

As soon as the Civil War broke out, Congress passed, July 22, 1861, the act establishing the national defense and it was again provided that each regiment should have a chaplain, to be appointed by the commander on a vote of the field officers and company. It further provided that "the chaplain so appointed must be a regular ordained minister of a Christian denomination."

This gave rise to widespread comment and agitation which was taken up by the newspapers and many public patriotic societies. From all parts of the country there arose a demand that the Acts of Congress should recognize that, as soldiers were accepted without religious discrimination, the brethren in faith of those who thus freely took upon themselves the defense of their country, and of whom many had already made the supreme sacrifice, should receive recognition of the American right to worship under leaders of their own faith and be afforded opportunities so to do. The then recently organized Board of Delegates of American Israelites presented to President Lincoln, and to both the Senate and House Representatives, a memorial setting forth the facts and praying that the Acts of Congress "be formally amended, so that there shall be no discrimination as against professors of the Jewish faith, in the several laws affecting the appointment of Chaplains in the service of the United States."

Rabbi Arnold Fischel went to Washington to interest President Lincoln in the situation. Dr. Fischel has described his interview with the President:

> I called this morning (December 11, 1861) at ten o'clock at the White House, where hundreds of people were anxiously waiting for admission, some of whom told me that they had been for three days awaiting their turn. I was, nevertheless, at once invited to his (the President's) room and was received with marked courtesy. After having read the letter of the Board and delivered to him several letters of introduction, he questioned me on various matters connected with this subject and then told me that he fully admitted the justice of my remarks, that he believed the exclusion of Jewish chaplains to have been altogether unintentional on the part of Congress, and agreed that something ought to be done to meet this case. I suggested that he might do for Jewish, what he had done for the Christian volunteers, and take upon himself the responsibility of appointing Jewish chaplains for the hospitals. He replied that he had done that at a time when Congress was not in session, deeming the subject to require immediate attention, but that, after the meeting of Congress, he would not be justified in taking the responsibility upon himself. Finally, he told me that it was the first time this subject had been brought under his notice, that it was altogether new to him, that he would take the subject into serious consideration, that I should call again to-morrow morning, and if he had five minutes to spare he would receive me and let me know his views. I thanked him for his kind reception, and expressed to him my best wishes for his welfare. In the course

of my remarks I gave him clearly to understand that I came to him not as an office-seeker but to contend for the principle of religious liberty, for the constitutional rights of the Jewish community, and for the welfare of the Jewish volunteers, which he seemed fully to appreciate.[2]

Invited to call again the following day, Rabbi Fischel was unable to see Mr. Lincoln, "as he had important public business to transact with the Governor of Indiana and foreign ambassadors." The President, however, sent him a note stating "he is not forgetting his case and will lay it before the Cabinet to-day." Next day this was followed up by a further communication:

Executive Mansion, December 14, 1861

Rev. Dr. A. Fischel.

My Dear Sir: I find that there are several particulars in which the present law in regard to Chaplains is supposed to be deficient, all of which I now design presenting to the appropriate Committee of Congress. I shall try to have a new law broad enough to cover what is desired by you in behalf of the Israelites.

Yours truly,
A. LINCOLN.

In the meantime, without official recognition, Rabbi Fischel took upon himself the duty of visiting camps and hospitals, ministering to the needs of Jewish soldiers. At the same time he continued activities in Washington, agitating against the discrimination by which many religious denominations received no recognition in the appointment of chaplains. Some opposition developed in the Committee on Military Affairs because it was feared that too broad a change might imply a positive repudiation of the Christian religion.

At last a bill was prepared and adopted by the Military Committee of the Senate and presented to that body. In the House of Representatives, in order to test public opinion, a resolution was introduced on January 20, 1861:

> That the Committee on Military Affairs be instructed to inquire into the expediency of changing the existing law as to the employment of chaplains in the army, so as to authorize the appointment of brigade chaplains, one or more of which shall be of the Catholic, Protestant and Jewish religion.

Showing the change of national sentiment, this resolution was unanimously passed, although in the previous Congress a similar resolution, proposed by Mr. Vallandigham, then an important member of Congress, had been rejected by a considerable majority.

On May 20, 1862, an act was finally passed authorizing the

> President of the United States to appoint, as he shall deem it necessary, a chaplain for each permanent hospital, whose pay, with that of chaplains heretofore appointed by him, shall be the same as that of regimental chaplains in the volunteer force.

This was followed by an amendment (July 17, 1862) providing:

> That so much of Section 9 of the aforesaid act approved July 22, 1861 and of Section 7 of the "act providing for the better organization of the military establishment" approved August 3, 1861 as defines the qualifications of chaplain in the army and volunteers shall hereafter be construed to read as follows: That no person shall be appointed a chaplain

in the United States Army who is not a regularly ordained minister of some religious denomination, and who does not present testimonials of his present good standing as such minister, with a recommendation for his appointment as an army chaplain from some authorized ecclesiastical body, with not less than five accredited ministers belonging to said religious denomination.

And also that:

The chaplains of the permanent hospitals appointed under authority of second section of the act approved May 20, 1862 shall be nominated to the Senate for its advice and consent and they shall in all respects fill the requirements of the preceding section of this act relative to the appointment of chaplains in the army and volunteers and the appointments of chaplains to army hospitals, heretofore made by the President, are hereby confirmed and it is made the duty of each officer commanding a district or post containing hospitals, or a brigade of troops, within thirty days after the reception of the order promulgating this act, to inquire into the fitness, efficiency, and qualifications of the chaplains of hospitals or regiments, and to muster out of service such chaplains as were not appointed in conformity with the requirements of this act, and who have not faithfully discharged the duties of chaplains during the time they have been engaged as such.

Thereupon President Lincoln appointed Rabbi Jacob Frankel of Philadelphia, Rabbi B. H. Gotthelf of Louisville and Rabbi Ferdinand Sarner of New York, hospital chaplains and they immediately entered upon the discharge of their respective duties. No Jewish regimental chaplains, however, were appointed during the war.

In the Spanish War the question of Jewish chaplains did not arise. For the war was comparatively short and the army was so largely professional that the volunteer forces played but a small part.

Even before the United States entered World War I, when the National Defense Act of June 3, 1916 was enacted, it contained amongst other provisions an immediate recognition of the necessity of increasing the corps of army chaplains:

> The President is authorized to appoint by and with the advice and consent of the Senate chaplains in the army at the rate of not to exceed, including chaplains now in service, one for each regiment of cavalry, infantry, field artillery and engineers, one for each one thousand two hundred men and officers of the coast artillery corps, with rank, pay and allowances as now authorized.

On October 6, 1917, that rabbis and Unitarian ministers might receive adequate recognition, the sixty-fifth Congress passed a further act:

> That the President may appoint to service, during the present emergency, not exceeding twenty chaplains at large for the United States army, representing religious sects not recognized in the apportionment of chaplains now recognized by law, provided no person shall be eligible to such appointment unless he, at the time of his appointment, be a citizen of the United States.

The following May, the National Defense Act gave further recognition to the liberalized religious viewpoint of the nation by a further amendment to provide:

That the President is authorized to appoint with the advice and consent of the Senate chaplains in the army at the rate of not to exceed, including chaplains now in service, one for each one thousand two hundred officers and men in all branches of the military establishment, with rank, pay and allowances as now authorized by law: Provided that there shall be assigned at least one chaplain for each regiment of cavalry, infantry, field artillery and engineers. Provided further, that the person appointed under this act shall be duly accredited by some religious denomination or organization and of good standing therein under such regulations as may be prescribed by the Secretary of War and under forty-five years of age.

Of the twenty new chaplains then appointed under the new law six were Jews and the remainder were selected from Unitarian and other sects which had not, up to that time, been recognized in the selection of regimental chaplains. Immediately, Rabbi Elkan C. Voorsanger was appointed by President Wilson the first Jew to serve as a regimental chaplain. Since he was already abroad as a volunteer with a hospital unit, he received his commission there, on November 24, 1917. He held his first Passover services in the war zone, at St. Nazaire, in 1918 — the first Jewish holiday celebration officially conducted by an officer of the United States Army.[3]

Ultimately twelve rabbis saw such active service as regimental chaplains, ten of them abroad.[4] Thirteen others were commissioned as First Lieutenant Chaplains and served in camps and cantonments with the army in the United States.

The duties which Jewish chaplains discharged were not confined to ministering to Jewish soldiers. Equally with all army chaplains, Jewish chaplains conducted these regimental religious services in so broad a spirit that all the soldiers of their post, irrespective of sect, shared in them. They gave that "spiritual ministration, moral counsel and religious guidance," without regard to creed, to all who came under their military jurisdiction, that by precept and example they might discharge to the full the duty of being "the exponent in the military establishment of the religious motive as an incentive to right thinking and right acting."

At this writing, ten months after the entrance of the United States into World War II, the number of Jewish chaplains approaches one hundred. It seems that before long the Army and Navy will require as many more.

4

THEODORE ROOSEVELT AND THE
RUSSIAN TREATY

IN APRIL, 1832, President Andrew Jackson sent James Buchanan as United States Minister to Russia to negotiate a treaty of commerce and navigation. Although the Russian Government was not anxious for such an arrangement a treaty was finally negotiated and signed by the representatives of the two governments, on December 18, 1832. By the following May it was ratified by both Russia and the United States.

ARTICLE I of the treaty provided that:

> There shall be between the territories of the high contracting parties a reciprocal liberty of commerce and navigation. The inhabitants of their respective states shall mutually have liberty to enter the ports, places and rivers of the territories of each party wherever foreign commerce is permitted. They shall be at liberty to sojourn and reside in all parts whatsoever of said territories, in order to attend to their affairs, and they shall enjoy, to that effect, the same security and protection as natives of the country wherein they reside.

As early as 1864 trouble arose under this treaty by Russia's refusal to recognize the right of an American Jew to enter Russia under an American passport.[1] From that time on there was a repeated exchange of diplomatic correspondence between our State Department and the Russian Government over such constant discrimination against American Jewish citizens. After the cruel May Laws of 1881 had driven vast hordes of Russian Jews to the United States, where they soon became good citizens, the issue became increasingly acute. Russia raised both the issues of Jew and of expatriation. When Jewish citizens sought to visit relatives in Russia, or their business affairs necessitated their going to Russia, our State Department found itself constantly embarrassed by being unable to guarantee a citizen the rights to which he was entitled under our Constitution and laws.

Finally, in 1907, in recognition of this fact, Elihu Root, as Secretary of State, issued instructions to the Passport Division under which, in issuing a passport for Russia, the applicant was to be informed that:

> Jews, whether they were formerly Russian subjects or not, are not admitted to Russia unless they obtain special permission in advance from the Russian Government, and this department will not issue passports to former Russian subjects or to Jews who intend going to Russian territory, unless it has assurances that the Russian Government will consent to their admission.

In effect this was a confession that the United States found itself powerless to protect its citizens in the enjoyment of the rights and privileges which the Constitution guaranteed to them. By this acquiescence and by the adoption of these departmental regulations, our Government was proposing to allow a foreign power, with which it was in friendly relations, to force it to abandon its treaty rights.

As soon as this became publicly known, there was widespread and spontaneous indignation that the United States

Government should officially recognize discrimination between its citizens on racial or religious grounds in issuing passports to which every citizen was equally entitled. To American Jews, whether they desired to go to Russia or not, this attitude of our Government was a serious menace because of its potentialities as a precedent. Their position was that this was not a Jewish question; it had become an American one.

For years unsuccessful agitation was carried on to stir the United States Government to take a firm stand and alter the situation. Our Department of State had from time to time attempted, by diplomatic negotiations, to induce Russia to change its attitude. Russia had been unyielding. In the meantime other governments, notably France and Germany, had succeeded in removing this discrimination against their Jewish nationals.

By 1911 the agitation for abrogating the Russian treaty assumed national proportions. It was not confined to Jews. Public meetings were held in many of our more important cities. Newspapers throughout the country were almost unanimous in voicing a popular demand for government action. Both the Republican and Democratic party platforms as early as 1904 carried planks favoring abrogation of the treaty and these were repeated in their platforms in subsequent years. Many state legislatures passed resolutions calling upon the authorities at Washington for speedy and positive action. It was so insistent a demand from so many quarters that Congress could not but give heed. Finally, in December 1911, a resolution for the abrogation of the treaty, originally introduced by Representative William Sulzer of New York, was passed with hardly a dissent.

President Taft immediately instructed the Honorable
Curtis Guild, American ambassador at St. Petersburg, to
serve formal notice on the Russian authorities that the treaty
of 1832 would be abrogated on December 31, 1912, because
it is "no longer responsive, in various respects, to the needs
of the political and material relations of the two countries."
With the approval of the President's action by both Houses
of Congress,[2] this chapter of American Jewish history was
brought to a close. It left the United States, however, without a treaty with Russia, and its Jewish citizens without a
chance to visit Russia. It was years before this could be
righted.

The memoirs of Count Witte, who was the chief Russian
plenipotentiary at the Peace Conference at Portsmouth,
New Hampshire, to negotiate the ending of the Russo-
Japanese War, have revealed a little-known and interesting
side light on an important incident in the history of the
efforts made by our officials to handle this situation. It also
shows the great personal interest which President Theodore
Roosevelt manifested in the question. When the Count was
returning to Russia in 1905, after a brilliant diplomatic
career in Washington, the President wrote to him:

Oyster Bay, Sept. 10, 1905.
Dear Mr. Witte:—

I beg you to accept the enclosed photograph, together with my hearty greetings.

I thank you sincerely for His Majesty's message,
which was transmitted to me, informing me of his
noble-hearted intention henceforth to interpret the
article about the most favoured nation in such a manner as to put America on an equal footing with the
other Powers.

Please convey to His Majesty my sincere gratitude for this act.

In the course of our conversation, which took place last evening, I urged you to give your attention to the questions of issuing passports to respectable American citizens of the Jewish faith. It seems to me that if that could be done, there would be eliminated the last cause of irritation between the two peoples, for the perpetuation of whose historical mutual friendship I should like to do everything in my power. You can always refuse to issue a passport to some American citizen, Jew or Gentile, if you are not quite certain that the issuance of the passport will not harm Russia. But if your Government found a way to permit respectable American citizens of the Jewish faith, whose intentions you do not distrust, to enter Russia, just as you permit it to respectable Americans of Christian faith, this would be, it seems to me, in every respect fortunate.

Assuring you again of my profound respect and renewing my felicitations to you and your country on the conclusion of peace, I beg you to believe me,

Sincerely yours,

(signed) THEODORE ROOSEVELT.

Mr. Sergius Witte
Hotel St. Regis, New York.

Count Witte adds:

Before I left the United States, President Roosevelt handed me a letter with a request to transmit it to Emperor Nicholas. The missive began by referring to the gratitude His Majesty had previously expressed to the President for his assistance in bringing about the peace. Now, the author of the letter went on, he was asking a favour of his Majesty. The commercial treaty of 1832 between the United States and Russia,

the President said, was interpreted by the Americans
as providing for the free entrance of all United States
citizens into Russian territory, it being understood
that limitations of that right were to originate exclusively from the necessity on Russia's part to protect
herself from harm, material and otherwise. As a
matter of fact, however, the Russians seemed to interpret the treaty in a different spirit. In recent years,
the President pointed out, it had become the practice
of the Russian Government to discriminate against
the American citizens on the basis of religion and
refuse admittance to Jews of American allegiance.
To this discrimination, President Roosevelt emphat-
ically asserted, Americans would never consent.
Therefore, the letter concluded, to continue the
friendly relations which had been inaugurated by my
visit to the United States, it was necessary for the
Russian Government to give up the reprehensible
practice of excluding the American citizens of Jewish
faith from Russia. This letter I transmitted to His
Majesty and in due course it reached the Minister of
the Interior. In my premiership a special commission
was appointed to study the matter. The commission
after long deliberations recommended to give up the
interpretation of the treaty clause which offended the
Americans, but this recommendation led to no practical consequences.[3] In the end the United States
Government abrogated the treaty, and we lost the
friendship of the American people.

JUDAISM IN AMERICA

5

WAS CHRISTOPHER COLUMBUS A JEW?

LEARNED researchers have spent years investigating ancient archives and examining rare manuscripts and remote records, trying to solve the mystery of Columbus' origin, only to leave it like a crossword puzzle with unbridged gaps and conflicting alternatives without a convincing conclusion.

Was there some secret bond or was it mere coincidence that on Columbus' first American voyage five[1] of the one hundred and twenty who manned his three tiny vessels have been identified as Jews? Was it accident that the great Marrano theologian, Diego de Deza, Bishop of Salamanca and professor in its university, gave him more than moral support when his project needed a champion? Abraham Zacuto, learned Jewish astronomer, publicly advocated the Columbus adventure and his astronomical tables guided the western course Columbus steered.[2] The Jews, Abraham Senior and Isaac Abravanel, royal contractors, gave their financial aid to the expedition. Juan Cabrero, Luis de Santangel, Gabriel Sanchez and Alfonso de la Caballeria, all Marranos, were his ardent advocates and supporters. Was it mere coincidence that so many Jews were thus associated with this enterprise? Indeed an unfriendly critic, struck by all this Jewish association of Columbus, has written:

> It is as though the New World came into the horizon by their aid and for them alone, as though Columbus and the rest were but managing directors for Israel.[3]

We ask whether the reference with which Columbus begins his journal has personal significance:

> After the Spanish monarchs had expelled all the Jews from all their kingdoms and lands in January,[4] in that same month they commissioned me to undertake the voyage to India with a properly equipped fleet.

Even from Columbus comes corroboration of Jewish affiliations. The first glad tidings of the success of the voyage, written off the Canary Islands on February 15, 1493, were dispatched to Luis de Santangel, Chancellor of the Royal Household and Controller-General of Finance in Aragon.[5] Santangel was a native of Calatayud, which in the fourteenth century had the richest Jewish community in Aragon. He himself had come from a Jewish family, members of which had been burned by the Inquisition for their Jewish faith. He had married Juana de la Caballeria, of a distinguished Marrano family. That Santangel was known as a Jew is evidenced by the fact that in 1497, as a mark of esteem, Ferdinand granted him, his wife and his children and heirs, exemption from all charges of apostasy, while the Inquisition in Valencia and elsewhere were admonished not to molest them or their descendants. Is there any significance that Columbus imparts his great news to his Jewish friend rather than to the king and queen direct?

It has been asserted that "the blood that flowed in Columbus' veins was three-quarters Jewish." Even apart from historical proof, there are those who see the Jew in Columbus' personal characteristics. In spite of the pronouncement of science that there is no Jewish type, one author insists that "it must be admitted quite frankly that all existing portraits of the discoverer gave him a Jewish cast of countenance."[6] While the famous German Jewish author, Jacob Wassermann, points out:

> He has many of the traits of the eager apostate who is nervously anxious to cover up the paths that he has trodden . . . . . A certain soft-heartedness in Columbus is a Jewish trait, in the best and worst sense of that adjective; Jewish, too, is his unmistakable inclination to find a sentimental solution for practical problems; Jewish likewise is his characteristic timidity in the face of far-reaching responsibilities — a timidity that springs from age-long fear of the irrevocable and of what has been decided from above.[7]

Christopher's son, Fernando Colombo, and his friend, Las Casas, in their biography of the discoverer, claimed a noble lineage for the family. They had in their hands all Christopher's papers, but they furnished no real information, much less proof, about the family and its antecedents.

> Their silence, under all circumstances, leads to the belief that they were intentionally mute and that, for some reason or other which we cannot fathom, they did not wish to convey to us what they knew, what indeed they could not help knowing on the subject.[8]

So we are fairly justified in agreeing with the conclusions of Justin Winsor that the only real information upon which we can rely is that "beyond his birth of poor and respectable parents we know nothing positive about the earliest years of Columbus."[9]

That his real name is Cristóbal Colón and that he was the son of Domenico and Susanna Fontenarossa Colón seems now fairly established. The date of his birth is still a matter of debate. Eighteen or twenty different Italian towns have put forth claims as his birthplace. Based partly upon contemporary documents from the local archives, but largely on the strength of his act of *Mayorazgo* (the formal legal document setting up a family property, which is a strange medley of will and declaration of trust establishing a hereditary estate), in which he declares he was born in Genoa, that city has generally been accorded the honor of being his birthplace. But in the light of critical analysis, that declaration is by no means conclusive. For a sailor of his day to boast that he came from Genoa was in the fashion of the hour merely to boast of superior seamanship,[10] like the artist of yesterday claiming to have studied in Paris, or a surgeon boasting of his European hospital training. In no documents has Columbus called himself a Genoese, while in some he has merely described himself as a foreigner. It has been pointed out that he called himself Colón, not Colombo.[11] If a native Italian, it is curious that in all Columbus' correspondence and in his literary work he used Spanish. It is said that there are extant only two of his letters in Italian, and those in that faulty Italian commonly called "macaroni Italian." While his Spanish is not always perfect, it is at least without Italian idioms and points to the dialect of the province of Galicia. Those who argue for his Spanish origin lay great stress on the anomaly of a Genoese sailor, learned and skillful in the nautical arts and science, being awkward in the use of his alleged native language.

About 1900 Don Garcia de la Riega, a Spanish historical scholar living in Pontevedra in Galicia, discovered in the local archives records of a family which had lived there in the fifteenth century by the name of Colón, whose members bore the same forenames as were found amongst the Colombos of Genoa — notably Bartolomé and Cristobo, brothers of Domingo, and a sister Blanca. He further located, at that date at Pontevedra, a Fonterossa family of Jews. The coincidence that Columbus' father was named Domingo and that he had a brother Bartolomeo and a sister Bianchinetta and had married a Susanna Fontenarossa was so striking as to suggest that, instead of Genoa, Columbus' birthplace was in Galicia, and that the secret which Columbus hoped to hide was his Jewish origin.[12]

This hypothesis necessitates several wide leaps. The name Colón was commonplace in Latin countries. Domingo and Bartolomeo appeared not infrequently in conjunction with the family name of Colón in Genoa and elsewhere. The hypothesis further assumes that Domingo Colón of Pontevedra married a Fonterossa and that she was named Susanna and that after the revolution in Galicia the family emigrated to Genoa and adopted the Italian form of Colombo as its name.

To bolster their argument the "Spanish" protagonists claim that the land which Columbus first saw in America he named San Salvador, which was the name of the parish in Galicia in which he had been born. To Cuba they claim he gave the name of Porto Santo after a Galician town. And so through the islands and bays and points, one after the other, they point to names, not Italian, but Spanish Galician.[13]

It is also asserted that Columbus' signature, as found in his letters, forms a hieroglyph which can only be deciphered with the help of the Galician dialect,[14] while the astute Mr.

David finds in the signature "a perfect triangle — a figure sacred to the Jews and used by them on the front of synagogues, on church vessels for sacramental wine, and on gravestones."[15] Nor do they neglect to point out that not only was he fond of quoting the prophets but himself wrote a book on prophecies.

To offset this it may be pointed out that, while there were Jewish Colóns in Italy as well as in the Spain of Columbus' day, there were also recognized Christian families of the name. Because the mother of Columbus had the biblical name of Susanna it is farfetched to reason that it proved her Jewish. Even more strained is it to travel to Spain to pick out the name of Fonterossa when just to the northeast of Genoa lies the valley of Fontenarossa with its considerable market town of that name.

Señor de Madariaga advances the hypothesis that the Colombo family were Spanish Jews who came to Genoa to escape religious persecutions. He accepts, therefore, the documents that Christopher was born in Genoa of a humble family of weavers and claims a Catalan Jewish origin for the family.

To accept the thesis of Columbus' Spanish Jewish origin blindly necessitates the rejection of so many Italian documents of recognized authenticity that many scholars are content to pass Don Garcia's contentions as merely an interesting interlude.

Like so many myths, the discovery of Columbus' being a Jew is perennial. Only lately an industrious researcher has boldly announced:

A casual research among the age-old and discolored letters hidden away for over four centuries in the archives of Spain — all written by the hand of the discoverer — have brought to light the sensational proof that the great benefactor of mankind, who opened a New World to the suffering and overcrowded Old World was:

1. A Spaniard and a Jew.
2. That he secretly remained a Jew in spite of all the spying of the inglorious Inquisition.
3. And that his name was Cristóbal Colón, and never, at any time, "Columbus."

Although Maurice David thus accepts as proven the theories of Garcia de la Riega, he demonstrates the Jewishness of Columbus from a totally different angle. Ingeniously, from a study of photographic reproductions of the autographed letters of Columbus, with enthusiastic conviction, he offers a "sensational find."

He points out that generally the letters written by Columbus, according to the fashion of the day, have a cross at the top of each letter as a symbol that the writer was a true believer. But Mr. David finds a different symbol on the thirteen letters written to his son.

On all of these thirteen intimate letters but one, the attentive reader can plainly see, at the left top corner, a little monogram which may seem cryptic to him, but which is, in fact, nothing more or less than an old Hebrew greeting or benediction, frequently used among religious Jews all over the world even to this day.

This monogram, consisting of two characters, *beth* and *hai*, the second and fifth letters of the Hebrew alphabet — written from right to left, like all Semitic script — is an abbreviation of the Hebrew words, *Baruch Hashem* (Praised be the Lord). Any hand-writing expert can confirm this.

I have stated that the Hebrew monogram appears on all, but one, of the thirteen letters from Columbus to his son. Its omission from that one is probably more revealing than its appearance on the others. Because, [although] this particular letter begins with the traditional: *Muy Caro fijo* (My dear son), [but] its contents show that it was intended to reach the eyes of Queen Isabelle. Colón therein advises his son that he is sending him by special messenger two bags of large gold nuggets, the first found in India by the Spanish explorers, and directs him to hand them over to the Queen together with the letter, adding: "To you, I am writing another long letter, which will leave here tomorrow."

What a powerful revelation in these four innocent words!—"together with the letter"— this very letter, which out of the thirteen remains the only one ad-dressed to his son *without* the Hebrew greeting; yet Colón, even in those letters which required more than one page, was careful to put the same Hebrew greeting on top of the second sheet, exactly as reli-gious Jews would do it at the present time.

No contemporary of Colón, knowing his secret — if he could come back to us and testify — would con-vince us more than does this Hebraic salutation and its omission on just the one letter that the father directs his son to pass on to the Queen. It leaves no doubt that, if ever we could find yet another letter, directed to the son, it would bear the same Hebrew greeting on top. But such a communication in the possession of Queen Isabelle could have easily fallen into the hands of the bitter enemies of the Jews — the Grand Inquisitor of Spain and his many accomplices — which would have ended everything for Colón.[16]

Fantastic as this "proof" may appear to some, it cannot be casually dismissed. Señor de Madariaga considers it at length and leaves it an open question. The scholarly Cecil Roth expresses himself as sceptical of it. He points out that, while it is "possible for the eye of faith to read the Hebrew letters *Bet He*, standing for *be-'Ezrat ha-Shem* (that is, 'with the help of God'— not *Baruch ha-Shem*, or 'Blessed be God,' as the author of the theory believes)," it may be "nothing more than a library sign; for all the letters bearing it come from the Beragua collection and the exception is from the Alba." At the same time Roth lends plausibility to the David argument by pointing out that "it was certainly usual among the Marranos for old religious customs to persist in an atrophied, meaningless form," so that a fifteenth century Marrano, remembering how his elders when writing used to make a certain mark on the top of a letter, might well have followed the practice without intending more than to follow a family usage.

To those with a "will to believe" there are provisions in Columbus' last will (1506) to add proof to the argument from another angle. In this will he orders his son, Don Diego, to pay debts named in a special list. In the list of persons thus designated he directs:

> I want to be given from my fortune the amount named in my list without changing anything of the amount etc. It must be given to them in such a way

that they do not notice wherefrom it comes . . . To a Jew who lived at the entrance of the ghetto in Lisbon, or to another one who may be named by a priest, the equivalent of one half mark in silver.

There are some who speculate that this was the remembrance of some kindly act of some fellow Jew who had befriended him when, as a down-in-the-pocket sailor lad, Columbus was sowing his youthful wild oats. If this were not so, why should he go to all this bother over some poor, unknown, unnamed Jew of Lisbon? Why, indeed, must the beneficiary be a Jew? Why Lisbon? One guess is as good as another.

Cecil Roth has added a further line of argument which he modestly offers as "something which must be taken into account in a final summing up of the problem," but which, when presented to Señor de Madariaga, that scholar felt clinched the argument. It centers on Columbus' use of Jewish viewpoints and expressions, so casually and naturally employed as to indicate his "study of Jewish literature at first hand." The Columbus note on Pope Pius II, *Historia Rerum Ubique Gestarum*, reads in part: "and from the destruction of the Second House according to the Jews to the present day, being the year of the birth of our Lord 1481, are 1413 years."

By "the Second House" Columbus means the Second Temple in Jerusalem. The words are a literal translation of the Hebrew phrase always used — Gentiles spoke of "the destruction of Jerusalem." But according to the Jewish tradition (quite inaccurate, it may be added) universally used in Jewish lore and chronology, that tragic event took place two years earlier, in the year 68 — the precise year that is indicated in this passage (1481 minus 1413 equals 68, not 70). Thus, in an all-important point of Jewish chronology, Christopher Columbus followed the inaccurate Jewish, not the accurate Gentile tradition, and used Jewish and not Gentile phraseology.[17]

Columbus ended his life under an eclipse, in obscurity and misery, forgotten and neglected by the Spanish crown. It was only long afterwards, when his accomplishments were better understood, that his true greatness appeared.

Italian, Spaniard, Jew, which was Columbus? Perhaps further research may discover some conclusive proof to settle the controversy. Today, as the historian assembles the facts, presents his arguments and replies to his adversaries, he is prone to overemphasize anything supporting his contentions and to reject as untrue, or at least to soft pedal, disconcerting evidence, and, as all the facts cannot be reconciled, he finds the answer as he wills.

> Trifles light as air
> Are to the jealous confirmations strong
> as proof of Holy Writ.

There are those who brush aside this controversy with the argument that it is inconsequential and that the significant Jewish role in connection with Columbus was the scholarly contributions of Jews to the advance in science which made possible the voyages of discovery of the fifteenth and sixteenth centuries. They point out that the discoveries of Vasco da Gama, Magellan, Columbus and the other great navigators of that age, were based on the contributions of Jews in perfecting the instruments and science of seamanship. The new astronomy with better astronomical tables, the improvement of the astrolabe and its successor the quadrant and the advance in map making, are all associated with the names of Jews such as Abraham Zacuto, astronomer royal of Portugal, Pedro Nunes, cosmographer, Jehuda Cresques, *el judio de las brujelas*, "the compass Jew," Abraham ibn Ezra, Joseph Vecinho, and numerous other Portuguese and Spanish Jewish scholars.[18]

6

THE MARTYRDOM OF FRANCISCO MALDONADO
DE SILVA

"Where the history of the Jews in Spain ends, their history in America begins; the inquisition is the last chapter of the confessors of Judaism on the Pyrenean peninsula and its first chapter on the continent of the western hemisphere."

M. Kayserling.

IT IS interesting to speculate whether, in the support which made possible the first voyage of Columbus to America, Louis de Santangel was not animated by more than a hope for the conquest of new markets. Treasurer of Aragon, head of a great business, Louis de Santangel, one of Spain's most eminent Jewish financiers, had at the time only lately been through the harrowing experience of seeing members of his own family burned for apostasy by the dread Inquisition. Already the expulsion of the Jews from Spain had long been forecast. At the end of March preceding this voyage of Columbus, the dread edict of expulsion of Jews from Spain was finally promulgated. Did Santangel dream of an enlarged world in which his fellow Jews might find a haven of safety?

The Spaniards, in preparing for a final desperate war to regain the Kingdom of Granada from the Moors, permitted their own prejudices to make them fear the Jews as a potentially dangerous element who might give comfort and support to the neighboring Granada when once the contest was under way. Jews had consequently been banished from Andalusia. As soon as the campaign was over, Ferdinand and Isabella, from religious zeal, extended the edict of banishment to force all Jews to leave Spain. Thus when Columbus sailed on that eventful voyage, not only had the civil government made the lot of the Jews of Spain a nightmare, but contemporaneously the activities of the Inquisition were stimulated to renewed vigor. State and Church were eager rivals for the glory of God and earthly prosperity in seizing goods and property which the harassed Jews had to abandon in a headlong and blind flight to distant refuges.

As knowledge of the newly discovered continent spread, Jews from Spain and Portugal were amongst the earliest settlers there. They sought not only an enlarged opportunity for commercial activity but some place where, safe from civil oppression and beyond the reach of the dread Inquisition, they might openly and safely profess Judaism. This hope was soon shattered. So many of these Jews, in the guise of "new Christians" (Marranos) from Spain and Portugal, sought this retreat, that repeated efforts were made to forbid their emigration. In 1518, the Spanish government prohibited Jews from departing from Spain for America. This prohibition proving ineffective, papal authority was appealed to. In 1537, Pope Paul III, by his bull *Altitude divini consilii*, forbade apostates' going to the Indies and commanded his colonial bishops to expel them. As early as 1519, Inquisition officials had been appointed for the Indies and, theoretically at least, the true faith in America was thus protected from the contamination of Jews, heretics and infidels.

By 1536 the long arm of the Inquisition was functioning in America. At first its efforts were sporadic and feeble, but gradually it managed to organize itself so that, while never operating as effectively as in Spain, it soon became a dominating power in Spanish and Portuguese colonies.

In the Spanish settlement of Peru there early appeared a considerable Jewish community made up of refugees from Brazil, Mexico, Granada, Puerto Bello and Buenos Aires. Jews became the masters of its commerce. No matter how great their worldly success or how far-flung their influence, these Jews did not dare openly to practice their religion. Outwardly they lived as staunch sons and daughters of the Church. Their children, ignorant of their heritage, were brought up as Christians, for the Inquisition had been established in Peru in 1570 under Don Diego de Espinosa as its Inquisitor-General. Between that date and 1806, when it became less active, thirty-four *autos de fé* had been held at Lima. It had as its victims over one hundred and twenty-five Jews, of whom twenty-four were burned at the stake.

Of all these *autos de fé* the greatest was in 1639. Indeed, its historian, an eye-witness of the event, begins the preface of his narrative with a dedication *Al Tribunal del Santo Oficio de la Inquisicion de los Reynos y Prouincias del Perù*. He boasts of the high rank which America had attained in this line of achievement, in that:

> Two *autos de la Fe*, the greatest, have taken place in "Hamerica." The first was held by God, the First Inquisitor, against the apostacy of Adam and Eve in Paradise (most probable is the opinion of those who would seek to place the site of Paradise in America), on Sunday, three days after the Creation of Man;

the second was held by you (The Tribunal of the
Holy Office of the Inquisition of Peru), on the 23rd
of January, 103 years after the discovery of Peru.

In the *auto de fé* of 1639, one of the chief victims was
Manuel Bautista Pérez, a Jew, reputed to be the richest
merchant of Peru, who was burned at the stake. But
beyond all others, the central figure of this event was
Francisco Maldonado de Silva, descendant of an old Jewish
family originating in Portugal. Francisco, by his bold and
courageous bearing in facing torture, has earned a place in
the long list of American heroes who have died for religious
convictions, and his story should not be lost.

Diego Nunez de Silva, the head of the de Silva family,
had had his experiences with the Holy Office of the Inquisition and had been reconciled to the Church in 1605. The
family then moved to Callao, where he established a reputation as a skillful surgeon. There Diego lived as a Christian
and brought up his family of two daughters and a son as
Christians. His son, Francisco Maldonado de Silva, born
in 1592, was also educated as a physician. He evidently
was of a poetical and philosophical bent of mind and became
greatly interested in theological discussion. When a boy of
eighteen, chance brought to Francisco's attention a copy of
Scrutinium Scripturarum, which he read eagerly. This was
a work written by Pablo de Santa Maria, born Solomon
ha-Levi and originally a learned rabbi. Rabbi ha-Levi, in
1391, was converted to Catholicism and soon, because of
his learning, became Bishop of Búrgos and a great figure in
the Church. In the State, too, he rose to positions of prominence and influence, becoming regent of Spain during the
minority of Juan II. He wrote this magnum opus, *Scru-*

AVTO
DE LA FE
CELEBRADO EN
LIMA A 23. DE ENERO
DE 1639.

*AL TRIBVNAL DEL SANTO OFICIO
de la Inquisicion, de los Reynos del Perù, Chile,
Paraguay, y Tucuman.*

POR EL LICENCIADO DON
Fernando de Montesinos, Presbitero,
natural de Ossuna.

CON LICENCIA DEL ILVSTRISSIMO
señor Inquisidor General, y señores del Consejo de
su Magestad, de la Santa, y General
Inquisicion.

*En Madrid. En la Imprenta del Reyno,
año de* 1640.

Title-Page of the Account of the *Auto de Fé* in which De Silva Figured

tinium Scripturarum, in 1394, to prove the truth of Christianity. It was a work so highly regarded and considered so unanswerable and convincing that it was much favored as a means of converting Jews.

The more young Francisco read and pondered over the words of the Bishop of Búrgos the more questions and doubts arose in his mind as to whether the learned author really had all truth in his grasp. He pressed his father for explanations to answer these doubts and difficulties. His father sought to avoid such discussions by advising him to read the Bible and to find his answers there. Francisco was persistent and refused to be put off. He sought to argue with his father about his perplexities and unbelief until his father finally revealed to him that he himself was a Jew and had always observed the law of Moses and had never inwardly accepted the Christian faith which he had so long outwardly professed. Thereafter they studied the Bible together, while father instructed son in Jewish traditions, beliefs and practices. Thus Francisco became an ardent convert to Judaism. Of necessity all this was guarded as a dangerous secret the least inkling of which, once suspected by their neighbors, would have exposed them to the greatest danger.

In 1615–16 the father died and was buried as a respected citizen and true son of the Church. Thereafter Francisco in secrecy pursued his Jewish studies alone.

Francisco continued to practice his profession and rose to a position of prominence in the community, winning a reputation as a skillful surgeon. Surrounded by wife and family, with his mother and a sister dependent on him, he was prosperous and happy. Especially was there devotion between himself and his sister.

One day, as a matured man of thirty-five, he thought that his sister, who was his junior by two years, should learn the family secret. He revealed to her that he believed in Judaism as had their father before him. His sister, brought up as a devout Catholic, was much shocked by this revelation and even more sorely troubled when he tried to prevail upon her to become a Jewess. She, in turn, sought to persuade him to readopt the Catholic faith in which both had been born. When he refused, in her perplexity she sought the advice of her father confessor. She was told of the mortal sin of apostasy and instructed that she could not hope for sacramental absolution unless she discharged her duty as a true daughter of the Church by denouncing heresy even though she would have to expose her brother. Reluctantly she obeyed her confessor's commands and denounced her brother to the Inquisition.

Francisco was immediately arrested, on December 12, 1626. It is a curious history which follows. Evidently Francisco was an attractive personality and an interesting controversialist who endeared himself to his grim inquisitors. He freely admitted that he was a Jew and observed the law of Moses. He defended his position with ingenuity, both orally and in writing, and refused to budge. Instead of being rushed through the ordinary steps of an ecclesiastical trial to final judgment, he was kept in prison for nearly thirteen years. The Inquisitional officials sought to argue and to reason with him and, even after no other course was left but to pronounce judgment, the proceedings were reopened that they might reargue everything all over again. Francisco was adamant. He persisted in refusing to swear on the cross. He repeated that he was a Jew and would live and die as such and that, if he had to swear, he did not wish to be contaminated by a Christian oath but would swear only by the living God, the God of Israel. A long sickness intervened, caused by an eighty days' fast, but it left him as stubborn as ever. We are told how he spent his time in prison writing books to fortify his position. He produced two of them, each of more than a hundred pages, written on scraps of paper pieced together with great ingenuity, with ink made of charcoal and pens cut out of egg shells by a knife manufactured out of a nail. The old narrative says he let his beard and hair grow like the Nazarenes and changed his name to Heli Hazares, "unworthy servant of God."

Finally there was nothing left for the authorities but, after a conviction of apostasy, to transport him to the prison at Lima, there to await execution with other condemned Judaizers.

In 1634 the Lima prison was sadly overcrowded with such victims. They were all facing the fearful fate of being burned alive. There were those who, in the face of such a threatened ordeal, weakened and sought, by renouncing their faith, to escape death. Francisco heard of this in his prison cell. He asked for maize-husks in place of his ration of bread and twisted these husks into a rope by which he escaped from his cell and made a round of neighboring cells urging the prisoners to be brave and to hold to their faith. Captured, he freely admitted what he had done and defied the authorities. He could only be sent back to his cell and kept a close prisoner. He then wrote letters and verses which were transmitted secretly to the other prisoners to inspire them to keep up their courage.

At last the eventful day arrived for the *auto de fé*. It was a gala occasion for Lima. Large crowds assembled, aug-

mented by an influx of folk from the surrounding country.
A great procession was formed with distinguished church
and government officials and sixty-three Jewish victims. Of
these, eleven were to be burned in the *auto de fé*, while the
others, "reconciled" to the Church, were to suffer lesser
degrees of punishment. As they proceeded to the square,
sixty-two of the prisoners carried green crosses[1] as part of
the pageantry. Francisco alone refused to do so, insisting
that he would go to his death as an impenitent, *por ir
rebelde*.

As they stood around the scaffold, the "sermon of faith"
was preached and the prisoners were turned over to the
secular authorities who thereupon pronounced the dread
sentence of burning. Fagots were piled about the victims,
bound to their stakes, and the fires were about to be set
when, says the Chronicler, "A strong wind arose that old
inhabitants of this city affirm [that] they had never seen
any wind so strong in many years. It tore away with great
violence the awning which darkened the scaffold at the
very spot where Francisco was standing, who, looking up
towards heaven, said: 'The God of Israel has ordained this
in order to see me face to face from Heaven.'"

So Francisco Maldonado de Silva went to his death for
his faith.

7

JEWS IN THE FRENCH COLONIES

TWO hundred years ago, when a virile France contended with its rivals — England, Spain, Holland, and Portugal — for empire in an expanding world, one spring day in Paris in 1741, grave scandal reached the ears of His Lordship, head of the French Admiralty, as he sat in his Ministry of Marine. From the ancient and important seaport of Bordeaux, seat of the great Catholic Archbishop, had come a shocking rumor to tarnish the fair scutcheon of his administration of the expanding French Colonial Empire of the western *Isles du Vent*.

It was reported that a Jew in St. Domingue (San Domingo), who had been long settled there, had some time ago sent to Bordeaux two mulatto daughters. Their mother was a free Catholic negress who was reputed to be his wife. She had consented to the children's coming to France only upon the condition that they should be educated as Catholics, in which religion she had brought them up. The father's relatives, Bordeaux Jews, to whom they had been sent, refused to respect the mother's desires and were proposing to bring up the girls as Jewesses. His Eminence the Archbishop had to intervene to rescue them from this terrible misfortune. So down sat the Minister of Marine, April 16, 1741, to demand from the governor of St. Domingue an investigation and, most important of all, a report as to how, in the face of His Majesty's royal decrees, it happened that there was a Jew on that island.

He called attention to the fact that his vigilance in preventing Jewish immigration to these western islands should have prevented an infiltration of Jews. The Jews of Bordeaux daily sought permission to go to the French Indies and he always refused to let them. He ordered that he be immediately informed of the number of Jews in the western isles, to supplement a former report, made in 1739, when mention was made of only two Jewish residents. It was then providently reported that these two had then already been converted to Catholicism. He warned the governor that he had reason to suspect that there had been an increase in the number of Jews there. He admonished him to prepare a census to show where Jews were and what they were doing, to the end that he might be instructed of the king's pleasure concerning the same.

More than two years passed (July 4, 1743) before any report was made. It is to be noted that the tone of the report was such as not to expose Jews to unfriendly official attention. This report records that after a careful investigation the officials could find in the colony only very few persons whom they recognized as Jews. They enumerate only three, two of whom, Messieurs Mirande and Mendès, famous Bordeaux merchants, had been settled at I'Isle à Vaches for more than fifteen or twenty years and there they carried on a large business. In self justification the reporting officials pointed out that these gentlemen were of great benefit to the community, especially as they were most honest men, and there never had been the least word of complaint against them. As a further badge of merit they naively add that neither of the Jews was married.

At Ville du Cap there was a merchant, Jacob Suarès, long established in the town, unmarried, and of a most excellent reputation. Formerly a person had been there, named Pereyre, whom the Jesuits had suspected of being a Jew, but he had died two years ago; and, besides, he had been purged of this suspicion by order of the town Church wardens.

There had also been a Jew at St. Marc; but he had returned to Europe.

This accounted for all Jews known in St. Domingue. Now as for that Bordeaux gossip, they passed it off as just dirty work of a Father Rhédon, recently returned to Bordeaux, who now wanted to pay off old scores on a Monsieur de Paz. While it was true that Monsieur de Paz was a descendant of a very distinguished Jewish family, they found that he himself was a very good Catholic.

Here in miniature are reflected the sidelights of a long history of struggle between Church and State over Jews in the French Colonies.

In 1615, by royal edict, Louis XIII had reaffirmed the banishment of Jews from all French soil.

> For these reasons we have said, declared, wished and ordered:
> We say, declare, wish, ordain, and it is our pleasure, that all the aforesaid Jews who dwell in this our Kingdom, country, domain, and seigneuries under our command shall under penalty of execution and confiscation of their property leave and depart from here forthwith, and this within the time and terms of one month after the publication of these presents.[1]

Although laxly enforced in France itself, as France expanded its American colonization no attention at all appears to have been paid to this law in the western world.

Settled in Martinique long before the French became its master in 1635, although never numerous,[2] Dutch Jews had established themselves as dominant factors in the island's commerce as well as in the cultivation and manufacture of its principal products: sugar and cocoa. Dutertre, the clerical historian who was the first to write the history of the French colonies, tells us that at the beginning of the year 1654 refugees from Recife arrived at Martinique and asked the Governor, M. du Pacquet, for permission to settle on the island. When the Governor proposed to grant such permission, the Jesuit fathers remonstrated, pointing out that it would be contrary to the king's desires, as most of them were Jews and others heretics, and secured a reluctant refusal of the permission. These Jews, however, apparently settled without formal permission and continued to live there unmolested. The French priest, Antoine Biet, visiting the island as early as 1652, complains that Jews "were permitted in the Island to judaize, and in sight of all the world to exercise their religion and observe their sabbath." He went on to say that: "The Jews have or had at this time their various shops at St. Pierre, the town or city of the island where vessels come to port. They are the principal merchants, and have found so much favor and credit with M. Parquet (the governor) and his wife, by means of their friends, that they have obtained from him the free exercise of their sabbath." Then he told how the island's market day had been transferred from Saturday to Friday to accommodate these Jews.[3]

Some nine hundred people, mostly Jews, fled to Guadeloupe after the Dutch surrendered Brazil to the Portuguese in 1654.[4] A Captain Languillet reported in 1660–61 that there were fifteen or twenty families of these Jews who were then planters at Cayenne.[5] Dutch Jews had settled at Cayenne as early as 1644. Although many of them left afterwards, when it was captured by the French, there is a fair basis for the assumption that this number was in excess of that mentioned by Captain Languillet.[6] Their importance was recognized by a concession granting them every protection and assistance to enjoy their property and possession and by assigning a place for the free exercise of their religion.[7]

Indeed, a French historian tells us that, when the French seized islands in the West Indies, they found there many Jews who were so important throughout the new colonies in commercial, industrial and agricultural life that their presence could not be ignored. As early as 1680 the newly appointed governor of Martinique had reported to his superiors that he had found Jews so active in every business that almost all trade was in their hands.

So conspicuously satisfactory was the position of the Jews in the French colonies that in 1655, in their petition to the Dutch West India Company to permit Jews to continue in New Amsterdam, the petitioners, Dutch Jews, called to the attention of the directors of the company that "the French consent that the Portuguese Jews may traffic and live in Martinique, Christopher and other territories, whither also some have gone from here, as your Honors know."

French Colonial policy towards Jews was largely determined by the interplay of events in the Island of Martinique. From the very earliest days of French rule a campaign against Jews was waged by the Religious Orders. The island government, backed by Colbert, *Controleur Général de Finance* of France, was adverse to any restriction against Jews. The Jesuits, zealous for the success of their missionary efforts, sought the banishment from the island of all Jews as heretics. The secular authorities, intent on the material success of the colony, recognized the commercial and industrial value of the Jews as powerful factors for its prosperity and gave them both friendly encouragement and covert support.

In 1658, over the active opposition of the colony's governor, the Church for the first time obtained from the French authorities an order restricting Jewish commerce. The island government ignored the order for the time being, and after a few months it was apparently repealed. However, from that time on the Jews continued to be increasingly the victims of the conflict between the two contending forces until finally, by a series of laws and decrees, a definite French anti-Jewish colonial policy was officially formulated and enforced.

Temporarily, in 1671, the pendulum swung in favor of the liberal policy of the civil government and, through the influence of Colbert, a charter of liberties was granted to the Jews under royal authority. This applied not only to Martinique but to all French islands and was a recognition of Jewish usefulness in agriculture and of their contribution to island defenses. It secured to Jews the same privileges

that other inhabitants enjoyed, including liberty of conscience, so long as they caused no scandal to the Catholic
faith.[8]

Mons debaas, ayant été informé que les Juifs
qui sont établis dans la Martinique et les autres
Isles habituées par mes sujets ont fait des dépenses
assez considerables pour la culture des terres et qu'ils
continuent de s'appliquer a fortiffier leurs établisse-
ments en sorte que le public en recevra de l'utilité,
Je vous fais cette lettre pour vous dire que mon intention est que vous teniez la main a ce qu'ils jouissent
des mesmes privilèges dont les autres habitants des
dites Isles sont en possession, et que VOUS LEUR
LAISSIEZ UNE ENTIERE LIBERTÉ DE CONSCIENCE
en faisant prendre néantmoins les precautions necés-
saires pour empescher que l'exercise de leur religion
ne puisse causer aucun scandale aux catholiques.
Sur ce, Je prie Dieu qu'il vous ayt, Mons debaas,
en sa saincte garde. (Signed): "Louis," (and below):
"Colbert."

Ecrit à Dunkerque le XXIII mai 1671.

After the death of Colbert, the Jesuits won final victory.
Le Comte de Blénac, a supporter of the Jesuits, became
governor of the island and, no longer restrained by the
influence of Colbert, joined in their anti-Jewish program.
In 1683 he visited Paris and through his influence an edict
for the expulsion of Jews was extracted from the king.
Two years later there was enacted the formal exclusion of
Jews from France's American island possessions, to become
famous as the decree of March 1685, known as the *Code
Noir*. Inserted as the first section of a code primarily
intended for the regulation of negro slavery in its *Isles
Françoises de l'Amérique*, and addressed particularly to

Martinique, Guadeloupe and Saint Christopher, was a provision extending to these American colonies the edict of Louis XIII of 1615 banishing Jews from French territory. This section, and it is the only one devoted to Jews, freely translated is:

> It is our wish, and we decree, that the edict of the late King of glorious memory, our greatly honored lord and father, dated April 23, 1615, be carried into effect in our Islands and, by these presents, We command all our officers to chase out of our Islands all Jews who have established their residence there whom, as declared enemies of the Christian faith, We command to get out in three months, counting from the day of the publication of these presents, upon penalty of the confiscation of their bodies and property.

Other provisions forbade any religion except the Roman Catholic and compelled the observance of Sundays and Catholic holidays and prohibited the teaching of Judaism to slaves.

Apparently, however, it was only a paper victory for the Jesuits, as the local authorities were so uninterested in its enforcement that Jews continued to be permitted illegally to reside in the colonies. From time to time the Jesuits succeeded in obtaining further regulations to strengthen their hands in their anti-Jewish drive. The same official laxity and indifference in enforcement continued in civil insular government circles notwithstanding these subsequent anti-Jewish regulations.

Such hostile legislation gradually and continually brought about the withdrawal of the Jews. Whenever fault was found with the negligent enforcement of these anti-Jewish regulations, the local civil authorities still persisted in reporting home that the Jews who thus withdrew were eagerly accepted by the neighboring colonies. They emphasized their loss in the removal of Jewish wealth, industries and commerce, and pointed out the benefits to be derived from a return of Jews to the French colonies.

Across all this hostility, legislation and official regulations, cut grants of special privileges. There were the *Lettres de Naturalité* granted by the Crown to favored Jews, investing them with the privileges of ordinary French citizens, which included rights of colonization. Then there were those who had a special license to go to a colony. In such cases the secular officials reasoned that, if the King had granted such permission to a Jew, he removed him from the class which the Crown, in the *Code Noir*, had described as enemies of the Christian name, and that therefore they might be encouraged to join any settlement they selected.

Then there were the great Jewish merchant princes of Southern France, Bordeaux, Bayonne, Marseilles and the other cities of the Provence, who were not considered as bound by any of these restrictions. Driven out of Portugal and Spain in 1492, the Marranos (new Christians) had there established themselves, taking with them the world trade which their genius and their fleets had created as the commercial center of Europe. Letters-Patent of 1550 and 1574 gave to these Jews freedom of residence, travel and trade throughout French territory.

Some of these leading merchants had taken advantage of the opportunities offered by the great American adventure. They sent their vessels to trade in the French West Indies. Among the earliest to realize the possibilities of these colonies, they not only set up commercial agencies but became interested in establishing plantations. They often sent the young men of their families to be their representatives. The powerful Gradis family of Bordeaux maintained establishments both in Martinique and in St. Domingue. When young Samuel Gradis died in Martinique in 1732, the priests made an exception by allowing him to be buried in the Catholic cemetery according to the Jewish rites. In 1783, upon the death of Abraham Gradis, of the firm of Gradis & Mendès *frères*, the civil authorities saw that his estate was distributed according to his Jewish will, notwithstanding a Christian claimant. In fact, six of the Gradis fleet of ships, the *Polly*, *David*, *Patriarch Abraham*, *le Parfait*, *l'Alliance* and *le Vainqueur*, maintained the official regular communication between the islands and France as well as between Canada and France. The decrees of banishment seem never to have been applied to such great Jewish families.

It thus resulted that the situation in the French American colonies was not altogether intolerable. When the Count d'Estaing was appointed governor of Martinique, in 1764, the Jews, in presenting an address to him, were able to say that although they had originally come from many different countries they had been well received by the inhabitants, treated with friendly goodwill and given permission to trade freely. They claimed that thus they had contributed to the prosperity of the colony by making it a shipping center, a market for all sorts of merchandise, as well as by financing those who needed assistance to carry on. They pointed out that they were manufacturing a variety of merchandise and operating sugar mills (refineries). They petitioned that in the interest of the colonies, as well as for their own welfare, the governor might continue this liberal policy.

To develop the colony, d'Estaing proceeded to impose upon the Jews special levies which, on their face, seem pretty heavy — 285,190 livres — apportioning the tax according to the means of the individual from 100 to 50,000 L. When some of these taxpayers protested, the governor sent to the Minister of Foreign Affairs and War, the Duke of Choiseul, an analysis and justification of what he was doing. Some of this report is sufficiently amusing to bear repetition.

M. DePas, head of his family, 7,000 L: He is a man with three different estates and 280 slaves; DePas, Junior: "an honest man," who is about to buy an estate with a hundred slaves near Bourg d'Aquin, has three other estates; Jean DePas has a plantation at Mangon with thirty slaves; Michel DePas, "a bad lot," 50,000 L to be paid in one and two years. Against him, it is added, there are all kinds of complaints. Besides all this, he is a mulatto and a bastard. He has a great estate, with one hundred and twenty slaves, on a big hill, another with thirty slaves, and he is a former broker for Gradis, who, incidentally, was presenting to the king the complaints of the Martinique Jews. M. S. J. DePas and his cousin, Antoine DePas, 10,000 L, and no remarks! Lewis, 10,000 L: He has two houses worth 10,000 L; has ruined many a resident by lawsuits in which he carries on a regular business, pretends to have been baptized, and claims the Duke d'Orléans as godfather. He has turned Jew in the colony. Altogether there are some thirty or forty Jews named, among whom the payments were thus apportioned.

There was open opposition to this program, both in the colony and at home. A protest, *sept points d'accusation,* was filed, claiming that "he [d'Estaing] has levied considerable taxes upon the Jews of the colony although the Portuguese Jews have the privilege of settling in any French territory as freely as in France." This was the signal for a showdown fight which continued for two years — a useless one it proved to be. In spite of all their opposition and the length of the struggle, in the course of which a court order was obtained to enforce the law banishing all Jews from the colonies, as was to be expected, the Jews paid up and the decrees of banishment were nullified. The Jews were patted on the back with the assurance that, in spite of a difference in religion, they were free men, very useful to the State and its colonies because of their industry as agriculturalists and their ability in commerce. They were told they would be permitted to continue their residence and activities as formerly.

Cayenne, originally a Dutch colony but captured by the French in 1664, had Jewish settlers as early as 1644. In 1654 the number was considerably augmented by the accession of those who fled from Brazil when the Dutch ceded that territory back to the Portuguese under the Treaty of Utrecht. David Nassy, in 1659, under a charter from the Dutch West India Company, founded a Jewish colony there, which was later joined by Italian Jews. At the end of five years, however, most of these colonists withdrew to Surinam. Dutertre states that the Dutch Jews introduced the cultivation of sugar and indigo to the colony; and there can be no question but that they were substantial factors in the agricultural and commercial development of the early colony and continued to be of importance after it became French. In 1725 the Jews of Surinam petitioned the King of France for authority to settle in Cayenne. This was denied.

The Jews therefore had no official status in the island, but continued there much as they did in other French possessions.

Neither in the Louisiana territory nor in Canada were the Jews noteworthy factors in the early settlements. It was only after the British conquest of Canada that Jews figure in its development. In Louisiana, the history of the early Jews is still a more or less unexplored field. Even though their numbers were insignificant, as early as 1724 a *Code Noir* was proclaimed for *la Province & Colonie de la Louisianne*. Differing from the earlier *Code Noir* in some particulars, it repeated in its first article the exclusion of Jews:

> The edict of the late King Louis XIII, of glorious memory, April 23, 1615, shall be carried into effect in our province & colony of Louisiana; this being done, we enjoin the Directors of that company and all its officers to chase out of said country all Jews who may have established their residence there whom, as declared enemies of the Christian name, we command to get out in three months, counting from the day of the publication of these Presents, under penalty of the confiscation of their bodies and property.

In 1774, on the accession of Louis XVI to the throne, in applying for a renewal of their ancient rights, upon the urgent solicitation of the colonial Jews and of their relatives in France, the French Jews, known as *Marchands portugais ou noveaux Chrestiens*, petitioned to have their privileges extended to include a right to dwell in the colonies. They based the plea on the ground that the privileges of residence granted them in 1550 extended *par terre et seigneurie de l'obéissance de Sa Majesté*, and that the only reason the colonies were not then expressly mentioned was that the date when France acquired colonies was two centuries later. They conceded that whenever their rights had been questioned in the colonies they had been protected by proper orders, but they thought they were entitled to obviate all such future difficulties by obtaining now an express mention of colonies rather than depending upon the goodwill of some government official.

After the problem thus raised was presented for the opinions of many different officials and evoked divided counsel, it was placed before the *Conseil du roi*. The decision was that the king should make no change to give Jews any legal standing in the colonies, but should allow the status of toleration to continue for them. At the same time, in that year 1776, ninety years after the promulgation of the *Code Noir*, when our Declaration of Independence was proclaiming to the world that all men are created equal and endowed by their Creator with unalienable rights, it was willing to record only that the provisions of that Code might appear too harsh.[9]

Such continued to be the status of Jews in the French colonies until the French Revolution.[10]

8

COTTON MATHER'S AMBITION[1]

AT A TIME when New England was still dominated by
a clerical hierarchy, Cotton Mather was not only head
of this theocracy but his intellectual and religious viewpoints represented popular opinion. Dynamic in preaching,
voluble and indefatigable in writing, tireless in all good
causes, he was militant Puritanism in its aggressive lustiness.
He enjoyed controversy. He fought not only religious
errors, but explored the divergent ranges of government and
science in which to exercise his intellectual alertness.
Cocksure, he believed in his Church and in his America.
Inspired by a firm conviction that he was the anointed
champion of truth, he went forth to combat human failings
and to lead the people in his day from America to the
Kingdom of God.

Traditionally we think of this commanding Puritan as
religiously intolerant. But he was modern and liberal in
his condemnation of religious persecutions and opposed the
use of punishment or violence to enforce conformity.

'Tis to be wished, that the *Mother of Abominations*,
that is to say, all Persecutions for Conscientious
Differences in Religion, may become *abominable*.[2]

As early as 1692 he wrote:

A man has a Right unto his life, his estate, his
liberty, and his family, altho' he should not come up
to these and those Blessed *Institutions* of our Lord.[3]

Twenty-five years later, in 1717, in laying down for Christians "The Grand Maxims to be United On," in his publication entitled *Malachi*, he reiterated:

> All men that would see Mankind in Peace, ought for ever to do all they can, that all *Persecutions* for *Conscientious Dissents* in *Religion*, may come under an Universal Detestion.[4]

As a Puritan clergyman, both by training and interest, Cotton Mather was deeply concerned with the Jew. This interest in them, their language, their Old Testament and their history, was insatiable and life-long. It is said that at the age of twelve he "entered upon his Hebrew Grammar" and "after his entrance into college he made as quick dispatch as before, mastering Hebrew perfectly."[5] He claimed an exact knowledge of Hebrew[6] and an acquaintanceship with the "Talmuds,"[7] and later himself trained his eldest daughter, Katharine, to "read Hebrew fluently."[8]

As early as 1714 he had written, in six monumental unpublished manuscript volumes, *Biblia Americana*,[9] a history of the Jews. This was not only the usual retelling of Jewish history of the biblical period in the unscientific dogmatic manner of the day; there was added "an elaborate and entertaining history of what has befallen the *Israelitish Nation*, in every place, from the Birth of an Great *Redeemer* to this very day."[10] It was the earliest attempt by an American author to write post-biblical Jewish history.

He had more than an academic interest in Jews. Jews represented to him the great unsolved human problem bound up in divine mystery. They alone had learned the word of God by direct communion. Even though later re-

jected by God for their denial of Christ and commanded ever
to wander over the face of the earth, somehow, to his
thinking, they still managed to preserve in the learning of
the Diaspora something of divine inspiration. He liked to
use Jewish stories to illuminate some point he wanted to
drive home. To illustrate the necessity that the communities
should be ever vigilant in keeping guard against enemies,
he tells:

> I remember, a notable Passage, reported in a
> Jewish History: That a Famous King of PORTUGAL
> finding himself unable to SLEEP in the Night, went
> and walk'd on the Top of his Palace; from whence he
> saw a couple of Wretches throw a DEAD CORPSE into
> the House of a poor Jew not far off. The next
> morning those Wretches, made a clamour about
> the City, that the Jew had Murdered the man who
> was missing; and the whole People of Jews in the
> City, had been Massacred, in the Tumult raised on
> this Occasion, if they had not been rescued by the
> Justice of the King, who had been an EY-WITNESS,
> how the PLOT was managed. The King then asked
> the Chief RABBI's of the Jews, how they translated,
> the FOURTH Verse of the HUNDRED & TWENTY FIRST
> Psalm. They Answered, HE THAT KEEPETH ISRAEL
> SHALL NEITHER SLUMBER, NOR SLEEP: He Reply'd,
> NAY, I TRANSLATE IT SO, He will not Slumber, nor
> will He Suffer to Sleep, the Keeper of Israel; WHICH
> (he added), YOU HAVE SEEN FULFILLED, IN YOUR
> DELIVERANCE BY MEANS OF MY WAKEFULNESS.[11]

Again he narrates a version of a famous Hillel story to
give point to his discussion of the Golden Rule.

> ... In the TALMUDIC Treatise, Entitled, SABBATH,
> we have a Story: That an Heathen proposed it unto
> Rabbi HILLEL, To teach him the WHOLE OF THE LAW,

in as little time as he could keep standing upon one Foot, on which he said, that he would become a PROSELYTE. Rabbi HILLEL immediately made him a PROSELYTE, and performed all he desired, in saying but this one thing unto him, THAT WHICH THOU WOULDEST HATE FOR ANOTHER TO DO UNTO THEE, DO NOT THOU THAT UNTO ANOTHER. THAT IS ALL THE LAW; ALL THE REST IS BUT AN EXPLICATION OF THIS.[12]

Judge Sewall relates with malicious pleasure, in his diary, under date of February 5, 1704, Mather's unsuccessful attempt to convert to Christianity a Boston Jewish merchant, one of the Frazon brothers — evidently by some jugglery with holy text. In the words of the diary:

> The forgery was so plainly detected that Mr. C. M. confest it, after which Mr. Frasier would never be persuaded to hear any more of Xianity.[13]

The ambition to be the means of converting a Jew to Christianity was so near an obsession on the part of Cotton Mather that it is easily possible to understand how he overstepped the bounds of propriety when one realizes his Puritan viewpoint. The Puritan settlers of America in the seventeenth and eighteenth centuries believed the millennium was something very near and real which every day brought measurably closer to hand. To them it was possible for any living man not only to have a chance to partake in that great event, but personally to hasten its coming. They accepted literally the words of prophecy that, as soon as the Jews had been dispersed throughout every land of the earth, there was to be a calling of the Jewish nation, their conversion to Christianity and then the millennium. It was a subject of active debate whether this conversion of the Jews was to be in mass or whether individuals were gradually, one by one, to embrace Christianity until all had disappeared as Jews. Whichever view was adopted, to be the means of converting a Jew was not merely a matter of personal glory, but another step accelerating the establishment on earth of the Kingdom of God.

Mather firmly believed that the conversion of individual Jews was the method to adopt. He hoped for a very active and personal share in such conversions. All through his life, each and every Jew within view was a potential prospect for his missionary success.

For years Mather had prayed and dreamed of a chance to convert a Jew. His *Diary* is filled with expressions of this desire on his part so strongly stated that it is incomprehensible today. Thus, his prayer of July 18, 1699, concretely voiced his desire:

> This day, from the dust, where I lay prostrate, before the Lord, I lifted up my cries: For the conversion of the Jewish Nation, and for my own having the happiness, at some time or other, to baptize a Jew, that should by my ministry, bee brought home unto the Lord.[14]

Before the Frazon incident, his missionary activities had been purely literary. In 1699 he published *The Faith of the Fathers*,[15] of which he gave the following account:

> April 9, 1699. This week, I attempted a further service to the name of the my Lord Jesus Christ. I considerd, that when the Evangelical Elias, was to prepare the Jewish Nation, and the coming of the Messiah, he was to do it, by bringing down the Heart of the Fathers before the children. And I considered, that would not only confirm us Christians in our

Faith exceedingly to see every article of it, asserted in the express words of the Old Testament, but that it would mightily convince and confound the Jewish Nation. Ye, who Knowes, what use the Lord may make of such an Essay? Wherefore, with much contrivance, I drew up a Catechism of the whole Christian Religion, and contrived the Questions to fit the answers, whereof I brought every one out of the Old Testament. I prefased the Catechism, with an address unto the Jewish Nation, telling them in some lively terms, that if they would but return to the faith of the Old Testament, and believe with their own Ancient and blessed Patriarchs, this was all that wee desired of them or for them. I gave this book to the Printer, and it was immediately published. Its Title is, THE FAITH OF THE FATHERS.[16]

The little volume was dedicated to the "Jewish Nation" and with a most tactless exhortation implored them to see the error of their ways:

To the Jewish Nation:
One thing that satisfied us Christians, in the Truth of Christianity, is your obstinate aversion to that Holy Religion; our Blessed Jesus, the Author of our Faith, foretold your continuance under the circumstances now come upon you until the Ties of the Gentiles in the four monarchies, just now expiring, are expired . . . Here is now put into your Hands an irresistible and inefragable demonstration that tho' you say, you are Jews you are not so . . . Be amazed, O ye Rebellious and rejected People of our Great Lord Messiah . . . Return O backsliding Israel!

The idea expounded was that, if the Jews would only return to the faith of the Old Testament, they would see the errors of their ways and be converted to Christianity, which is in fact only the true, complete Jewish religion developed through Jesus. The work consisted wholly of passages of the Old Testament so arranged as to prove Jesus the Messiah of the Jews.[17]

Undoubtedly *The Faith of the Fathers* had been inspired by Mather's acquaintance with some Boston Jew, possibly this same Frazon. At all events, as soon as the book had appeared in print, he hopefully dispatched a copy of the new volume to this Jewish friend.

> April 28, 1699. And whereas, I have now for divers years, employ'd much prayer for, and some discourse with, an infidel Jew in this Town; thro' a Desire to glorify my Lord Jesus Christ in the Conversion of that Infidel, if Hee please to accept mee in that Service. I this day renew'd my Request unto Heaven for it. And writing a short letter to the Jew, wherein I enclosed my, Faith of the Fathers, and, La Fedel Christiano, I sent it unto him.[18]

Prayerfully he awaited the results.

> May 21, 1699. I had advice from Heaven — Yea, more than this; That I shall shortly see some Harvest of my Prayers and Pains, and the Jewish Nation also.[19]

Although he was doomed to local failure, he was later able to rejoice over the report of the successful influence of his book in Carolina.

> September 2, 1699. This Day, I understand by letters from Carolina, a thing that exceedingly refreshes me, a Jew there embracing the Christian faith, and my little book, The Faith of the Fathers, therein a special instrument of good unto him.[20]

We are, however, without further information as to this Carolina incident, who the Jew was, or whether the achievement was mere gossip manufactured for export for the New England trade.

The following year, 1700, Cotton Mather published his second tract intended to influence the conversion of the Jews.

> October 28, 1700. AMERICAN TEARS UPON THE RUINS OF THE GREEK CHURCHES. Moreover, a very charming relation of Conversion made by a Jew, one Shalom Ben Shalomoh, at his joining lately to a Congregational Church in London falling into our Hands, I foresaw many advantages to glorify the Lord Jesus Christ by Reprinting it. Wherefore, composing a preface to make the Transition agreeable, I procured this to be added as an appendix to the book of the Greek Churches.[21]

The appendix was, in fact, only a reprint, with omissions, of a London edition of the previous year of a "conversion sermon" of an apostate Jew.[22] Perhaps the inspiration of this appendix came from Sewall, who had imported copies of the pamphlet from London.[23]

It is almost ten years before the next reference to the Jews occurs in Mather's *Diary*. This omission in his *Diary* does not mean that Mather had lost interest in Jews during this period. The American Antiquarian Society, of Worcester, Mass., has a manuscript, finished December 25, 1703,[24] which deals in part with the conversion of the Jewish nation. In this he indorsed the view of his father, Increase Mather, as expressed in the latter's *Mystery of Israel's Salvation*.[25] A second undated manuscript, *Triparadisus*, also in the possession of that Society, is not unlikely of this period. In Chapter XI of *Triparadisus*, dealing with the national conversion of the Jews, Mather concluded that the millennium is not to come until the Jewish nation has been "brought in." As the nations showed evidences of being destroyed, the Jewish people were to come into the "Happy State" as the Gentiles had done.

Under date of February 12, 1710–11, he prayed:

> February 12, 1710–11. Song of Jubilation. And that the Lord may be glorified in the Conversion of that poor Jew, and where I was concerned now 16 or 17 years ago; and towards whom the Dispensations of Heaven have been singular and wonderful.[26]

Again, a little later he prayed once more:

> April 11–12, 1711. Vigil-prayer. I cried unto the Lord, that I might yett see one (opportunities) and a very Rich one, in the conversion of that poor Jew, for whose conversion and salvation we have been for 6 or 7 years more than waiting on him.[27]

Two years later he still seemed to be praying for this same Jew:

> July 4–5, 1713. Vigil-prayer. For the conversion of the poor Jew, who is this Day returned once more unto New England, and who has now for 19 years together been the Subject of our Cares and Hopes, and Prayers.[28]
>
> August 29, 1713. Prayer. For the conversion of the Jew for whom I have been so long and so much concerned![29]

In 1716, Mather was strongly moved by reading a report of the conversion of Jewish children in Berlin.

> October 15, 1716, A. D. A late and strange Impression of Grace, on the Jewish Children, in the

City of Berlin: May I not improve it, and an Excitation of Piety in my flock, and sway the young people of it.[30]

Mather wrote to John Winthrop, August 15, 1716, that in a letter received from "a famous German Divine" two days before, he was told of

a strange and miraculous motion from God upon the minds of the Jewish children in the City of Berlin. The little Jews, from eight to twelve years of age, fled to the Protestant ministers, that they might be initiated into Christianity. They embraced it with such rapture that when they saw the name of Jesus, in a book, they kissed it a hundred times, and shed floods of tears upon it. No methods used by their parents to reduce them are effectual; but they say to their parents, "We shall not return to you; it is time for you to come over to us!" This German divine saw happy auspices in this rare occurrence.[31]

The following year he wrote an account of the incident, and requested the Master of the Grammar-School in Boston to call it to the attention of his scholars.[32]

Shortly after this he resolved to publish his manuscript:

I do accordingly give these things unto the Bookseller, under the title, FAITH ENCOURAGED, a brief relation of a Strange Impression of Heaven, upon the Minds of some Jewish Children at the City of Berlin, (in the upper Saxony), and an Improvement made of so marvellous an occurrence.[33]

It tells of three young Jewish girls, Sprintz, Guttel, and Esther, daughters of Isaac Veits and Sophia Moses, Jews:

the eldest of 'em was twelve; (tho' the mother gives out she is but nine) the youngest was eight; or as the mother pretends, but six.

These precocious infants of Berlin cast off their parents and insisted, in spite of all discouragements from the Protestant minister and the efforts of a royal commission of three distinguished clergymen appointed by the King of Prussia, on embracing the Protestant religion. The story could only have been an inspiration to a generation which seriously read the remarkable infant professions of faith in the *Magnalia*. Cotton Mather not only offered this relation as a warning and inspiration to his own people, but he took occasion to address the "Jewish nation" with a pious wish that this brave example might not be lost upon them:

> How is it possible to publish the Relation of the Jewish Children at Berlin, without an Address unto the Jewish Nation; and a Tender unto them of Things that should be more thought upon?
>
> If but one Soul of all that Beloved People, should be found, and reach'd, and touch'd, by the Things to be now laid before them it will be well worth while the Pains of these Expostulations. It may be, the same Spirit, who wrought upon the Babes at Berlin, will fall upon some of that Beloved People, while they have these Words before them. We will Prophesy over these Dry Bones, and see what the Spirit of Life will do upon them!
>
> What considerations are there, which would mightily Convince them, that they do they know not themselves in their Infidelity; and which, Men and Brethren, Oh! that you would shew yourselves Men, and suffer them to awaken you.

Mather was eager for more than abstract activity in converting Jews. He wanted to meet and converse with the occasional Jews with whom he came into contact. His *Diary* shows this:

> G. D. I hear of a Jew in this place. I would seek some conversation with him.[34]
>
> G. D. I am this week entertained, with surprising advice, concerning the Jew, with whom and for whom we were so much concerned three and twenty years ago.[35]

There is evidence to suppose that he frequently preached upon the subject of converting Jews.[36]

It is but reasonable to suppose that he enjoyed the friendship of Judah Monis, Harvard's Hebrew instructor, who was the most famous converted Jew of the day.[37] Although Monis' conversion is credited almost wholly to Increase Mather, it would be strange if Cotton Mather had not been of some assistance to his father in so notable an achievement. Cotton Mather's *Diary*, however, contains no mention of Monis. It records no personal triumphs of Jewish conversions. Beyond the enumerated casual personal contact with isolated Jews, Cotton Mather's Jewish activities were scholarly and wholly literary.

As a theologian Cotton Mather abominated what he regarded as Jewish religious errors and ever aimed to be a means of ultimately redeeming all Jews to the true faith of Christianity. As a humanitarian on principles of ethics he demanded that Jews should be free from religious persecution.

9

ARARAT — A CITY OF REFUGE FOR THE JEWS

IN THE early days of our republic there was no more flamboyant figure in Jewry than Mordecai Manuel Noah. He was born in Philadelphia in 1785. Of his father little is known beyond his having been a native of Mannheim, Germany. His mother came of the distinguished Portuguese-Jewish Phillips family, early settlers in America. Left an orphan in childhood, he was reared by his maternal grandfather, Jonas Phillips. First apprenticed to a carver and gilder to learn that trade, he proved an industrious and studious youth who educated himself by his own efforts. It is said that his earnestness so attracted the attention of the great Colonial financier, Robert Morris, that he obtained for Noah, then a mere lad, an appointment as clerk in the Auditor's Office at the United States Treasury.

Restless, ambitious, and versatile, Noah made for himself careers as journalist, playwright, author, politician, judge, sheriff, diplomat and philanthropist, not to mention his military office of major and his appointment by President Jackson as surveyor of the Port of New York.

The highlight of his career came when, after he had declined an appointment as consul at Riga, President Madison in 1813 appointed him consul for the kingdom and city of Tunis, an important diplomatic post in the days when the Barbary pirates, preying on American vessels, gave rise to ticklish international problems.

He was a Quixotic medley of the theatrical, the ridiculous and the wise, a man of fine presence, real eloquence, but obsessed by his own importance and the conviction that he was a great genius and a personage of vast importance to his country; a dreamer of dreams, a visionary and an enthusiast, and yet withall, in spite of his foibles, a man of action, talent and ability — a curious, pompous, likeable combination of contradictions.

A Jew, sincere and reverent, devoted to his people, Noah conceived himself divinely appointed their leader and protector. In 1825, in his fortieth year, he made up his mind that the time had arrived when, as the Captain of Israel, he should realize his long cherished scheme to solve the Jewish problem by leading the Jews into a new promised land. His was the ambition and dream of a restored Israel, anticipating by almost a century the Zionism of today. He proposed to renationalize the Jews in a land of their own where the persecuted of all countries, Gentiles as well as Jews, might be welcome to enjoy political freedom and religious liberty under the protecting aegis of the United States — a republic within a republic.

The Erie Canal, then opening up the rich farming country of western New York, directed the attention of land speculators to the great opportunities for profitable ventures in that territory. On this western border there was at this time what we later came to know as a real estate boom.

It is now known that, as early as 1820, Noah had already had his attention directed to a small island, called Grand Island, of about five miles broad and thirteen miles long, in the Niagara River, opposite the present City of Ton-

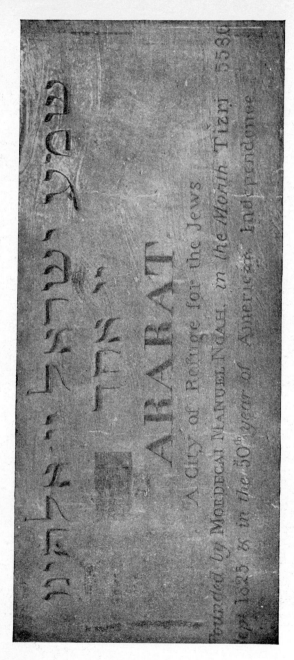

Cornerstone of Ararat

New York Apr 27 /864

Dear Sir

with you have the kindness to
inform me whether the survey of France Island
has been completed and what the land has
been valued at. I am also desirous of learning at what price you will fix for the
sale of the same —

Very respectfully yours

awanda. In that year he petitioned the New York Assembly
to sell him Grand Island

> for the purpose of attempting to have the same
> settled by emigrants of the Jewish religion from
> Europe; that he not only considers the situation of
> Grand Island as well adapted for the contemplated
> purpose, but that the obtaining of the title from the
> State would be very advantageous in inducing the
> emigration of capitalists, as well as others.[1]

After a favorable committee report introducing "an act
directing the commissioners of the land office to survey and
sell Grand Island, in the Niagara River, to Mordecai M.
Noah," the matter seemed to have dropped from sight.

By 1825 friends of Noah had interested themselves in
the development of this same island. Whether to help his
friends realize on their land speculations or to use the
opportunity to develop his cherished plan for the benefit
of his fellow Jews may always be a matter of argument,
but Noah decided to launch his plans for an asylum of
freedom for the Jews[2], not as their final resting place, but
merely as a temporary step to assemble the Jews, preliminary to the ultimate goal and the final establishment of
a Jewish state in Palestine.

It was his firm conviction, often reiterated, that the Jews
must do something for themselves, move onward to realize
their repatriation in the Holy Land so long promised and
foretold. "When they *do* move, that mighty power which
has for thousands of years rebuked the proscription and
intolerance shown to the Jews, by a benign protection of
the *whole* nation will still cover them with His invincible
standard."

So he issued in grandiose terms, in his newspaper, *The*

National Advocate, a call for all the Jews of the earth to assemble on the Niagara frontier, to participate in the founding of a "City of Refuge" for the Jews and named September 15, 1825, as the day for the great event.

With his devoted friend, A. B. Seixas, he made elaborate preparations for the ceremonies. Unfortunately, however, Grand Island proved not accessible for the event. Noah therefore chose the nearest available place — Buffalo. In 1825, Buffalo was a small settlement of some 2,500 people, hardly more than a growing frontier village in Indian territory. Noah had a single acquaintance there, the Reverend Addison Searle, who was settled as the clergyman of the little Episcopal Church of St. Paul. He prevailed upon him to lend his church for the ceremony as the most available meeting place for a large assembly in Buffalo. When the eventful day arrived, Noah was on hand bedecked in a self-designed uniform of ermine and silk, which was a glorious combination of judicial and regal splendor. He was by no means discouraged because no Jews had appeared to take part in the ceremony. His plans did not make their presence a necessity so long as his fellow Masons loyally turned out for a procession, made colorful by their full regalia, before crowds of onlookers to applaud the Major, the self-appointed Judge of Israel, the cynosure of all eyes.

First there came the great parade through the town:

Grand Marshall, Col. Potter on horseback
Music
Military
Citizens
Civil Officers
United States Officers
State Officers in Uniform

President and Trustees of the Corporation
Tyler
Stewards
Entered Apprentices
Fellow Crafts
Master Masons
Senior and Junior Deacons
Secretary and Treasurer
Senior and Junior Wardens
Masters of Lodges
Past Masters
Rev. Clergy
Stewards, with corn, wine and oil

Globe { Principal Architect with square, level and plumb Bible } Globe

Square and Compass borne by a Master Mason
The Judge of Israel [Noah himself]
In black, wearing the judicial robes of crimson silk,
trimmed with ermine and a richly embossed golden
medal suspended from the neck.
A Master Mason
Royal Arch Masons
Knight Templars

Into the church they crowded to the strains of the Grand
March from *Judas Maccabeus*. The first sight to attract
attention as one entered that edifice was a large stone,
from the sandstone quarries at Cleveland, standing on the
communion table — a stone destined to be the cornerstone
of Ararat inscribed:

"Hear O Israel, the Lord is our God — The Lord is one."
ARARAT
A City of Refuge for the Jews
Founded by Mordecai Manuel Noah,

in the month Tizri, 5586, Sept. 1825 & in the 50th year of
American Independence."

The church ceremonies were opened by the Reverend
Mr. Searle reading the Episcopal morning service. Then
Noah arose and delivered an address, a sort of Jewish
Declaration of Independence, a mélange of religion, idealism,
politics, history, patriotism, boastfulness, real estate and
theatrical nonsense. He called on all the Jews to gather
together in a

> land of milk and honey where Israel may repose in
> peace under his "vine and fig tree" and where our
> people may so familiarize themselves with the science
> of government and the lights of learning and civiliza-
> tion as may qualify them for that grand and final
> restoration to their ancient heritage, which the times
> so powerfully indicate.

He then went on to expound the attractions of the state
of New York, and of Grand Island in particular, as a site
for a City of Refuge to which both Jews and others "of
every religious denomination" were invited to foregather
and there dwell in peace and happiness. He continued a
long rambling talk covering such widely diverse topics as
the Indians being the lost tribes of Israel and the necessity
of neutrality in the impending war between the Greeks and
Turks, the abolition of polygamy among the Jews of Africa
and Asia and the desirability of charity, goodwill, toleration
and liberality amongst all the brethren of every religious
denomination.

Then, in the crowded little Episcopal Church of Buffalo,
Noah proceeded with great formalities and Masonic ritual
to lay the cornerstone of Ararat — upon the communion
table. The Chronicler then relates: "The ceremonial, with

its procession 'Masonic and Military,' its pomp and magnif-
icence, passed away." Major Noah had had his day. This
was the beginning and end of Ararat.

Without ever setting foot on Grand Island, the Major
returned to his home in New York, from which he caused a
"Proclamation to the Jews" to be issued to the world and
widely circulated, announcing the great achievement of the
establishment of Ararat:

> I, Mordecai Manuel Noah, Citizen of the United
> States of America, late Consul of said States for
> the City and Kingdom of Tunis, High Sheriff of New
> York, Counsellor at Law, and, by the grace of God,
> Governor and Judge of Israel, have issued this my
> proclamation, announcing to the Jews throughout the
> World that an asylum is prepared and hereby offered
> to them, where they can enjoy that peace, comfort
> and happiness, which have been denied them, through
> the intolerance and misgovernment of former ages.
>
> In His name do I revive, renew and re-establish
> the Government of the Jewish Nation, under the
> auspices and protection of the constitution and laws
> of the United States of America, confirming and per-
> petuating all our rights and privileges, our name, our
> rank, and our power among the nations of the earth
> as they existed and were recognized under the govern-
> ment of the Judges. And I hereby enjoin it upon
> all our pious and venerable Rabbis, our presidents
> and Elders of Synagogues, Chiefs of Colleges, and
> Brethren in authority throughout the world, to
> circulate and make known this my proclamation,
> and give it full publicity, credence and effect.

After repeating much of Noah's dedicatory address, the
proclamation proceeded to decree a census to be taken of
the Jews of the world and established a "capitation tax of

three shekels in silver per annum" on each Jew, to defray
the expense of reorganizing the government and of aiding
emigrants to establish themselves in Ararat. The Governor
and Judge of Israel appointed as his commissioners to carry
into effect the provisions of his proclamation some of the
most distinguished Jewish leaders of Europe:

> The most learned and pious Abraham de Cologna,
> Knight of the Iron Crown of Lombardy, Grand Rabbi
> of the Jews, and President of the Consistory at
> Paris; likewise the Grand Rabbi Andrade of Bor-
> deaux; and also our learned and esteemed Grand
> Rabbis of the German and Portugal Jews, in London,
> Rabbis Herschell and Mendola, together with the
> Honorable Aaron Nunez Cardoza, of Gibraltar,
> Abraham Busnac, of Leghorn, Benjamin Gradis, of
> Bordeaux, Dr. E. Gans and Professor Zunz, of
> Berlin, and Dr. Leo Woolf of Hamburgh.

No sooner had Noah departed from Buffalo than the
"cornerstone" was removed from the church and deposited
against its rear wall outside. There it remained exposed
to the weather, a thing of curiosity, never to reach its
destination on Grand Island. Finally it has come to a
resting place in a glass showcase of the Buffalo Historical
Society.[3]

Promptly, as soon as they learned of his assumption of
authority, the learned rabbis and leaders of Europe not
only repudiated his self-appointed leadership and his
scheme but some even went so far as to denounce him as a
charlatan.

After the tumult and the shouting had died and the
pageant had faded away, Noah went serenely on his busy
way, too much preoccupied with newer affairs again to give

an hour to the realization of his promises and his pre-
dictions of the salvation of Israel through a City of Refuge.

So, out of a vanished past, Ararat survives only as a dim
memory, an American legend of long ago, dream, comedy
and tragedy.

His talented biographer, Isaac Goldberg, sums up the
story:

> It is interesting that, though the futility, the
> vanity, the self-seeking of Noah's "Ararat" have
> not been forgotten, his position in the history of
> Jewish self-determination is on the whole a highly
> honored one. The intention has been taken for the
> achievement. He emerges as an eccentric, surely,
> but none the less as an important pioneer in the
> story of Zionistic endeavor. If his descendants in
> the struggle for a Jewish homeland cannot honor his
> head, they do all honor to his heart.[4]

Today, as the traveler speeds on his way from Buffalo
to Niagara Falls over the magnificent bridges and highways
which cross Grand Island, he cannot but speculate — what
if this dream of Noah's had come true? What if, after that
September day of 1825, to this fair island had come a
stream of liberty-seeking Jewish settlers from old world
ghettos? Would Jewish history have been changed? Would
our beloved America have been a richer land by enlarged
contributions of Jewish learning and culture?

"For of all sad words of tongue and pen,
  The saddest are these: 'It might have been!'"

10

THE DEDICATION OF MASSACHUSETTS' FIRST SYNAGOGUE

A HUNDRED years ago, in 1842, just three hundred and fifty years after the first Jew had landed on American soil, when John Tyler was President of the United States and the great Daniel Webster his Secretary of State, Boston was a growing city of 80,000, beginning to take on the ways of a metropolis. An English visitor of that day wrote:

> The general aspect of the city, as you approach it by land or by sea, is imposing, for the rising slopes of the buildings, the numerous steeples of the churches, and the crowning dome of the lofty State House, which stands on the highest ridge of the city, is rendered strikingly prominent in every view of the picture and forms a most appropriate, beautiful elevation in the center of the whole.

In striking contrast to most American cities, Boston was becoming famous and excited envious comment for its clean streets, "well paved, well lighted, swept and drained free from mud and dust," lined by stores or dwellings well built and carefully maintained with but few vacancies. Fed by a constant influx of eager youth drawn from neighboring small towns and surrounding farms, it was still a homogeneous community of alert and energetic Yankees. Its 1842 directory, politely segregating in a separate appendix its resident "people of color," presented a long roster of names with a remarkable predominance of scriptural and markedly Hebrew-Christian names with a good New England twang. There were but few indicating foreign origin.

Boston enterprise was building its neighboring territory into new industrial and manufacturing centers. It had just completed the Boston and Albany, or Western Railroad, as it was then called, so as to be a step ahead of other eastern cities in affording access to the midwest into which the sons and money of New England were pouring, opening up that promising territory and spreading the seeds of its sturdy anti-slavery faith.

While visitors remarked that the commerce of Boston had ceased to be so extensive or so varied as that of New York, still its great merchants appeared "more substantially opulent, and their operations were on a larger and more comprehensive scale." Its shipping overshadowed all its other commercial activities; and its fast clipper ships sailed the seven seas and made its Yankee traders famous throughout the world. Boston numbered twenty-nine banks, was the home of twenty-eight insurance companies and was not only a busy retail center but the wholesale market of New England and the West.

In 1842 New England had been, on the whole, almost untouched by the immigration which came to America during the post-Revolutionary era. The famines in Ireland, which were soon to send so many of its sons and daughters to settle in Boston, were still in the future. If you ventured on Boston streets you saw a crowd of men and women, rather above middle stature, pale and thin, well dressed, without foppery, remarkably neat, of a serious countenance, pursuing their unhurried way with dignity.

Jewish history in Boston began in 1649, when the prospect of a Jew settling in the nineteen-year-old town so alarmed its pious citizens that they offered a substantial bribe to induce Salomon Franco to depart. From that day, although Jews had made Boston their home, their number was small and, as they learned of better opportunities or greater hospitality elsewhere, they had deserted Boston. German Jewish immigration to America had never been attracted to New England.

In 1840 the Damascus ritual-murder accusation, and the attendant crass cruelty and persecution to which the Jews had been subjected, had not only stirred the Jewish communities of the world but had shocked all Christendom. As a repercussion to meetings held in New York and Philadelphia, calling American attention to these outrages against the Jews, there were reverberations in the missionary circles of Boston. A meeting was held on September 21, 1840, at the Clarendon Street Chapel, "to take into consideration the condition of the Jewish nation as respects both their present and future welfare," and resolutions were unanimously passed. These, after piously expressing hopes and plans for the conversion of Jews to Christianity, culminated in a resolution to extend an invitation

> to the suffering Jews of other nations, to come to this country, and would now particularly invite them to our city, where we presume they might do as well as in other cities in the world, though at present we have very few with us.[1]

Although the resolutions were directed to be well advertised, evidently they attracted little Jewish attention. So, as we approach the year 1842, the number of Jews living in Boston was still small, many of them only recent newcomers, almost all of them young men and women then just beginning in a modest fashion to make a place for themselves in its busy community life.

From time immemorial Jewish communities date their beginning from the dates on which they established their first *minyan*, that coming together of at least ten men to join in the practice of their religion. In earlier days Boston Jews had gone to Newport, New York, or to Albany for a rabbi to officiate at marriages or burials, and often they journeyed to those cities to join their brethren in services for the high holidays. As early as 1703–4, Judge Sewall records in his dairy: "Joseph Frazon, the Jew, dyes at Mr. Majors . . . Satterday, is carried in Simson's coach to Bristow, from thence by water to Newport where there is a Jews-burying place."

The Boston of 1842 was conspicuously a religious city. It had sixty-eight churches, one for every twelve hundred of its inhabitants. These were still the center of the social life of the people. When, in that year, Charles Dickens landed in Boston on a beautiful wintry Sunday morning, he writes:

> I am afraid to say, by the way, how many offers of pews and seats in church for that morning were made to us, by formal note of invitation, before we had half finished our first dinner in America, but if I may by allowed to make a moderate guess, without going into nicer calculations, I should say that at least as many sittings were proffered us, as would have accommodated a score or two of grown families. The number of creeds and forms of religion to which the pleasure of our company was requested, was in very fair proportions.

Indeed, just at this time, Boston was the center of a new religious excitement which had gripped New England and western New York with such high emotionalism that one read almost daily reports of persons driven insane by the strain. With militant zeal, a sect called "Millerites" were prophesying the first resurrection and day of judgment to take place in April 1843. Already they were erecting a great Millerite Tabernacle in Boston which, in fact, was only finished in May 1844. In the meantime their leaders from time to time postponed the millennium to farther and future dates.

The Catholics had already established four places of worship in Boston. In such an atmosphere it is most probable that from time to time, as opportunity offered, the Boston Jews had been in the habit of coming together for sporadic religious observances. It is, therefore, not surprising that in the religious atmosphere of the day, in 1842, a little group of eighteen families of Boston Jews was moved to establish a Jewish congregation. Repeated in many other American cities from the Atlantic to the Pacific, what was done in Boston, with changed names and dates, is but the story of the founding of many another American synagogue. Thus, as immigrant Jews came to realize that they had at last found a home for themselves in this new land, they testified to their sense of permanence by establishing a temple for their most precious heritage.

In 1842,[2] as the Jewish New Year approached, a meeting was held at 5 Wendell Street, on Fort Hill, to arrange for holiday services. This had been the home of the Oliver Wendell Holmes family and was then occupied by several families, one of which was Peter Spitz's, a cap maker. Amongst those assembled at Peter Spitz's were the proprietor of the

Railroad Hotel on Church Street, William Goldsmith; his
assistant, Bernard Fox; Hyman Spitz, associated with
Peter; Jacob Norton, a furrier and hat presser; Abraham
F. Block, a manufacturer and dealer in soap; Isaac Wolf, a
peddler; Charles Heineman, a peddler; and Moses Ehrlich,
in the dry goods business on Washington Street, together
with others whose names have not come down to us. They
arranged both for services for the coming holidays and for
continuing to come together for weekly religious services.
Thus was organized Boston's first Jewish institution,
originally called *Oheb Shalom* (which they translated
"Friends of Peace"), to assume more formal organization the following February. Then Moses Ehrlich was
chosen its first president and William Goldsmith, vice
president. They were soon joined by others: Levi Ondkerk,
dealer in laces (1843), Samuel Rosenberg, peddler (1843),
Julius Bornstein, cap maker (1845), and Alexander Saroni,
cap maker (1846).

In Boston's religious circles this organization, so important to these modest citizens, created not a ripple in
the busy life of the city. Even as late as 1846, in the list
of churches and ministers published in the Boston directory,
they were ignored. The community was too excited over
politics to have its attention distracted from the attack
upon its favorite son. Daniel Webster, as Secretary of
State, had just negotiated a treaty with Great Britain,
which the foes of the administration claimed "had sold the
United States down the river." To give an opportunity to
their Whig hero to justify himself and the new treaty and
overwhelm his detractors, a committee of prominent leaders
in the city, this holiday season, was engaging Faneuil Hall
to tender him a public reception.

It is said that one Bernard Wurmsar, keeper of a variety store, who first came to Boston in 1846, temporarily acted as the first rabbi for the little group. Shortly thereafter they were able to secure Abraham Saling to act as rabbi. In default of better accommodations, Saling's house on Carver Street became the congregational headquarters.

How unpretentious was the small congregation may be gathered from a description contained in a letter published September 23, 1844, by the Reverend E. M. P. Wells of the Episcopal City Mission Chapel, in the *Boston Mercantile Journal*. He tells of his surprise in learning that there was a synagogue in Boston, when invited by "a son of Abraham" to accompany him there to witness the "feast of trumpets." He found it "an upper room," "not a comfortable or decent place for the performance of that service which thousands of years ago swelled through the arches of Solomon's Temple." He reported that, "the service was performed with more solemnity, earnestness and apparent devotion than I have seen in a far better synagogue. I was surprised that so many (there were about forty present) could read the Hebrew so fluently and in most cases with a good degree of understanding, as apparent from their manner. Every man took a part in their service, and there was far more voice used than is often heard in the beautiful responsive service at Trinity or St. Pauls." Told that there were no rich men among the members of this synagogue, the reverend gentleman appealed to his fellow Bostonians "if we cannot in some way aid them to a synagogue." "Is there no one in Boston of whom the Jews shall hereafter say with gratitude, as they did of old, 'He loveth our nation and hath built us a synagogue'?"[3]

In 1844 the congregation received its first public recognition when it was granted by the city the privilege of establishing a cemetery in East Boston. A petition had been first presented to the City Council, April 29, 1844, asking that to them, as "Trustees of a religious society of the Israelitish denomination," there might be appropriated, for the exclusive use of this society, a piece of ground of one hundred square feet in one corner of the East Boston City cemetery. There was opposition to the petition. Possibly the ancestors of George Appleby and of H. M. Pulham, Esq. felt called upon patriotically to defend the land of their birth. Who had ever heard of a Jewish burying ground in Massachusetts?[4] The spirit of "Know-Nothingism" was still rife in Boston. Was there fear that, even from a cemetery located in suburban East Boston, Jewish corpses might disturb the sanctity of the soil old Puritan ancestors had cultivated? So the city fathers denied this petition. But the petitioners persisted and filed a second petition showing that they had themselves arranged to purchase a plot of land, asking the right to establish a cemetery there. On July 25th, the City Council was induced to allow the new petition. On the same day title was taken to a plot of land in East Boston for the burial ground.

In the following year (March 22, 1845), having officially forty members, the congregation obtained a charter from the state as a religious corporation calling itself, not *Oheb Shalom*, but *Ohabei Shalom* (Lovers of Peace), with authority "to hold and manage estate, real and personal, to an amount not exceeding ten thousand dollars which shall be applied to the payment of the debts of the corporation and to the support of public worship."

As an offshoot of the Congregation, in 1847, were organized Boston's two earliest Jewish societies: The Hebrew

Literary Society of Boston and The Ladies' Hebrew Benevolent Society. By 1854 they had as auxiliary societies The Brotherly Love Society and The Sisterly Love Society.

So satisfactory was the progress of *Ohabei Shalom* that, in 1849, under the leadership of J. W. Ezekiel, lately come to Boston from Philadelphia, a group formed a second congregation for Polish Jews, *Beth Israel*. That year, under Rabbi P. Rosendale from New York, it held holiday services in a hall over the Boylston Market on Washington Street. They claimed a hundred members. Inasmuch as the best estimate is that there were probably not more than 125 Jewish families living in Boston in 1851, this number is obviously exaggerated. *Beth Israel* had only a very brief existence.

Up to 1851 *Ohabei Shalom* held its services in a large room in Washington Street. It was then estimated that there were at least a hundred and twenty-five Jewish families in Boston, "who, though mostly in moderate circumstances, are able to support themselves; and if we understood aright, there are few or none, either here or in other northern towns, who require charity for their support."[5]

By 1851, *Ohabei Shalom*, now grown to "eighty male members and their families," felt itself sufficiently prosperous to invest $3,417.23 in the purchase of a plot of land on Warren (now Warrenton) Street and to plan the erection of what was to be, in the pious phrase of the day, Boston's first "Israelitish Synagogue." Many of their Christian neighbors showed their interest in the project by generous subscriptions. This contribution by Christians to help a synagogue was not the first of its kind in America. In 1788, the congregation *Mikveh Israel* of Philadelphia had found itself in financial straits because "many of their number at the close of the late war returned to New York, Charleston and elsewhere, leaving their homes (which they had been exiled from and obliged to leave on account of their attachment to American measures), leaving the remaining few of their religion here, burthen'd with a considerable charge consequent from so great an undertaking." An appeal by the congregation addressed to its "worthy fellow citizens of every Religious Denomination" was answered, amongst other subscribers, by Benjamin Franklin £5, David Rittenhouse (the famous astronomer) £2, and William Bradford (the printer) £3.[6] Again in 1843, when the Jews of Montreal (a German and Polish congregation) proposed to erect a synagogue, Sir Charles Metcalf, Governor General of Canada, gave £10 towards the building.[7]

On the other hand, when, in 1711, Trinity Church, New York, built a steeple, seven New York Jews contributed £5.12.3 out of a total of £312.13.7 then raised.[8] Then, too, the story of Judah Touro, the philanthropist, coming to the rescue of a Christian Church by purchasing its building and permitting the congregation to occupy it rent free for years, is an oft-told tale of New Orleans' history.[9]

A total fund exceeding $7,000 was thus raised by the little Boston group, and slowly they proceeded to the actual building of a Temple.

By spring, Samuel Jepson, the South Margin Street carpenter, had completed the building, and the modest wooden structure was ready for its congregation.

On the day of its dedication an enthusiastic local newspaper reporter wrote, as for the first time he saw a Jewish synagogue:

The lot upon which it stands is 35 feet by 75 deep. The building itself is 46 by 30 feet. It ranges east and west. In the rear of the place of worship is a room used as a schoolroom in which every afternoon the children of the congregation are instructed in the Hebrew and German languages. Over this is another room, in which the Trustees who manage the affairs of the Congregation hold their meetings. There are about 30 children who attend this school regularly.

The portion of the building appropriated for public worship will seat about 400 persons. It is finished in a very neat but plain manner. In the east end is the ark, in which are deposited the Sacred Scrolls of the law. This ark is in the form of a large case, 8 feet by 12 feet 8 inches high. The inside is lined with blue silk. It is closed by sliding doors in front of which, and hiding them from view, are richly wrought curtains. On the top of the ark, engraven in gilt letters in Hebrew upon a white marble slab are the ten Commandments. Several varieties of choice flowers in pots also ornamented the top of the ark.

Directly in front of the ark is a small desk, upon which is placed a copy of the Scriptures. There is then a passageway of 3 or 4 ft. and then a stand raised some 2 ft. from the floor, on which the minister stands with his face to the east and chants the Psalms used in the service. At the four corners of this stand, as well as at the corners of the balustrade in front of the ark are large gas lamps in imitation of candles, which are kept burning during service.

Friday, March 26, 1852, the ceremony of dedication was held. About half past three in the afternoon there gathered in the body of the synagogue a goodly assembly, headed by His Honor Benjamin Seaver, Mayor of Boston, members of the City Government and Boston's leading clergymen, amongst whom was the illustrious Theodore Parker. Then in marched the trustees of the congregation: Moses Ehrlich, Alexander S. Saroni, L. Ondkerk, Charles Heineman, B. Fox, A. Price and J. Bornstein, with Rabbis Strouss and Morris J. Raphall and Ansel Leo. The two latter rabbis were of the New York congregation, *B'nai Jeshurun*, which had not only lent its rabbis to grace the occasion but also its *Sefer Torah* (scroll).

Our Christian reporter found the services of dedication, "though novel," "of an interesting character." The program of exercises is a modest outline of the proceedings.

> The Rev. Dr. Raphall, followed by the Trustees and past officers of the Congregation, bring the sacred scrolls of the Law to the door of Synagogue, where, standing under a Canopy, he exclaimed:
> > Open unto us the gates of righteousness, we will enter them, and praise the Lord.
> The doors being opened, the Rabbi Preacher and the Readers enter in procession with the scrolls, saying:
> > How goodly are thy tents, O Jacob! Thy tabernacles O Israel!
> > O Lord! I have ever loved the habitation of thy house, and the dwelling place of thy glory.
> > We will come into thy tabernacles, and worship at thy footstool.

READER

> Enter into his gates with thanksgiving, into his court with praise
> Come let us worship and bow down, let us bend the knee before the Lord our maker.
> Worship the Lord with gladness, come into his presence with exulting sound.

CONGREGATION

Come, let us sing unto the Lord, sing aloud
to the Rock of our salvation, Let us approach his presence with thanksgiving, and
sing joyful hymns unto him.
Blessed be he who cometh in the name of
the Lord; we bless ye from the house of
the Lord.

Then, led by the three rabbis, the Rev. Dr. Raphall,
assisted by the Rev. Strouss and the Rev. Ansel Leo, a
procession of members, "proceeds to circumambulate the
Synagogue seven times." During each circuit a different
psalm was chanted by one of the rabbis and the congregation. After the seventh march, the sacred scrolls were
placed in the ark by Rabbi Leo, who chanted the age old
wish: "May the Lord grant power unto his people; the
Lord bless his people with peace."

Then the Reverend Rabbi Raphall preached the dedication sermon on the text, "How lovely are Thy tabernacles,
O Lord of Hosts." This sermon, preached in English, was
for the time an unusual departure from the customary
service. After expressions of congratulation on the occasion
which had brought them together, the rabbi proceeded to
expound the meaning of the command, "They shall prepare
Me a sanctuary." He pointed out that it was the duty of
the members of the synagogue to "do justice, love mercy,
and walk humbly before God." He closed by imploring
the divine blessing upon the building, the congregation and
all assembled there, upon our country, and its rulers.

The Jews of Boston thus dedicated their first synagogue.[10]

ISRAELITISH SYNAGOGUE,

WARREN STREET.

This building, which was erected in 1851, is a small wooden structure, tastefully decorated and pleasing in its appearance. It will seat about 500 persons, and has connected with it, rooms for a school and for business meetings of the trustees of the society, and for other purposes. There are, also, in the rear, bathing rooms for the females of the society, after the ancient customs of the Israelites. The galleries of the church are set aside for the use of the females of the congregation, the body of the church being occupied exclusively by the males.

The Synagogue of Israelites were first organized in Boston in 1843, and consisted at that time of ten members with their families. There are at the present time belonging to the society about 120 families. The name which the Synagogue adopts, and by which they are incorporated, is " Ohebei Shalom," which being interpreted is, " Friends of Peace."

Connected with the Church is a school for their children, where they are taught in the ancient Hebrew as well as in the English language.

There are, also, two charitable associations made up of members of this Synagogue, the one for males and the other for females.

The services in their church are all conducted in the Hebrew language, and with all the ancient forms and ceremonies. They have the five books of Moses written on parchment, from which their Rabbi reads as part of their Sabbath service. At the present time the Rev. Joseph Sachs officiates as their religious instructor, and also as teacher of their children in the Hebrew tongue. They give him the ancient title of Rabbi. Their Sabbath commences on Friday at Sundown, and ends at the corresponding hour on Saturday. Their numbers are quite rapidly increasing. They have a burial ground at East Boston.

Boston's First Synagogue

There they worshipped until 1863, when the needs of a growing community demanded larger quarters. *The Boston Herald* of February 8 of that year announced:

> A Church to be Converted into a Synagogue.
> The first Hebrew Congregation (*Ohabei Shalom*) worshipping in Warren Street have purchased the Church of the First Universalist Society in Warren Street, which will in the course of next summer be altered to adapt it to the worship of the Israelites' ritual.

There the Congregation prospered. In 1861, an anonymous writer, commenting that the number of Jews in Boston was "quite rapidly increasing," describes the Congregation as "Polish Jews" under the leadership of Rabbi B. E. Jacobs. He describes the synagogue as "tastefully decorated," seating about five hundred persons, and having "in the rear, bathing rooms for the females of the society, after the ancient customs of the Israelites." He tells us that there was maintained "a school for their children where they are taught in the ancient Hebrew as well as in the English language." "There are, also, two charitable associations made up of members of this synagogue, one for males and the other for females."

FIGHTERS FOR PRINCIPLE

11

ASSER LEVY VAN SWELLEM

JACOB BARSIMSON, one of a party of emigrants from Holland sent by the Dutch West India Company in the vessel *The Peartree* (*de Pereboom*), landed in New Amsterdam on August 22, 1654, to become New York's first Jewish settler.

At the time Jacob Barsimson was disembarking at New Amsterdam, a little ship, *The St. Charles*, after a narrow escape from pirates, was making its slow, uncertain way towards the same port. The following month it reached its destination with twenty-three Jewish passengers who had fled from Brazil after the Dutch had turned that territory back to its old Portuguese masters.

A more distinguished immigrant than these Jews had but recently been welcomed in New Amsterdam. This was Dominie Johannes Theodorus Polheymus, sent by the Classis of the Dutch Reformed Church of Amsterdam to join the Reverend Johannes Megapolensis in caring for the souls of the growing colony of New Netherlands. Consequently, when winter was past and shipping afforded an opportunity for Dominie Megapolensis to submit his report to his church authorities, thanking them for the addition of a "good clergy-man," his sentiments were divided between gratitude to the "Lords-Directors of the Dutch West India Company and your Reverences" and alarm over this influx of Jews of which he felt in duty bound to complain:

Some Jews came from Holland last summer, in order to trade. Later a few Jews came upon the same ship as De Polheymus; they were healthy but poor ... Some of them have come from Holland this spring. They report that still more of the same lot would follow, and then they would build here a synagogue.

He then proceeded to point out that it was bad enough to have "servants of Baal" concealed under the name of Christians, without allowing "obstinate and immovable Jews come to settle here."

The good Dominie was not the only one disturbed over the prospect of having those who did not share his religious views live in the colony. The testy old governor-general, Peter Stuyvesant, undertook personally and officially to give vent to his prejudice. When the Jews refused to be persuaded by him that there was no room for them on Manhattan Island, he immediately (September 22, 1654) petitioned the directors of the Dutch West India Company for authority to expel them:

The Jews who have arrived would nearly all like to remain here, but learning that they (with their customary usury and deceitful trading with the Christians) were very repugnant to the inferior magistrates, as also to the people having the most affection for you; the Deaconry also fearing that owing to their present indigence they might become a charge in the coming winter, we have, for the benefit of this weak and newly developing place and the land in general, deemed it useful to require them in a friendly way to depart; praying also most seriously in this connection, for ourselves as also for the general community of your worships, that the deceitful race — such hateful enemies and blasphemers of the name of Christ — be not

allowed further to infect and trouble this new colony,
to the detraction of your worships and the dissatisfac-
tion of your worships' most affectionate subjects.

This was soon (March 1, 1655) seconded by the action of
the magistrate of the town:

> Fiscal van Tienhoven informed the Burgomaster
> and Schepens, the Director General and Supreme
> Council have resolved that the Jews who came last
> year from the West Indies and now from the Father-
> land, must prepare to depart forthwith, and that they
> shall receive notice thereof, and asked whether Burgo-
> masters and Schepens had anything to object thereto.
> It was decided No, but that the resolution relating
> thereto should take its course.

Alarmed at this prospect of expulsion, the Jews of New
Amsterdam had appealed to their brethren in old Amsterdam
to intercede in their behalf with the directors of the Company. Accordingly a petition in their behalf was presented.
It asked why Jews, Dutch subjects, who had resided and
been settled in Holland for years, many of whom were
burghers, should be excluded from the privilege of emigrat-
ing. It called attention to the fact that the French and
English allowed Jews to emigrate to their colonies and
pointed out that Jews were large stockholders in the Company and had stood by it even when things had not gone
well. It urged that transportation be not refused to Jews
to a country where land was extensive and spacious and
where the greater the population the better the chances for
success.

Under date of April 26, 1655, the official answer was made
from Amsterdam by the directors of the Dutch West India
Company to Peter Stuyvesant:

We would have liked to effectuate and fulfill your wishes and request that the new territories should no more be allowed to be infected by people of the Jewish nation, for we foresee therefrom the same difficulties which you fear, but after having further weighed and considered the matter, we observe that this would be somewhat unreasonable and unfair, especially because of the considerable loss sustained by this nation, with others, in the taking of Brazil, as also because of the large amount of capital which they still have invested in the shares of this company. Therefore after many deliberations we have finally decided and resolved to apostille upon a certain petition presented by said Portuguese Jews that these people may travel and trade to and in New Netherland and live and remain there, provided the poor among them shall not become a burden to the company or to the community, but be supported by their own nation. You will now govern yourself accordingly.

Still unconvinced, Stuyvesant argued to his masters:

To give liberty to the Jews will be very detrimental there, because the Christians there will not be able at the same time to do business. Giving them liberty, we cannot refuse the Lutherans and Papists.

To this the directors replied with a curtness which closed the discussion:

The consent given to the Jews to go to New Netherland and there to enjoy the same liberty that is granted them in this country was extended with respect to civil and political liberties, without the said Jews becoming thereby entitled to a license to exercise and carry on their religion in synagogues or gatherings. So long, therefore, as no request is presented to you to allow such a free exercise of religion, any consideration relative thereto is too premature, and when later something shall be presented about it, you will be doing well to refer the matter to us in order to await thereon the necessary orders.

Either among the "healthy but poor" Jewish passengers who arrived with Dominie Polheymus or arriving at that time from another vessel fleeing from Brazil, was Asser Levy van Swellem, a native of Amsterdam.

As soon as the controversy over the right of Jews to dwell unmolested and to pursue their lawful occupations in their new home had been settled by the directors, Asser resolved to perform the duties of a burgher and to claim burgher rights. He objected to the discriminatory tax which was levied upon Jews as a compulsory substitute for the customary military service exacted from all other inhabitants. Accordingly, on November 5, 1655, together with Jacob Barsimson, he proceeded to petition for the right to stand guard in defense of the town, like other burghers. They met with a prompt refusal and were further informed that, if they thought this denial was injurious, permission was granted "to depart whenever and whither it please them."

Not to be discouraged, Asser proceeded to perform his military duties. Apparently his services were accepted, for he presented a second petition to the Court of Burgomasters and Schepens (April 9, 1657) to the effect that, since now he had kept watch and ward (*tocht en wacht*) in common with other burghers, he requested to be admitted a burgher, representing that he had been a burgher in Amsterdam. Again the court denied his request. This time, however, the opportunity was left open for him to appeal to the Director-General and Council of the colony. They allowed his appeal and he was admitted a burgher. Thus Jews first won full rights of citizenship in New York.

In the meantime, Asser had established himself as a trader. In those days trading with Indians for furs was the "big business" of the community. He soon extended his activities into regions as distant as Albany (Fort Orange), much to the dislike of its local traders. They tried to stop him; and when he still persisted, they appealed to the authorities in Holland to cut off his competition. The Amsterdam authorities seemed to be sympathetic to the objectors. Asser, however, forestalled any adverse action from them by bringing in the local authorities to keep the trade open to all alike. Thus Asser and his associates finally established the rights of free trade throughout the colony.

By this time Levy had gained sufficient standing to be selected by the New Amsterdam authorities one of six licensed butchers for the community. He took "the oath that Jews are accustomed to take" and was expressly excused from killing hogs, on account of his religion. Later, in 1678, he was granted leave to build a slaughterhouse at the east end of Wall Street, which became known as the Broadway Shambles.

In 1662 Levy acquired an estate on William Street and thus became the first Jewish real-estate owner in New York, if not the first such in the United States. Later he also owned a celebrated tavern near his slaughterhouse. He also acquired land in Albany. On the whole Asser Levy prospered and won for himself a recognized position in the Dutch community, so that in 1664 he was rated amongst "the wealthiest inhabitants" who were called upon to confer with the burgomaster and Schepens respecting the rebuilding of the defenses of the city. For that purpose he advanced one hundred florins to the authorities.

Asser had now won for himself an assured standing in the community and, like a good citizen, took upon himself many neighborly duties for Christian and Jew alike. In 1673 the court called upon him to act as custodian of the merchandise over which two of his Christian neighbors were in litigation. On occasions he acted as executor for Christian friends. In 1671, when the Lutherans built their first church, he advanced them the funds.

Once, when a Jew, who had been fined for Sabbath-breaking by the Connecticut authorities, appealed to Asser to intervene in his behalf with the magistrates, it is recorded that on his application the court abated the fine of five pounds "as a token of their respect to the said Asser Levy."

When the English succeeded the Dutch and New Netherland became New York, Levy was one of those who, in 1664, took the oath of allegiance to the king of England. Asser Levy died in 1680, leaving what was for the times a substantial estate (£553) of which his wife, Maria, was administratrix. Unfortunately, his estate became involved in considerable litigation in the courts of New York. After his death it is supposed that his family removed to Long Island. A grandson, Asser Levy, served as an ensign in the first New Jersey regiment in the Revolutionary War.

On the whole, his is not a record particularly headlined by the ordinary writers of American history. It is, perhaps, too typical of the lives of many pioneers, Jew and Gentile, who shared in the small beginnings of our country. Still, Asser Levy stands out as a man of determination, a bold, energetic and resourceful adventurer and useful citizen whose life work made its small contribution to the upbuilding of a new continent. His was a career honorable and creditable to the individual and serviceable to his fellows, especially to his fellow Jews as a protagonist of Jewish rights and liberty in America. His efforts helped to lay the foundation for the abolition of the limitations imposed upon Jews by the civic authorities of a less tolerant age and forced the recognition of Jews in New York as human beings entitled to share, on the same basis as all others, in the common benefits and burdens of citizenship.

12

MR. HAYS SPEAKS OUT[1]

AS THE uprising against Great Britain progressed through the thirteen colonies into an organized rebellion, public opinion was by no means unanimous. All who were satisfied with the existing order of things — the government office holders, the clergy of the Established Church, substantial merchants, property owners and the prosperous aristocrats — made up a Tory party. As has been pointed out "the great majority of men could be regarded as indifferent, ready to stampede and rush along with the successful party; yet, even among the masses, this traditional love of kingship had to be reckoned with and combatted. Loyalty was the normal condition, the state that *had* existed, and *did* exist: and it was the Whigs — the Patriots, as they called themselves — who must do the converting, the changing of men's opinions to suit a new order of things which the revolutionists believed necessary for their own and their country's welfare."[2]

Until 1776 all shades of opinion continued to exist: moderate Whigs and extreme Whigs, moderate Tories and extreme Tories, with a large group on the borderline of indecision. Even the bloodshed of 1775 had not crystallized the issue. When first the Continental Congress assembled in 1776, leaders like Washington, Jefferson and Adams still clung to a hope of reconciliation.

From the radical Whig point of view the opposition was a combination of perverse enemies, described by Thomas Paine as "interested men who are not to be trusted, weak men who *cannot* see, prejudiced men who *will not* see, and a certain set of moderate men who think better of the European world than it deserves."[3]

So Sons of Liberty, Committees of Correspondence, Leagues, and kindred organizations were speedily organized to spread patriotic propaganda, to arouse enthusiasm for the Revolution and to terrorize the opposition. Threats, extravagant political abuse and even physical violence were the order of the day. Factional feeling ran high. Tory and Whig, patriot and loyalist, engaged in a constant partisan battle of intolerance, vilification and personal conflicts. Rumor and suspicion arrayed neighbor against neighbor.

With the spread of the revolt through the colonies, the Whigs seized control of the local governing bodies and organized and regulated social order in each community. The persecution of Tories as enemies of the popular cause then assumed an official character.

Even before the Declaration of Independence, in June 1776, the Rhode Island Assembly passed, if not the first, certainly one of the earliest acts requiring of its inhabitants an oath of loyalty to the Revolutionary cause.[4] It provided that any male inhabitants over sixteen years of age, "suspected of being inimical to the United American Colonies and the arduous struggle in which they are engaged against the force of Great Britain," might be haled before a member of the Assembly and called upon to subscribe to a prescribed oath. The penalty for refusal was the issuing of a warrant authorizing a sheriff to search out and seize all arms, ammu-

nition and warlike stores of such person and turn them over
to the militia. The following July two additional acts were
adopted. The first punished, as guilty of a high misdemeanor
under penalty of a fine of £100, any person who acknowledged the King of Great Britain as sovereign. The second
took from "any male of twenty-one years, being an inhabitant or resident of this state," the right of petitioning the
Assembly for review or for a stay in a lawsuit, and also
deprived him of the right to vote in a town meeting until
the prescribed test had been subscribed. Actually, in practice, additional punishments were meted out by removing
a suspect from his residence to some designated town, there
to be detained under the supervision of local authorities.

No sooner had the first of these Acts been adopted than
a petition from Newport was presented to the Honorable
Metcalf Bowler, Speaker of the Lower House, by the officers
of the Rhode Island Brigade. It listed seventy-seven inhabitants of Newport suspected as "enemical to the United
Colonies in America" and requested that the Declaration
or Test ordered by the General Assembly be tendered to
these suspected persons. Amongst those named were four
Jews: Isaac Hart, "Parson Tororo Jew Priest," Moses M.
Hays, and Myer Pollock. A subpoena was issued to the
sheriffs to summon all the persons named to appear before
the Assembly on Friday, July 12th next.[5]

Already before this, the previous June, Moses M. Hays
had subscribed to the Test as follows:

> We, the subscribers, do solemnly and sincerely
> declare that we believe the War Resistance and oppo-
> sition in which the United American Colonies are now
> engaged against the fleets and armies of Great Britain
> is on the part of said Colonies just and necessary and

that we will not directly nor indirectly afford assistance of any sort or kind whatsoever to the said fleet
and armies during the continuance of the present
War, but that we will heartily assist in the defense of
the United Colonies.

1776, June, Session of Assembly, M. M. Hayes[6]

On July 11, 1776, four members of the General Assembly
met at the Colony House at Newport and tendered the
persons summoned to assemble there the Declaration and
Test in the above form. Of the Jews present, first "Rev. Mr.
Tororo[7] appeared and refused to sign the test as he has not
been naturalized and it's against his Religious Principles and
likewise he is a subject to the States of Holland." Then
Isaac Hart appeared and refused to sign the Test until it
was required from all alike. Myer Pollock refused to sign
because it was "contrary to the custom of Jews." When
Moses Michael Hays was called, the record proceeds:

He refused to sign the Test and called for his accusers. He was then told there was a number present
whom he there saw. He likewise called for his accusation which was read. I have and ever shall hold the
strongest principles and attachments to the just rights
and privileges of this my native land, and ever have
and shall conform to the rules and acts of this government and pay as I always have my proportion of its
exigencies. I always have asserted my sentiments in
favor of America and confess the War on its part just.
I decline subscribing the Test at present from these
principles first that I deny ever being inimical to my
country and call for my accusers and proof of conviction, Second that I am an Israelite and am not allowed
the liberty of a vote, or voice in common with the rest
of the voters though consistent with the Constitution,

and the other Colonies, Thirdly because the Test is
not general and consequently subject to many glaring
inconveniences, Fourthly, Continental Congress nor
the General Assembly of this nor the Legislatures of
the other Colonies have never in this contest taken
any notice or countenance respecting the society of
Israelites to which I belong. When any rule, order
or directions is made by the Congress or General
Assembly I shall to the utmost of my power adhere to
the same.[8]

So that there should be no error in recording his protest,
Hays wrote out what he had thus said and left with the
Assembly a signed copy of his refusal.

Evidently humiliated and smarting under the indignity
and injustice of having his loyalty thus challenged, and convinced that the hysteria of patriotism would destroy the
liberty of the individual, Hays was unwilling to let matters
drop with this. Showing initiative and independence, characteristics which were to prove so distinctive of his subsequent career, he demanded of the Assembly a further
investigation by presenting the following petition:

To the Honorable The General Assembly of Rhode
Island Now Sitting at New Port

Moses M. Hays of New Port, Begs leave humbly
to represent to your honors, that he hath ever been
warmly and Zealously attacht to the rights & Liberties of the colonies & ever uniformly conducted himself consistant with the rest of the Good & friendly
people of these colonies, & always despised inimicall
principles, & as farr as one person can testify for
another, numbers of creditable persons can testify.—
Yet on the 12th inst. was sighted by the sheriff to
appear at the court house on that same day at 2

o'clock in the afternoon when I attend'd accordingly,
& being called was informed by your honorable
speaker that an information had been lodged against
me among a number of persons of being inimicall to
the country (Mr. Sears, Mr. Fowler & Mr. Geo.
Wanton & some officers present). I denied & do still
deny holding or entertaining such principles, & desired
to know my accusers and accusations: — I was an-
swered by Mr. Bowlers reading a paper purporting to
be a complaint from the officers that there were many
suspected inimicall persons in town & naming them;
desired they might be called on.— And no other alle-
gations appearing against me I declined signing the
Test then for reasons I gave in writing, which will no
doubt be laid before your honors and trust they will
appear justifiable.

I ask of your Honors the Rights & Privileges due
other free citizens when I conform to everything
generally done & acted and again implore that the
justice of your Honors may interfer in my behalf and
will give me leave again to call for the cause and my
accusation of Inimicalty, that I may have an opportunity of vindication before your Honors. I am with
Great Respect

Your Honors most ob. & most h[ble] Serv[t]

New Port July 17, 1776   M. M. Hays"

So far as the records disclose, this ended the controversy.

It is perhaps superfluous to comment on this brave stand
which Hays took. It can well be compared to that historic
fight which Asser Levy had made in New Amsterdam, more
than a century before, for Jewish civic rights. Although,
like most of the Newport Jews, ardently attached to the
American Cause, he must have fully realized that in the
inflamed state of patriotic passions his public refusal to sub-

scribe to the Test was liable to misconstruction and exposed him to unpleasant consequences. However, his stand dramatically challenged those who with patriotic fervor were fighting in the name of liberty yet failed to live up to the enlightened standards of religious freedom and the right of personal liberty to which the founders of Rhode Island had dedicated the Rhode Island Colony.

In the ensuing years there was never again any question of Hays' patriotism. When, in November 1779, a list of fifty alleged Tories of Newport was again filed by the authorities with the General Assembly, his name was not among them. The only Jewish names which that list contained were Higham (Haim) Levi, Simeon Levi, Benjamin Myers (with the annotation "gone"), Isaac Elizer and son, Isaac Isaacs, and Ja(cob) Isaacs.[9]

At the time of his appearance before the Rhode Island Assembly, Hays was but an inconspicuous young man of thirty-seven. Born in 1739, son of a New York merchant, Judah Hays, he had started life as a watchmaker and had been admitted a freeman in New York in 1769. Moving to Newport around 1770, he set up a modest shop as a general merchant "on the Point near Holmes Wharf." He had gone through years of hard sledding. An entry in the Diary of the Reverend Ezra Stiles, under date of September 5, 1771, illustrates Hays' Jewish loyalty:

> I was told last week that Mr. Hayes, a Jew of Philad[a], was lately converted to Christianity, was baptized by Rev. Morgan Edwards & became a member of the Baptist Chh. at Philadelphia. Mr. Hays Brother lives here in Newport. Two days ago I asked him about it. He said he knew nothing of it, and did not believe it: and added, if his B[r] had become a

Xtian it was only to answer his ends, he was not sincere, for he never knew one sincere in changing his religion and becoming Christian — & added there were many convert Xtian Jews in Spain & Portugal — & that the Jew was spread among them all — & that it could be proved that the King of Spain or Portugal was of Jew Extract. But I suppose the thing is true; for Mr. Edwards is now here at Commencm^t at Providence, and told this story in Town last week. It is said that the other of Mr. Hays (the family lived in N. York) once became a Xtian but afterwards renounced Xtianity for Judaism.[10]

When later he moved to Boston, he attained wealth in the insurance business and a position of prominence in the community and lived much respected amongst his Yankee neighbors.[11] He became a prominent figure in Masonic circles, serving as Grand Master of the Grand Lodge of Masons of Massachusetts, with Paul Revere as Deputy Grand Master under him. The distinguished Unitarian Minister, Reverend Samuel J. May, has left a charming picture of Hays' domestic life:[12]

There was but one family of the despised children of the House of Israel resident in Boston — the family of Moses Michael Hays: a man much respected, not only on account of his large wealth, but for his many personal virtues and the high culture and great excellence of his wife, his son Judah, and his daughters — especially Catherine and Slowey. His house, far down in Hanover Street, then one of the fashionable streets of the town, was the abode of hospitality; and his family moved in what were then the first circles of society. He and his truly good wife were hospitable, not to the rich alone, but also to the poor. Many indigent families were fed pretty regularly from his table.

They would come especially after his frequent dinner parties, and were sure to be made welcome, not to the crumbs only, but to ampler portions of the food that might be left.

Always, on Saturday, he expected a number of friends to dine with him. A full-length table was always spread, and loaded with the luxuries of the season; and he loved to see it surrounded by a few regular visitors and others especially invited. My father was a favorite guest. He was regarded by Mr. Hays and his whole family as a particular friend, their chosen counsellor in times of perplexity, and their comforter in the days of their affliction. My father seldom failed to dine at Mr. Hays's on Saturday, and often took me with him; for he was sure I should meet refined company there.

Both Uncle and Aunt Hays (for so I called them) were fond of children, particularly of me; and I was permitted to stay with them several days, and even weeks, together. And I can never forget, not merely their kind, but their conscientious care of me. I was the child of Christian parents, and they took especial pains that I should lose nothing of religious training so long as I was permitted to abide with them. Every night, I was required, on going to bed, to repeat my Christian hymns and prayers to them, or else to an excellent Christian servant woman who lived with them many years. I witnessed their religious exercises — their fastings and their prayers — and was made to feel that they worshipped the Unseen Almighty and All-merciful One.

On the death of Hays, in 1805, the *Boston Centinel*, in publishing his obituary, wrote: "He walked abroad *fearing* no man, but *loving* all — He was without guile, detesting hypocrisy as he despised meanness! Take him for all in all, he was indeed a man."

Robert Treat Paine, Jr. of Boston, son of a signer of the Declaration of Independence, added his poetical tribute:

> Here sleep't thou, Man of Soul! Thy spirit flown,
> How dark and tenantless its desert clay!
>
> ———
>
> Alas! 'Tis all thou art whose vigorous mind
> Inspiring force to Truth and Feeling gave,
> Whose rich resources equal power combined,
> They gave to brighten and instruct the grave![13]

He was buried in the ancient Jewish cemetery in Newport. A Hebrew inscription on his tombstone reads in translation:

> The exalted Moses Michael, son of Judah, liberated for Paradise on Friday the 11th day of Iyar 565.[14] And the days of his life were sixty-six years. The Memory of the Just is blessed. May his soul be bound in the bands of life.

JEWS AND BOOKS

13

THE TEN TRIBES LOST AGAIN

WHAT became of the lost Ten Tribes of Israel? Today we believe that when Sargon II (719 B.C.E.) deported the people of the Northern Kingdom en masse, these Hebrews either were completely assimilated and incorporated into the general population of Assyria and Babylonia or of the nations which later conquered those lands, or identified themselves with their Judaean fellow Hebrews. This was not always the general belief. When the reading of the Bible was a daily requirement for serious Christians, the assurance of the words of prophecy was accepted literally. It was then the unquestioned belief that at the appointed time the Jews would be called from the ends of the earth to be converted. It was inherent, therefore, in the logic of the situation that these ten lost tribes must somehow have escaped from Assyria and, in the meantime, be hidden away somewhere awaiting this calling of the Lord. But where? This puzzle was long the favorite mystery-story of Christendom. Fascinating solutions had a sure-fire popular appeal. To find the answer, the public eagerly swallowed many a traveller's tale or even waded through ponderous theologians' discourses to have their imaginations stirred by the discovery of the lost tribes in distant lands amongst strange peoples. It was evident that they were more interested in these missing Jews than in Jews close at hand.

In 1650, John Eliot, a young minister, was preaching the gospel to the Indians in a small settlement south of Boston, Massachusetts, known as Roxbury. In order to get the English public interested in providing funds for the support of these missionary labors, the Reverend Thomas Thorowgood of Norfolk, England, in that year published a book entitled, *Jews in America, or Probabilities that the Americans are of that Race. With the removall of some contrary reasoning, and earnest desires for effectual endeavors to make them Christian.* It proved that, at long last, the lost ten tribes had been found in America. By sure proof the Indian redskins were identified as Jews. This was not an original discovery. As early as 1585, Father Duran, in a history of New Spain, basing his conclusions upon a fancied resemblance between the religious rites of Jews and American Indians, wrote: "My opinion and supposition is confirmed that these natives are of the ten Tribes of Israel that Salmanasser, King of Assyrians, made prisoners and carried to Assyria in the time of Hoshea, King of Israel."[1] The Thorowgood book, however, as if disclosing a new discovery, won the formal approval and license of the official censor.

Septem. 4, 1649.

I have perused this learned and pious discourse concerning Americans, and thinking that it will much conduce to that most Christian worke of their conversion to the faith of the Lord Jesus Christ, I doe approve it as very worthy to be printed and published.

John Downame.

By 1650 Charles I had been beheaded and the Puritan hierarchy had taken control of the English government. Englishmen's thoughts had turned back again to the Old

Testament and their interest in Jews had been reawakened — an interest not merely in the Old Testament Jews but in living Jews. Taking literally the promise that the Millennium would come when the Jews shall have been dispersed to all the ends of the earth and "called" (converted), the Puritans looked for that happy time as very near at hand, possibly an event to occur within the lifetime of those then living. So this was a timely book on a live topic, this finding and identification of the ten lost tribes of Israel in another end of the world! It was a further strange confirmation of the truth of prophecy, and an assurance that the Millennium was really closer at hand than had ever before appeared.

The book is a typical seventeenth century religious polemic seeking to prove its contentions by citations and interpretations of holy text. That was considered stronger proof than any presentation of actual personal observations identifying the customs and traits of the Indians with those of the Jews. To the present-day reader, trained in thinking based on scientific investigation, this presentation is naturally wholly unconvincing.

As an adjunct to his work, Reverend Thorowgood added "An Epistolicall Discourse of Mr. John Dury to Mr. Thorowgood. Concerning his conjecture that the Americans are descended from the Israelites. With the History of a Portugall Jew Antonie Monterinos, attested by Manasseh Ben Israel, to the same effect." There was appended a translation of an affidavit from which it appeared that this Mr. Monterinos, or more correctly Antonio de Montezinos, is just plain Aron Levi. He has a long and complicated story to tell. Boiled down, what Aron Levi says is that, while traveling in South America, he met a race of savages who recited the *Shema‛*, practiced Jewish ceremonies and claimed to be of the tribe of Reuben. He had appeared before the authorities of the Amsterdam synagogue; and the author submitted the attestation of Rabbi Menasseh ben Israel that "the author Monterinos is a vertous man, and separate from all manner of worldly interests & that hee swore in my presence that all that which he declared was a truth."

The interest aroused in England by Thorowgood's book evidently suggested the idea to Rabbi Menasseh ben Israel that this theory of the Indians being Jews could be made use of for the benefit of real Jews. For some time the Amsterdam Jewish merchants had hoped to be able to bring about the repeal of the ban against the admission of Jews to England which had existed since 1290. To further that end, Menasseh ben Israel wrote a Spanish pamphlet which, in the same year, was translated into Latin and published under the title of *Spes Israelis*. The Latin edition was addressed "To the Parliament, the Supreme Court of England." Then it was translated into English and became that landmark of Anglo-Jewish history published in London, in 1650, entitled:

The
Hope of Israel:
Written
By Menasseh Ben Israel,
an Hebrew Divine, and Philosopher.
Newly extant, and Printed in
Amsterdam, and Dedicated by the
Author to the High Court, the
Parliament of England, and to the
Councell of State.

Translated into English, and
published by Authority.
In this treatise is shewed the place where the ten
Tribes at this present are, proved, partly by
the strange relation of one Antony Monte-
zinus, a Jew, of what befell him as he travelled over the Mountaines Cordillaere, with
divers other particulars about the restoration of
the Jews, and the time when.
Printed at London by R. I. for Hannah Allen.
at the Crown in Popeshead
Alley, 1650.

It is a subtle appeal to the Puritan hopes for the Millennium. The letter from Menasseh ben Israel to Dury,
quoted in Thorowgood, is a fair summary of the tract:

I declare how that our Israelites were the first
finders out of America; not regarding the opinions
of other men, which I thought good to refute in few
words onely; and I thinke that the ten Tribes live
not onely there, but also in other lands scattered
every where; these never did come backe to the
second Temple, & they keep till this day still the
Jewish Religion, seeing all the Prophecies which
speake of their bringing backe unto their native soile
must be fulfilled: So then at their appointed time,
all the Tribes shall meet from all the parts of the
world into two provinces, namely Assyria and Egypt,
nor shall their kingdome be any more divided, but
they shall have one Prince the Messiah the Sonne of
David. I do also set forth the Inquisition of Spaine,
and rehearse diuers of our Nation, & also of Christians, Martyrs, who in our times have suffered
seuerall sorts of torments, & then having shewed
with what great honours our Jews have been graced
also by severall Princes who professe Christianity,

I proue at large, that the day of the promised Messiah
unto us doth draw neer, upon which occasion I
explaine many Prophecies.

Of course no party in a controversial religious field has
it all to itself. So, no sooner was Thorowgood's book well
launched on its way to popularity, than the opposition
made itself heard. Sir Hamon l'Estrange, a well-known
theologian, was the first of the opposition to join issue. In
1652 he published *Americans no Iewes, or Improbabilities
that the Americans are of that race.* With many Latin quota-
tions, and on the authority of many and various authors
and by a showing of chapter and verse from Holy Script,
he demonstrates, to his own entire satisfaction, that the
Americans are just simple Indians and never Jews at all.

This proved a good start; and the heat of controversy only
confirmed all contestants in their preconceived opinions.

In the meantime events marched forward and by the
year 1660 the Stuart dynasty was restored to the English
throne and His Majesty, Charles II, reigned. In that
year, Thorowgood decided to publish a new edition of his
book. Instead of merely republishing, he entirely rewrote
it. He even changed the dedication. This time it was
addressed "To the King's Most Excellent Majesty" and a
certificate from witnesses appended to show that the 1650
edition was originally to have been so dedicated, had not
God at that time permitted violence to prosper. This new
tract was entitled

Jews in America,
or
Probabilities, that those Indians were Judaical,
made more probable by some additions to the former
Conjectures. An accurate *Discourse* is premised of

Americans no Iewes,

OR

Improbabilities that the
Americans are of that race.

---

*They shall be scattered abroad, and their remem-
brance shall cease.* Deut. 32. *v* 26.
*Vntill the fulnesse of the Gentiles be come in,
and so all Israel shall be saved.* Rom 11. 25.
*For through their fall Salvation commeth to
the Gentiles, to provoke them to follow them.*
Rom. 11. 11.

By HAMON l'ESTRANGE, K^t.

LONDON,
Printed by *W. W.* for *Henry Seile* over against
St. *Dunstans Church in Fleetstreet,* 1 6 5 2.

Title Page of l'Estrange's *Americans no Iewes*

Mr. John Eliot (who first preached the Gospel to the Natives in their own Language) touching their Origination, and his Vindication of the Planters.

Omitted are Dury's discourse and Mr. Aron Levi Monterinos' affidavit. Instead we have the "learned conjectures of Reverend Mr. John Eliot" himself.

With actual contact with Indians and long acquaintance with them, one might well have expected from Eliot a recital of personal observations and experiences; but, true to tradition, he only repeated the same old arguments from Bible texts in the same old way.

Thus was launched another chapter in this age-old puzzle and a new element introduced into the controversy proving that the poor American Indians were the ten lost tribes.

For two hundred years numberless books and pamphlets, learned and foolish, in many languages, pro and con, continued to appear perpetuating this controversy, now only to find their resting place on the dusty and neglected shelves of libraries and to testify to the passion of past generations, excited over what they regarded as a vital issue.[2] Today, satisfied to accept the word of science that, while ethnology assigns an Asiatic origin to the American Indian, he is far removed from anything Jewish, the world turns to problems more vital to the Jews, to the Indians, to America, and to humanity.

14

LITERARY AMERICA ADOPTS A JEW

WITH the appearance, in 1779, of Lessing's *Nathan der Weise*, the idea of the Jew as a living personality in the contemporaneous world forced itself upon the consciousness of Christians. From the pen of Germany's foremost literary figure, this daring challenge to the age-old misconception of the Jew, based on ignorance and prejudice, startled Europe. As the eighteenth century drew towards its close and as the ferment of the new French social philosophy, the influence from England of Locke's reasoning, and the example of our American political experiment in civil liberty, directed the thinking of Europe in new democratic channels, the shameful civil status of the Jews began to stir the conscience of certain Christians as a humanitarian issue. Christian Wilhelm von Dohm, for example, in 1781, appealed to this humanitarian and moral sensibility of his countrymen by means of a startling polemic, *Über die bürgerliche Verbesserung der Juden*. It was a provocative and challenging demand that, as Jews were human beings, they should be treated as such in a civilized state. In 1785 the Royal Society of Arts and Sciences of Metz offered a prize for the best answer to the question: Are there ways to make Jews happier and more useful in France? Two years later the prize was divided amongst three widely circulated essays. The first was written by Abbé Grégoire, the liberal Catholic;[1] the second by Thiery, the famous lawyer and politician,

Avocat au Parlement de Nancy;[2] and the third by Zalkind Hourwitz, a Polish Jew.[3]

The first tangible results of all this agitation came in 1790 when, for the first time, Jews were made full citizens of a European state. In that year, Jews of southern France — *les Juifs Portugais, Espagnols & Avignonois* — were, by royal *Lettres Patentes*, issued under a decree of the National Assembly, invested with all rights of *citoyens actifs*.

Even Tory England was not immune to the reverberations of this new spirit of the times. Although Catholic emancipation was still years away and complete Jewish emancipation was over half a century distant, the sway of the fox-hunting country squire was about to be challenged by a newly arising democracy led by city magnates and industrialists. The power of the rotten boroughs could not stem the tide before the increasing importance of Manchester, Birmingham and Lancashire. The mill, mine and factory workers were to supersede farm laborers as England's breadwinners. Before she fully realized the significance of the change, England was finding itself with a middle class socially, politically and intellectually aggressive in asserting new democratic ideals.

In 1782 a translation of *Nathan der Weise* was published in London. In 1794 Richard Cumberland wrote *The Jew*,[4] and his "Sheva" set a fashion in Jewish heroes. The play continued to hold popular favor for years and ran through seven editions. Within two years, in 1796, George Walker used another Jewish hero to captivate the English reading public with *Theodore Cyphon, or the Benevolent Jew*. With the rise of the romantic movement in English literature, the mysterious Jew and beautiful, sable-tressed, almond-eyed Jewesses made a sure-fire appeal to readers. By 1815

the popular idol of fashion, Lord Byron, wrote his sentimental *Hebrew Melodies* which, in spite of the handicap of
the weak, tinkling tunes of Isaac Nathan, stirred Jewish
sympathy in haunting appealing pathos:

> Oh, weep for those that wept by Babel's stream,

> Tribes of the wandering foot and weary breast,
> How shall ye flee away and be at rest!
> The wild-dove hath her nest, the fox his cave,
> Mankind their country — Israel but the grave!

or again in a wailing note for Israel's woes:

> She walks in beauty, like the night
>   Of cloudless clines and starry skies;
> And all that's best of dark and bright
>   Meet in her aspect and her eyes:
> Thus mellow'd to that tender light
> Which heaven to gaudy day denies.[5]

In this atmosphere Scott's *Ivanhoe* (1819) made its bid for
popular favor with his Isaac of York and the fair Rebecca.
Without enumerating the minor story-writers in the
Annuals which flourished during the period and commanded
a fashionable following, and lesser authors of popular fiction,
by mid-century, Grace Aguilar, Sir Edward Bulwer, Dickens,
Amelia Bristow, Disraeli, Maria Edgeworth, Anthony
Trollope contributed their share to make the Jew a stock
figure of romance. Caricatured, overdrawn, idealistic, im-
possibly benevolent or unnaturally wicked, unaccountable,
mysterious and exotic, villain or hero, in a flamboyant haze
of romantic unreality, Fagin, Leila, Mr. Levi, Alroy, Sidonia,
Mr. Riah, Miss Moses led a host of other Jews to haunt the
pages of English literature with the mystery of an ever
unsolvable and imperishable Israel.

The United States, at this period, largely imported its literature and literary ideals from England. Cumberland's *The Jew* was played in Boston (twice), New York, Providence, Hartford, Charleston and Philadelphia within a year of its first appearance in London; and, before another year was passed, it was republished five times in America, three editions appearing in Boston, and one each in New York and Philadelphia.[6] It scored the same smash hit with American audiences as it did in England. As late as 1806 the Boston Theatre advertised: "This evening, Dec. 3, will be presented, for the first and only time these two years, a favorite comedy in five acts, called THE JEW or BENEVOLENT HEBREW." Evidently a kindly Jew still held such popular appeal that the following week, as an afterpiece to *School of Reform*, they offered *Jew and Doctor, or a Prescription for Happiness*. Scott, Dickens, Disraeli, Trollope, Bulwer and the other English novelists, enjoyed the same popular following in America as in their native land. Their books were not only imported as soon as printed, but pirated for American readers. Thus America came to have a literary acquaintance with the European Jew and the romantic aurora in which his mysterious shadows cast spells of charm and color.

Prior to the German Jewish immigration of the forties, the average American, outside of a few Atlantic coast cities, had little or no Jewish contacts. When the itinerant convert, the Jewish missionary Frey, came to preach and gather funds in their local church for the conversion of the Jews,[7] the residents of the neighborhood turned out in goodly numbers in order to behold a living Jew, like unto those they had read about in their Bibles and their novels. Thus, by and large, the American public was imbued with a theoretical

and impersonal attitude of sentimental sympathy and
charity for Jews in the abstract and, at the same time, har-
bored towards them a kind of awesome antipathy arising
partly from inherited religious traditions and partly from
narrow prejudice against all foreigners who did not belong
to the crowd.

It was for this America that the poet Longfellow transmuted his acquaintance, Isaac Edrehi, a staid Boston Jewish
merchant, into:

> A Spanish Jew from Alicant
> With aspect grand and grave was there;
> Vender of silks and fabrics rare,
> And attar of rose from the Levant.
> Like an old Patriarch he appeared,
> Abraham or Isaac, or at least
> Some later Prophet or High-Priest;
> With lustrous eyes, and olive skin,
> And, wildly tossed from cheeks and chin,
> The tumbling cataract of his beard.
> His garments breathed a spicy scent
> Of cinnamon and sandal blent,
> Like the soft aromatic gales
> That meet the mariner, who sails
> Through the Moluccas, and the seas
> That wash the shores of Celebes.
> All stories that recorded are
> By Pierre Alphonse he knew by heart,
> And it was rumored he could say
> The Parables of Sandabar,
> And all the Fables of Pilpay,
> Or if not all, the greatest part!
> Well versed was he in Hebrew books,
> Talmud and Targum, and the lore
> Of Kabala; and evermore
> There was a mystery in his looks;

An Example of the English and American Evangelical Sentimentality about the Jew
in the Middle of the Nineteenth Century

THE SORROWING JEW.

(FOR ONE VOICE.)

He is mourning a-lone, for no kind friend is near, His woe-stric-en spirit to com-fort and cheer; Nor ev-er de-scends blessed sym-pa-thy's dew To re-fresh the sad heart of the sor-row-ing Jew.

1

"He is mourning alone, for no kind friend is near
His woe-stricken spirit to comfort and cheer;
Nor ever descends blessed sympathy's dew
To refresh the sad heart of the sorrowing Jew.

2

He thinks of the land where his forefathers lie
Beneath the warm smile of their own eastern sky,
And he wishes perchance, he were laid by them too,
For earth has no house for the sorrowing Jew.

3

He thinks of that holy and high honored fane,
Where Jehovah would stoop to hold converse with men;
He thinks of the glory Jerusalem knew,
And thinks of himself... a poor sorrowing Jew.

4

O hushed be thy sorrow, unheard be thy sigh,
And bid the warm tear trickling down from thy eye;
There are that would mock at thy grief and thy woe,
And scoff at the tear of the sorrowing Jew.

5

Yet woe to the man, though a prince on his throne,
Who shall mock at a people God still calls his own!
For he, whose great name is the Holy and True,
Hath sworn to avenge the poor sorrowing Jew.

6

Rouse, rouse ye then; Christians; if christians indeed,
Your hearts for the sorrow of Judah will bleed;
Ye will mourn for her temple, her glory laid low,
Ye will mourn for her son, the poor sorrowing Jew.

7

O! think ye, with fear, on the curse and the woes,
Jehovah has threatened on Abraham's foes;
O remember that He who was offered for you,
In the days of His flesh was a sorrowing Jew.

8

And thou, blessed spirit, whose life-giving power
Alone can the feet of the wanderer restore;
O teach them their own pierced Messiah to view,
And bring to his fold the poor sorrowing Jew.

His eyes seemed gazing far away,
As if in vision or in trance
He heard the solemn sackbut play,
And saw the Jewish maidens dance.

In this same period, catering to this same American taste, the Reverend Joseph H. Ingraham turned out the best sellers of his days in rapid and prolific exuberance. Beautiful Jewish maidens, noble Jewish youths and wicked Jewish villains were stock in trade, ready to his hand. When Ingraham abandoned the yellow-covered "blood and thunder" literature and turned to writing religious novels, he struck a new high in popular favor. *The Prince of the House of David* (1855), *The Pillar of Fire* (1859), *The Throne of David* (1860), all romanticizing the biblical Jews and "the grandeur of Hebraic history," immediately captured the reading public. Some idea of their popularity may be gathered from the fact that not only did publishers outbid one another in paying Ingraham a previously unheard of sum of $10,000 and royalties for a book, but that some twenty-three editions of the *Prince of the House of David*, nine of *The Pillar of Fire*, and twelve of *The Throne of David* were published, and as late as 1900 there was still a demand for the books. This being the state of American literary diet, a Jew or two judiciously scattered over the pages of a story served as piquant literary tidbits.

In 1862, James R. Newhall, a staid and sober historian, produced an unexpected Jew amongst the earliest settlers of his native Lynn. Did he intend this as a joke on the philo-Judaic attitude of his neighbors? Was Manasseh Guatolf an imaginary personality and his story invented as an exotic incident to serve the historian Newhall's purpose of arousing interest in the early history of Lynn? Or was he really some lonely wandering Ishmael who, in his goings and comings in the early Colonial days, found peace and companionship in the proximity of the learned Hebraist, the Reverend Samuel Whiting?

Often such odd fragments, strange incidents or some quaint individuals, do turn up to puzzle the historian. Sometimes they furnish leads to unexpected finds. At other times they are only misfit details which do not belong in the picture. By the serious researcher, however, nothing can be ignored as too insignificant or extraneous. This is particularly true in searching out our American Jewish history.

For the story we must rely on the pages of *Lin, or Jewels of the Third Plantation*, which James R. Newhall published under the pseudonym of Obadiah Oldpath in 1862. The authoritative history of Lynn by Lewis and Newhall contains no mention of him. The records of the First Church of Christ in Lynn for this early period no longer exist. The ancient burying ground where Guatolf is described as interred has disappeared. Nor is he listed in the vital records of ancient Lynn. Indeed, his very name, "Manasseh Guatolf," does not carry conviction as authentic for a Spanish Jew. The absence from other contemporary sources of any corroborating records of so notorious a conversion is suspicious.

The ancient diary of Obadiah Turner is not now to be located, and it is from alleged entries in this journal, purporting to cover the years from 1630 to 1681, that Newhall, writing as Obadiah Oldpath, presents the story. Obadiah describes how, while ransacking the garret of an aged relative, "the journal of Mr. Turner fell into the hands of the writer by one of those fortunate turns that sometimes happens to a man, to wit, the turning over of a barrel of old

papers." Is this romance of an old New England attic also
the elaborate hoax of a serious historian amusing himself
at the expense of the less learned?

Whatever the facts the story is intriguing.

In 1636 the Congregational Church in Lynn, the fifth to
have been established in Massachusetts, installed Samuel
Whiting as its second minister. Son of the mayor of Boston,
England, graduate of Cambridge, for forty-three years in
that community of sturdy New England farmers, he was
universally acclaimed the "Father of Lynn." Preacher,
author and scholar, of whom Cotton Mather says, "Especially he was accurate in Hebrew, in which primitive and
expressive language he took much delight."

> One, who for learning, wisdom, grace and years,
> Among the Levites hath not many peers.

A quotation from the Turner journal, in recording the
death of "ye dear and reverend Mr. Whiting," December 12,
1679, adds: "Hys learning was great. In ye Hebrew yt hath
been said none this side of ye water could come up to him."

Our tale begins with a statement that Guatolf was a
Spanish Jew, son of parents "conspicuous for their wealth
and proud of their Hebrew lineage." We are told that he
had received a superior education "especially in all the learning calculated to confirm and strengthen him in the ancient
faith." To escape persecution he was forced to flee and,
after years of wandering along "the coasts of the Mediterranean" and a journey to the Holy Land, finally sought our
shores. After residing in Boston for a year or two, Manasseh
and the Reverend Whiting, "both being among the best
Hebrew scholars in the country," met in the higher literary
circles of the town. "Charmed by the benignant character

of his new acquaintance," Manasseh made frequent visits to Lynn to which he finally removed in order to be nearer his friend. "By degrees, his adherence to the old religion weakened and, finally, on a serene Sabbath morning in early summer, the venerable pastor had the blessed privilege, before a great congregation, who had assembled from far and near, of baptizing this son of Abraham into the religion of the Nazarene. It was a marked occasion, and much talked of among the good people throughout the colonies."

The author then goes on to describe how Guatolf's "zeal and devotion may well have put to the blush many who had till then looked upon themselves as foremost in the godly race. He visited the widow and fatherless in their affliction and kept himself from the contaminations of the world. The fountains of grace that had sprung up within him seemed pure and unfailing. He was constant in attendance on the services of the sanctuary, and took great pains to lead thither others who had been accustomed to range the woods and fields on the Sabbath. And possessing well trained musical powers, he delighted to join, with his melodious voice, in the sacred song."

The death of Mr. Whiting cast a great gloom over Manasseh. He and the succeeding minister, Mr. Shepard, were not congenial. During the ensuing three years Guatolf gradually lost his interest in his new religion until, finally, he bade "an everlasting adieu to all his Christian hope and inspiration. But he did not return to his old Jewish faith. No, he wandered into the frigid wilds of Atheism." So the author points the sad moral: "About this time the withering hand of consumption was laid upon him. He was soon confined to his home, and then to his bed. And it was a sorrowful thing to the good people who came to visit him to find not even one ray of light glimmering in his darkened soul. And so he died; died, denying not only the great High Priest of the Christian faith, but also the great Jehovah whom his fathers worshipped. Of all people on earth, one would think, an educated Jew would be the last to die an infidel."

Manasseh was buried in 1685 in the old Lynn burying ground, his grave separated by but a few yards from that of Obadiah Turner, until time erased all traces and memory of both.

More elaborate and more plausible than most such tales of this period found in novels, verses, or amongst the miscellaneous literary mélange of decorative sentimental gift-book *Annuals*, it is typical of American tales of mysterious Jews. Again and again mystical wandering Jews pass and repass in the annals of family traditions and local Colonial history. James Russell Lowell persistently asserted that the genius of the Lowells was accounted for by the inheritance of the blood of a remote Jewish ancestor.[8] Perennially the story of a stray Jewish Pilgrim settler joining the Plymouth Colony[9] renews its vogue alongside of tales of Jewish pathfinders, such as the one who left his phylactery in the fair Berkshire hills of western Massachusetts.[10]

Thus was told the tale of the Jew, Manasseh Guatolf.

15

JEWS IN THE FIRST OLD FARMER'S ALMANAC

O N September 15, 1792, Robert Bailey Thomas, a youthful and enterprising Boston bookseller, signed the introduction to a new almanac on which he had been working for months and sent it to the printer. Modestly he wrote:

> I have thought proper to entitle (it) *The Farmer's Almanac*, as I have made it my principal aim to make it as useful as possible to that class of people.

Thus was launched the famous *Old Farmer's Almanac* which today is the oldest continuous publication in the United States.

In early America almanacs played an important role not only in disseminating information, in formulating opinion, but also in stimulating interest in many unexpected and varied directions. The very first book printed in America by its first printer, Stephen Day of Cambridge, was an almanac for the year 1639. Previous to the appearance of the *Farmer's Almanac* in 1793, a considerable number of almanacs had already been published in the colonies. The incomplete Congressional Library list alone lists almost 1700 of them.[1] Some of them attained extraordinary popularity and remarkable circulation. *The Ames Almanac*, begun in the year 1726, reached an astonishing sale of 50,000 copies for a single year. Indeed, Cotton Mather, in his introduction to his almanac for 1683, was well within bounds of moderation in writing: "Such an anniversary composure comes into almost as many hands as the best of books." They were the "best sellers" of the day. It has been pointed out that in North America, between the years 1639 and 1700, excluding religious books and pamphlets prepared for government use, eighty of the less than one hundred and fifty titles of American publications were almanacs.[2] Even through the lean years of the Revolution the contest for popular favor between competing almanac publishers continued unabated.

In the rivalry of such a highly competitive trade, almanac publishers vied with one another to cater to public taste with a sensitive and almost intuitive appeal to whatever was for the moment the predominating public fancy.

During this period the almanac had a hold on popular imagination as something which spoke with oracular wisdom and authority, predicted the future, revealed the past and advised about the problems of everyday life. Thus its contents received a serious attention no longer accorded to such publications by the sceptical reading public of today. In a discriminating article on the almanacs of Massachusetts, Dr. Charles L. Nichols[3] has divided early almanac publishing into three distinct periods on the basis of reading content which the almanacs stressed in their appeal for public patronage: the first, from 1639 to 1700; the second, from 1700 to 1800; and the third, extending to 1850. The earliest period was distinctly religious; the second devoted itself to practical, instructive and literary entertainment; while the third was predominately political.

In 1793 the pages of popular almanacs supplemented their serious expositions with historical extracts, biographical material, anecdotes, quaint bits of wisdom, moral maxims and miscellaneous information. A genius like Benjamin Franklin gave his *Poor Richard's Almanack* the spice of originality. The ordinary editor, however, gathered his material from the odds and ends of his reading or lifted it bodily from neighboring newspapers which had stuffed their often gaping columns with trivialities filched from any odd source when, as they went to press, their meager resources and unorganized means of getting news failed them.

The publication of his proposed almanac in 1793 was Thomas' great literary adventure. Born in 1766 on a farm in West Boylston, Massachusetts, Robert Thomas had received only the limited schooling of a New England rural district school. He had supplemented this by diligent and miscellaneous reading in the library which his father had inherited from his grandfather, an English university man. For a short term Robert was the village schoolmaster in his native town and then learned the trade of bookbinding. In 1793, Thomas established himself as a bookbinder and bookseller. Previously, in the summer of 1792, in order to fit himself to realize his ambition of publishing an almanac, Thomas came down to Boston to study in a "mathematical school" conducted by Osgood Carleton. Here he is supposed to have worked out the calculations for his first almanac, although in its preface he claims that he had "for several years past, paid some attention to that divine science, astronomy, the study of which must afford infinite pleasure and satisfaction to every contemplative mind."

He proposed that his almanac, besides "the large number of astronomical calculations" which were "fitted to the town of Boston but will serve for any part of the adjoining states," was to offer "as great a variety as are found in any almanac of new, useful and entertaining matter." Printed by Belknap and Hall at the Apollo Press in Boston, the almanac was offered for sale "at their office, State Street; also by the author and M. Smith, Sterling at sixpence for a single copy, 4s per dozen and 40s per groce."

The almanac attained an instant popularity and launched Thomas on that successful career which fifty years later he contemplated with self-conscious modesty as having accomplished "what has seldom been done in this or any other country, as we believe, the getting up and publication for half a century of a manual edited by the same person, even as unpretending as our modest and homely annual."

Whether Thomas had any special interest in the Jews is left entirely to conjecture. Perhaps in his boyhood days in Boylston he had heard the country gossip and had come in contact with the great Jewish merchants in the neighboring town of Leicester, whom the coming of the British army into Newport had forced to take refuge on the hilltop of that attractive Worcester county community. That he had at least a theoretical and sympathetic interest in the political fortune of Jews is amply evidenced by the fact that in the almanac for 1842, in his retrospect of the world's progress during the fifty years he had been publishing the *Old Farmer*, he singled out as one of the high lights of that progress that "the Turk has recognized the Jew as a human being and a brother."

As "new, useful and entertaining matter," his first number of *The Farmer's Almanac* contains two Jewish items. The first, on page 40, under the heading of "Memorable Accidents, Occurrences, and Events," reads:

> *The Royal George* of 100 guns overset at Portsmouth, (Eng.) by which misfortune Admiral Kempen-

felt, with the crew were lost; there were near 100 women and 200 Jews on board, June 28, 1782.

Launched in 1756, *The Royal George* had been the pride of the royal English navy for its first seven years, and thereafter had continued one of its great vessels. In 1782 it was still a useful ship. While undergoing repairs at Portsmouth, on August (not June) 28th, it sank at its dock. Although the actual number lost was never ascertained, it was currently reported that it carried down in the disaster some 900 of the 1200 persons aboard. Of these it was estimated 250 were women and children who, according to custom, were permitted to remain aboard with their sailor relatives until official sailing orders were received. In the investigation of its captain at the court-martial, there was nothing to indicate that 200 Jews had perished.[4] It is hard to believe that so large a number could have been present at the time.

Perhaps some of the press gangs of the day, through which the navy recruited its crews, had impressed a number of Jewish youths into *The Royal George's* crew; but that could account for but a small number. While some of the local Jewish dealers of Portsmouth, who sold naval supplies as "Licensed Agents for Petty Officers and Seamen," may at the time have been aboard the ship on business, this at best could account for no such number as two hundred. It is impossible to figure out how as many as two hundred Jews could have gone down with the vessel. Such a community disaster would have left an indelible record in Anglo-Jewish history, which registers no such loss.

The second Jewish item, which appears on page 41, is of greater importance. It is, we believe, the first narration of post-biblical Jewish history printed in America.[5] It covers more than a page of the forty-eight which make up the almanac. Although entitled "A brief account of the Persecution of the Jews," it reads to some extent more like a narration of Jewish persecutions of Christians. It is a curious mélange of misinformation and inaccuracies selected from a history of more than two thousand years.

A BRIEF ACCOUNT OF THE PERSECUTION OF THE JEWS

THE seventy years captivity of the Jews began 606, before Christ; they about Cyrene, headed by one Andreas, murdered about 100,000 Greeks and Romans, they eat their entrails, and covered themselves with the skins of those they assassinated, 115 after Christ. Above 580,000 destroyed by the Romans 135. First arrived in England, 1079. Thinking to invoke the divine clemency at the solemnization of the Passover, sacrificed a young lad of twelve years old, the son of a rich tradesman at Paris, by first whipping his flesh from his bones, and then crucifying him; for which cruelty the criminals were executed, and the rest banished France, 1180; from this circumstance the Jews have been ever since held in detestation. Massacred, Sept. 3, 1189. Seven were condemned to pay the King 20,000 marks, or suffer perpetual imprisonment, for circumcising a Christian child at Norwich, and attempting to crucify him, 1235. Two hundred and upwards were apprehended for crucifying a child at Lincoln, eighteen of whom were hanged, and the rest heavily fined, 1255. Seven hundred were slain in London, because a Jew would have forced a Christian to pay him more than two shillings per week for the loan of 20, 1262. Every Jew, who lent money on usury, was commanded to wear a plate upon his breast, signifying that he was an usurer, or to quit the realm, 1274. Two hundred and sixty-seven were hanged and quartered for clipping, 1277; the same year the Jews crucified a child at Northampton, for which fifty were drawn at horses' tails, and hanged. All the synagogues were ordered to be destroyed, 1282. All the Jews in England were apprehended in one day, their goods and chattles confiscated to the King, and they, to the number of 15660, banished the realm, having only sustenance money allowed, 1287; they remained banished 364 years, till Oliver Cromwell restored them. A general massacre of them at Verdun, (France) by the Peasants, who, from a pretended prophesy, conceived the Holy Land was to be recovered from the infidels by them; 500 of these Jews took shelter in a castle, and defended themselves to the last extremity, when for want of weapons, they threw their children at the enemy, and then killed each other, 1317. Driven out of France, 1394. Driven out of Spain, to the number of one hundred and fifty thousand, 1492; they retired to Africa, Portugal, and France. It was against them that the inquisition was there first established. There was not a Jew in England from 1610 to 1624. An act passed to naturalize, 1753; but was repealed on the petition of all the cities in England, 1754. Four were executed in London for murdering a servant, 1771.

To trace the possible source of this article presents an interesting puzzle. A search of the Worcester and Boston newspapers of the day, to which Thomas had access, shows that he did not get anything of this sort from their pages. That summer, Isaiah Thomas, the famous printer and bookseller of Worcester, had been advertising in the *Massachusetts Spy* an elaborate prospectus of a proposed American reprint of *Josephus*. This new edition promised to add to the text of *Josephus* a continuation of Jewish history by

Maynard's *Josephus.*

PROPOSAL

For Printing by Subscription,

Enriched with superb Engravings, Maps, Notes and Marginal References, as well as every other advantage of elegance and utility,

[To be completed in only *Sixty Numbers,*]

THE genuine and complete Works of FLAVIUS JOSEPHUS, the celebrated, learned and authentick Jewish Historian.

CONTAINING,

I. The Antiquities of the Jews in twenty Books; with their wars, memorable transactions, authentick and remarkable occurrences, their various turns of glory and misery, of prosperity and adversity, &c. from the creation of the world.

II. The wars of the Jews with the Romans, from their commencement to the final destruction of Jerusalem by Titus in the reign of Vespasian. In seven Books.

III. The book of *Josephus* against Apion, in defence of the Jewish Antiquities. In two Parts.

IV. The Matyrdoms of the Maccabees.

V. The Embassy of Philo from the Jews of Alexandria to the Emperour Caius Caligula.

VI. The life of *Flavius Josephus,* written by himself.

VII. The testimonies of *Josephus* concerning our blessed Saviour, St. John the Baptist, &c. clearly vindicated.

The whole newly translated from the original in the Greek Language, and diligently revised and compared with the writings of cotemporary authors of different nations on the subjects; all tending to prove the authenticity and real value of the work.

To which will be now first added,

A CONTINUATION of the HISTORY of the JEWS, From *Josephus* down to the present time, including a period of more than 1700 years.

Containing an account of their dispersion into the various parts of Europe, Asia, Africa, and America, their different persecutions, transactions, various occurrences, and present state throughout the known world.

Together with

Copious indexes of the Countries, Cities, Towns, Villages, Rivers, Mountains, Lakes, &c. where the principal transactions took place; and every other striking Matter recorded in this Genuine and Complete Edition of the Works of the celebrated JOSEPHUS. Also Tables of the Jewish Coins, Weights, Measures, &c. used in the time of the Author. With a great Variety of other interesting and authentick particulars never given in any Work of the like kind either in the English or any other Language.

By GEORGE HENRY MAYNARD, LL.D.

Illustrated with

MARGINAL REFERENCES, and Notes Historical, Biographical, Classical, Critical, Geographical and Explanatory,

By the Rev. EDWARD KIMPTON,

Vicar of Rogate in Suffex, and Author of the Complete Universal History of the Holy Bible.

CONDITIONS of PUBLICATION.

I. THIS work shall be printed on a superfine paper, on a particularly large, elegant and new type, cast on purpose by Mr. *John Baine,* Philadelphia.

II. It shall be completed in sixty numbers, in large folio; but if it should unavoidable exceed that quantity, the overplus shall be delivered gratis.

III. Every number of this work shall contain Three Sheets of letter press, and be adorned with one or more copperplates, illustrating some remarkable transaction recorded in the work.

IV. One number to be delivered regularly once a week, until the whole is completed.

V. The price to subscribers will be One Shilling and Two Pence a number, and those who choose, may have them in quarter volumes, by advancing one dollar when the first number is published, Two Dollars when each of the two succeeding quarters are delivered, and the remainder when the whole is completed.

VI. Those who shall obtain twelve subscribers, and become accountable for the money, shall have one copy gratis; and Booksellers the usual allowance.

*** A list of the subscribers' names will be published.

SUBSCRIPTIONS for the above Work, the two first numbers of which are already published and ready for delivery, are received by I. THOMAS, at his Bookstore in *Worcester.*

Advertisement of a New Edition of *Josephus*, 1793

George Henry Maynard L. L. D., bringing it down to the present time. It proposed to narrate the dispersion of the Jews in Europe, Asia, Africa and America, and their different persecutions and present state throughout the world. It also offered "a great variety of other interesting and authentic particulars never given in any work of the like kind either in the English or any other language" and promised marginal references and notes from "the Rev. Edward Kempton Vicar of Rogate in Sussex and author of the *Complete Universal History of the Holy Bible*."

This proposed edition was a reprint of the English edition of 1790. Although advertised by Thomas, it was in reality a New York enterprise which William Durell had begun printing in 1792. In sixty parts, it was completed by 1794.[6] Even assuming that Thomas' intriguing advertisement led Robert Thomas to have recourse to either the English edition or to advance sheets of the unpublished parts of the American edition, no basis for the almanac account is found either in Maynard's contribution of modern Jewish history or in the Reverend Kempton's marginal notes. Nor do the contemporary English magazines, such as *The Annual Register* or *The Gentleman's Magazine*, which had American circulation, furnish in their welter of miscellaneous information the source for the almanac's Jewish history.

The leading authority in English to which at that time one would have turned for the post-biblical history of the Jews was a translation by Thomas Taylor of *The History of the Jews from Jesus Christ to the Present Time*, by the learned Protestant pastor, Jacob Christian Basnage, which was published in London in 1706–1708. This huge quarto was well worthy of a place in the library of a graduate of an English university such as Thomas' grandfather had been. But a comparison of any of the incidents given in the almanac with Basnage shows at once that it could not have been Thomas' source of information. Thus the almanac tells of little Saint Hugh of Lincoln:

> Two hundred and upwards were apprehended for crucifying a child at Lincoln, eighteen of whom were hanged, and the rest were heavily fined 1255.

The narration from Basnage is:

> . . . the Jews of Lincoln were accus'd of murthering a child. There were three particular circumstances in this accusation — one was, that the inhabitants of Lincoln had invited four Jews from every city in England to assist at this sacrifice. A second, that the murderer confess'd, when his life was promised him, that this sacrifice was renewed every year, tho' it was not always discover'd, and that the earth had cast out the body of the child. The third was that the King refusing to ratifie the promise of saving the Jews arrested ninety one prisoners at London, and punish'd many others of 'em capitally.

Yet here is this history of post-biblical Jews from Thomas' pen, garnered some time somewhere from his miscellaneous reading, calling this sordid page of human history to the attention of an American public, most of whom at that time had probably never been in personal contact with a Jew. Does he add incidents of alleged wrong-doing by Jews in order to preserve an air of impartiality? Is he a conscious apologist, or is he only a harried editor, uncritically filling an unexpected void from some potpourri of cuttings collected promiscuously against the time of need? The oft repeated advertisement of the forthcoming history of the Jews in the most widely circulating newspaper in his home county had perhaps inspired him to make capital of the curiosity which still could be aroused in rural New England over the Jews as the ancient people of the Book. Perhaps it was merely a vainglorious and ostentatious display of assumed knowledge in order to steal a neighbor's thunder.

Be this as it may, it is fair to say that, at least, such an article directed attention both to the sufferings and persecutions of the Jews whom the widely scattered clientele of the almanac otherwise associated only with far distant biblical times. As New England, which had only so recently had its own experience of fighting for freedom from what it had regarded as tyranny and persecution, read this new American oracle throughout 1793, if this article did not arouse sympathy for the Jew, it could not have failed to have stimulated interest in him as a modern human being.

16

AMERICA'S FIRST JEWISH BOOKDEALER[1]

TO OWN books has ever been the ambition of all cultivated gentlemen, but when setting out to settle a new country, in the small vessels of the sixteenth and seventeenth centuries, it is not to be expected that even the most devoted booklover would find much cargo space at his disposal for such impractical baggage. Bibles and prayer books comprised in large part all that the early settlers counted as necessities. It is, however, surprising to see how soon after the first settlements secured a foothold an avid interest was manifested, in addition to the Bible and prayer books, in other books which began to make their appearance both in Pilgrim Plymouth and in the Puritan Bay Colony.

While most of these books were of a theological nature and make dull reading today, the classics were well represented and other literature was not absent. As early as 1629 the governor and company of the Massachusetts Bay accepted eight books from William Backhouse "to be sent for New England." It well may be a matter of debate whether the desire for a library, quite apart from the ambition to found an institution to educate clergymen, was not a considerable contributing influence in the founding of Harvard College. The beginning of its library was contemporaneous with the first building of the college. In 1638, in writing of its start, the Reverend Edmund Browne informed his correspondent: "Wee have at Cambridge heere, a college erecting, youth lectured, a liberary, and I suppose there will be a presse this winter."[2] It is recorded that in that same year "the Honoured Magistrates and Reverend Elders gave — out of their own libraryes books to the value of £290" to the college.[3] When the youthful Rev. John Harvard of Charlestown died, he, as its first benefactor, left the college his library of over four hundred volumes. This gift consisted of a truly imposing list of books. Professor Morison points out that John Harvard's collection was a distinctly modern library for the day in that over a quarter of the books had been printed since 1630.[4]

In 1657, when William Bradford died in Plymouth, he left a library of a hundred volumes. In 1673, Governor Thomas Prince left one hundred and eighty-seven volumes and the Reverend Cotton Mather is reputed to have had a library estimated at four thousand volumes. In 1693, thirteen hundred volumes of the Reverend Samuel Lee's library were offered for sale in Boston. An inventory of the stock of the Boston bookdealer, Michael Perry, who died in 1700, showed seventeen hundred separate titles.[5] These were not wholly isolated cases of early Colonial book collecting.[6]

Hardly two years elapsed after Harvard College had made its first feeble start in 1636, when "Mr. Joss. Glover gave to the college a font of printing letters, and some gentlemen of Amsterdam gave towards furnishing of a printing press with letters forty-nine pounds, and something more." Stephen Daye was engaged in 1638 to superintend its printing, with three servants to work the press; and printing in America began. The third item published in 1640, the famous *The Bay Psalm Book*, contained words printed in Hebrew as well as a Hebrew alphabet. It is generally accepted that this Hebrew type was handcut by the printer in his establishment, as it bears all the earmarks of local American workmanship. We know that until Abel Buell of Killingworth, Connecticut, in 1769, cast a font of type, there were no professional makers of type in America, and that in 1735, when Harvard College decided officially to publish a Hebrew grammar, the work of Judah Monis, its first "instructor in the Hebrew Language," it was unable to locate Hebrew type in America and was obliged to appeal to its English patron, Thomas Hollis, to send it a font of Hebrew letters from Europe.[7]

It was not until 1693 that William Bradford was induced to move from Pennsylvania to set up New York's first printing press. After 1698 he also became a bookdealer.

Among the Jews, people of the Book, it was a religious necessity not only to possess copies of the Bible but to be familiar with the commentaries and treatises of their learned scholars, which for ages had been passed down first in manuscripts and later in print.

From the earliest days of printing, Jews had set up presses and their early printers had produced books which still rank not only amongst the great incunabula, but are outstanding achievements of all times in the art of printing. There is no evidence of Jews in Colonial times engaging in printing in America. The *Evening Service of Roshashanah and Kippur*, the first volume of prayers for Jewish holidays' use to be printed in America, was published in New York by W. Weyman in 1761, while Isaac Pinto's translation of *Prayers for Shabbath, Rosh-Hashanah, and Kippur, or The Sabbath, the Begining* (sic) *of the Year, and the Day of Atonements; With The Amidah and Musaph of the Moadim, or Solemn Seasons. According to the Order of the Spanish and Portuguese Jews*[8] was likewise printed by a Christian, John Holt, of New York, in 1766.[9] In 1773 the sermon, *The Salvation of Israel,* which Rabbi Karigal preached at Newport, was "printed and sold by S. Southwick, in Queen-Street" Newport.[10] It is probable that it was not until the early days of the nineteenth century that Jews owned and operated printing establishments here.

It is said that the first vestige of Jewish literature in America appeared in 1636, "when some Brazilian Hebrews, in dispute about liturgical questions, sought counsel from Rabbi Chayim Sabbathai of Salonica, in whose responses, *Torat Ḥayyim,* part III, no. 3, the query and reply are printed in full."[11] In 1646 an anthology of hymns and jubilee psalms was compiled by Jews to celebrate the liberation of Brazil from the Portuguese yoke. From this early beginning, from the small scattered Spanish and Portuguese communities in America, there were Jewish poets, scholars and authors who contributed to the literature of the day.

At first, in British America, the selling of books was in the hands of peddlers (chapmen) and hawkers who toured the country, dealing mostly in ballads and chapbooks with a side line of Bibles and theological works. Perhaps the earliest American reference to bookselling is a passage in Cotton Mather's diary, under date of 1683, where he wrote:

> There is an old Hawker, who will fill this Countrey with devout and useful books, if I will direct him.

Evidently light literature was easier to sell and a more profitable commodity than "devout and useful books," for in 1713 the provincial legislature enacted a law restricting such peddlers; and Mather further records:

> I am informed, that the Minds and Manners of many People about the Countrey are much corrupted, by foolish Songs and Ballads, which the Hawkers and Pedlars carry into all parts of the Countrey.

and

> I must also assist the Booksellers, in addressing the Assembly, that their late Act against Pedlars, may not hinder their Hawkers from carrying Books of Piety about the Countrey.

In spite of hampering legislation such book peddling continued even after American book publishers and dealers were established in most of the larger cities. Thus the famous Parson Weems, as an agent for Matthew Carey of Philadelphia, peddled books through the southern states, along with his preaching, until well after the Revolution.

Like other Colonial merchants, the early Jewish shipowners and commission agents often received miscellaneous consignments of books as part of a speculative cargo to be sold for the account of some European merchant. Mostly such consignments came from England which, sharing a common language with the colonies, had a surer market for its wares in the larger eastern cities, but they had by no means a monopoly of the trade. In 1704, a Madame Rebecca Overton of London sent over to an agent in Boston, "to be by him disposed of for her Most advantage," a consignment of nearly fifty books, largely theological.[12]

It was not uncommon to advertise in the newspapers auction sales of books to be held in some popular coffeehouse. Thus:

> A valuable Collection of Books, consisting of Divinity, Physick, Mathematicks, History, Classicks,

Belles Lettres, in Latin, English and French, to be sold by Public Vendue or Auction, at the Crown Coffee-House in Boston . . . Printed Catalogue may be had gratis.[13]

A Collection of choice Books, Ancient and Modern, in several Languages, upon most of the Arts and Sciences, few of them to be had at the Stationers, and Books very neatly bound, to be sold by way of Auction . . . at Mr. Sibly's Coffee-House . . . King-Street, Boston.[14]

Sometimes the consignees sold them at their shops as part of a miscellaneous stock of merchandise "just imported."[15]

There were, however, from very early times, those who specialized as bookdealers. Hezekiah Usher, who died in Boston in 1676, had managed to amass a fortune as a bookdealer. When John Dunton, a London bookseller, visited Boston in 1686, he gave an amusing account of its four bookdealers: Samuel Phillips, "very just and (as an effect of that) thriving," young, witty and the "most beautiful man in the whole town of Boston;" Mynheer Joseph Bruning, the Dutch bookseller at the corner of Prison Lane, "well vers'd in the knowledge of all sorts of books. A compleat bookseller;" the Scotch Campbel, a brisk young fellow who dresses *a la mode*, and John, son of Hezekiah Usher, "very rich and very witty."[16]

Probably Boston was rather exceptional in affording at so early a date such opportunities for bookselling. In 1719, Daniel Neal, visiting America, remarked that while all around the Exchange in Boston there were booksellers' shops, in New York there was but one and "in the plantations of Virginia, Maryland, Carolina, Barbadoes and the Islands none whatever." Not long after this, booksellers must have found New York a more favorable market, for Evans discloses a constantly growing list of New York printers and publishers.[17]

As early as 1726, the Rev. Thomas Prince attempted unsuccessfully to raise a fund for a lending library in Boston. In 1779, Thomas Jefferson drew a bill for establishing a public library in Virginia. Probably the earliest circulating library in America was that of John Mein in King (State) Street, Boston, where, in 1765, "at the London Book Store, Second door above the British Coffee-House," he advertised a circulating library of 1200 volumes, "in most branches of polite literature, arts & sciences," where memberships cost subscribers one pound and eight shilling a year and those living in the country were invited to pay double and take "two books at a time."[18] Later, in 1784, William Martin advertised, from his shop near Seven Star Lane, Main Street, Boston, a "Library of Bibles and other Books."

Other New England cities, such as Salem, Hingham and Portland, Maine, followed at early dates. Philadelphia had the first American lending library in 1731. By 1754 a library had been established in New York City. In 1794, J. Fellows, of 131 Water Street, was advertising that he had added between 500 and 600 volumes to his circulating library, "making in whole upwards of 1,000 volumes" of French and English novels, romances and miscellaneous works available to his patrons.[19] Three years later, his successor, H. Caritat, having removed to 93 Pearl Street "a little below the old Slip," informed the public that he had added another 500 volumes, "chiefly novels and intend to purchase every new work of the kind that can be had in this city."[20]

With this background, indicating in America a growing

reading public and a fairly wide marketing of books, in 1791, a Jew first became bookseller as a separate and distinct trade which he combined with a kindred line of "stationery."

Benjamin Gomez, son of Matthias and Rachel Gomez, born in New York, September 17, 1769, came from perhaps one of the most distinguished of our early American Jewish families. He traced his ancestry to Isaac Gomez, a Spanish nobleman, who about 1660 was forced to flee from Spain by the Inquisition. When Isaac Gomez found refuge in France, in gratitude to the King for the kindly reception he and his family received, he caused his son, Moses, to assume the name of Lewis (Louis, Luis) Moses Gomez. This Lewis Moses later left France for England to escape the persecutions which followed the revocation of the Edict of Nantes in 1685. Towards the close of the seventeenth century he emigrated with his family to New York. In New York the family were important merchants and shipowners and assumed a position of leadership in the Jewish community. It was a member of this family, Gershom Mendes Seixas, who was rabbi of the Congregation Shearith Israel when George Washington was inaugurated and who, it has been said, took part in his inaugural ceremonies.[21]

Benjamin Gomez's father was a son of the fifth son of Lewis Moses Gomez.[22] Benjamin Gomez first appeared in the New York directory of 1791 as a bookseller, when he was located at 32 Maiden Lane, "near the Fly-market," where also his brother, Isaac M. Gomez, carried on business as a broker. This was apparently the Gomez family residence, used by both brothers as business headquarters. It is surprising how wide a choice of books Benjamin Gomez offered:

BENJAMIN GOMEZ,

BOOKSELLER AND STATIONER,

No. 32 Maiden lane, near the Fly-market,
Has received by the late arrival from Europe,
and by the *Union*, Capt. Snow, late from Dublin,
an addition to his former assortment of
BOOKS, amongst which are,

Raymonds, Plowdens, Mosseys, Cooke, Durnford
and East, Vernon, Dallas, and P. Williams Reports,
Hales pleas of the Crown, Powell on Powers, ditto on
devises, Morgans Law Essays, Lillies entries, Woods
conveyancing, Blackstones commentaries, Vattles
Law of Nations, Montesquieu's Spirit of Laws, Kid
on awards, Barrifier Lawyers Magazine, and a number of other valuable law Books; Whitfield, Blair,
Swift, and Muir's Sermons, Oftervald's quarto bibles,
with plates, quarto bibles with and without apo-
craphy, and a number of religious books too tedious
for insertion; Humes history of England, Millots
elements of History, Priestley's lectures on ditto,
Elegant Extracts, being a selection of the most approved authors, in verse, prose, and epistles, Robert-
sons history of India, do. of Charles the fifth, Gillies
Greece, Adams history of Rome, Brydon's tour
through Sicily and Malta, Bruces, Cooks, Seventons,
Marittis, Youngs and Bartrams Travels, Bligh,
Ansons, Boule, Cooks, and Sparmans Voyages;
Romance of the forest, Desmond, Celefina, rock of
Modree, Baronese, Old Manor House, Clarissa Har-
low, Delineations of the heart, Sidney Castle, and
many other new novels, Arabian night entertainments,
do. Tales, Tom Jones, or history of a foundling, and
many other new books too numerous for an advertisement; Chifeldens anatomy, Bell on ulcers, Douglass
on the muscels, Gregorys conspectus, Cullens first

lines with Rotherdams notes, do. Materia Medica;
Shakespear's works, with notes; Burke on the Sublime,
Devil on two sticks, Sterne's work, complete, Par-
nells and Pomphrets poems; quills slates, slate pencils, sealing wax, primmers, chap books, demi, folio,
quarto, post, and foolscap writing paper, wrapping
do. journals, day books, and ledgers, &c. &c.

July 6. m w s o

The following year, 1792, Benjamin extended his bookseller and stationer activities to include publishing. He
brought out an edition of *The Christian Economy*. This pur-
ported to be a translation from an ancient Greek manuscript
"found in the Island of Patmos where St. John wrote His
Book of Revelations." The first English translation had
appeared in London in 1760, published by T. Waller, and
its popularity is attested by several subsequent editions by
other publishers. It was first reprinted in America in 1773
in two editions, one by Hodge & Shober of New York, and
the other by James Humphreys Jr. of Philadelphia. Later,
in 1788, it was republished by Hough & Spooner of Windsor
and, in 1790, two further editions were issued, one from
Albany and one from Concord. In 1792, Matthew Carey of
Philadelphia got out a sixth American reprint. The printer
of the Gomez edition, the seventh American reprint, is not
known, its modest forty-eight pages indicating only that it
was printed for Benjamin Gomez of 32 Maiden Lane. The
success of this publishing experiment is indicated by his
publishing later in the same year a second book printed for
him by J. Harrison, "*Female Policy Detected*: or the arts of
a designing woman laid open, by E. Ward. Author of *The
London Spy*, and *A Trip to Jamaica*. Teaching:

I. Of her allurements, inconstancy, love, revenge, pride and ingratitude.

II. A pleasant and profitable discourse in defence of married men, against peevish, fretful and scolding wives; with several notable examples of the mischiefs which have attended their lust and pride.

III. A true character of a virtuous woman, or wife indeed. To which is added, a poetical description of a widow, wife and maid."[23]

The original had first appeared in 1695. It is coarse and strained eighteenth century humor from the pen of a forgotten prolific author of passing popularity in England. It was a worldly-wise sanctimonious guide to the art of managing women, what you might expect from an author who graduated into literature from tavern-keeping.

From this time on Gomez became an active book publisher. In 1794 he published a volume of 131 pages, combining Doctor Priestley's *Letters to the Jews inviting them to amicable discussion of the evidences of Christianity*, together with *Letters to Dr. Priestley in answer to those addressed to the Jews inviting them to an amicable discussion of the evidences of Christianity*, by David Levi, author of *Lingua Sacra, The Ceremonies of the Jews*.[24] Both were the "First American edition from the Second British edition." The original Priestley letter had been published in London in 1786–7. The Gomez edition bears the imprint "Reprinted by J. Harrison for B. Gomez, Bookseller and Stationer, No. 97 Maiden Lane, 1794."

The fact that Gomez, as a loyal Jew and prominent member of the Shearith Israel synagogue, should have chosen to publish this particular work raises an interesting speculation. Was he, as a shrewd businessman, publishing this merely because he hoped it might prove a best-seller of the day, or did he think that David Levi had the better of the argument and thus he might do the Jews a service by educating his Christian neighbors to the reasonableness of the Jewish viewpoint?[25]

At this period Gomez advertised "a great allowance will be made to those who buy to sell again. Binding of all kinds done with neatness, accuracy and dispatch" and that his stock in trade included; "Quills, slates and slate pencils, sealing wax, primmers, chap books and spelling books, demi folio, quarto, post and foolscap writing paper, wrapping do. journals, day books, & ledgers, invoice books, etc."

The following year he published *Captain Cook's Third and Last Voyage* and an abridged edition of *Robinson Crusoe*.

In 1795, in publishing an edition of Benjamin Keach's *Travels of True Godliness*, he made use of the title page to advertise his business:

> Books and Stationery (*sic*), for sale by Benjamin Gomez, No. 97, Maiden–Lane. Among which are the following: The Practical Navigator, and Seaman's New Daily Assistant, Latest London Edition. Seaman's Journals. Blank Books, different kinds. Pocket memorandum Books, Receipt Books, Copperplate Copy Books, best gilt Quarto Writing Paper, Common do. best foolscap do. common do. Wafers, Sealing Wax, Quills, Ink-Powder, Black Lead Pencils, Ink-Stands, Slates, Playing Cards, &c. &c. A great variety of New Plays and Farces. Book-Binding carried on with neatness and dispatch.

Evidently Gomez's success as a publisher was sufficient to cause Naphtali Judah of New York, in 1795, to enter the trade as America's second Jewish bookseller.

Gomez, now twenty-six years of age, married to Charlotte, daughter of Uriah Hendricks, moved to a new location at 97 Maiden Lane from which he published, amongst other titles, a four volume edition of *Captain Cook's Voyage to the Pacific*, Bunyan's *Pilgrim's Progress*, Bunyan's *Visions* and a translation of Goethe's *The Sorrows of Werther*. In his bibliography Mr. Vail has tabulated twenty-one books published by Gomez between the year 1792 and 1799.[26]

In 1798, Gomez became interested in promoting lotteries. In 1801 he established the "Fortunate Lottery Office" and gave up his other business to devote himself wholly to this then respectable occupation. Evidently the fortunes to be won there must have been only for his customers, as shortly thereafter he found it necessary to add to lottery-ticket selling a side line of dry goods. In 1805 his place of business was moved to 33 Warren Street. In 1806 he removed again, this time to 74 Maiden Lane, where again he resumed bookselling in connection with his lottery office. Later, with various changes of address, he added to these lines of business that of grocer and tobacconist.

Like so many members of his family Benjamin Gomez served the Congregation Shearith Israel in various offices, including that of treasurer and of president. Leaving a widow who survived him many years, three daughters and a son, Matthias (killed in a duel in New Orleans), he died in his fifty-ninth year. An old family Bible of Isaac Gomez records:

> 1828, August 14, My cousin, Mr. Benjamin Gomez died. He was taken sick on the Thursday previous with what the Doctor called the Deague (Dengue) Fever but I considered to be the Typhus. He had

been attacked once or twice before with Paralysis but he appeared to have got quite recovered. Such is the uncertainty of life that "when we are in life we are in death"— and all we have to do is to submit to the dispensation of Him who maketh darkness his pavilion. May peace be to his manes and may his soul be in everlasting bliss is my sincere prayer. He was buried in the Chatham Street Burial Ground about 7 oclock of same day and for which $250 was paid as the fine as usual in such cases.

to which he adds:

> He has the debt of nature paid,
> In the grave I've seen him laid;
> Fifty-nine years was just his age,
> I therefore mark it on this page.
>
> He was good to everyone.
> He finished life as he begun.
> In friendship, honor, and being just
> In God alone he placed his trust.
>
> As husband, father, friend,
> None were superior, you may depend
> In all his actions — He was the same
> Which has procured him a good name.[27]

JEWS IN AMERICAN SOCIETY

17

AMERICA'S FIRST JEWISH CLUB

THE men's social club is peculiarly an English institution. It developed through more or less informal meetings of convivial spirits at London taverns. As such meetings gradually assumed regularity the English sense of social orderliness evolved formality and ceremonials which gave individuality both to different groups and to their favorite taverns. Gatherings which originally came together in a particular corner of a tavern, or in some private compartments of an inn, formed themselves into club groups, some devoted to literary conversation, others to politics, some to the more material pleasures of dining, while still others retained their heterogeneous character of social congregations liberally stimulated by liquid refreshment.

Such gatherings of parsons, lawyers, military men, city men, gangsters, young bloods, Scotchmen, wits or whatnots, each in its group, at their favorite haunt in one of the thousands of London coffee-houses, taverns, or inns, assumed the status of organized clubs and became known under the name of the meeting place. In the early years of the eighteenth century London became conscious of this new development; and its social life, politics and literature were replete with references to White's, Boodle's, Arthur's, Crockford's, Almack's, Brook's, Lloyd's and The Royal Exchange.

In this country, the earliest club which is still in existence
is the famous Schuylkill Fishing Club, founded in 1732. The
Friendly Club was founded in New York on the eve of the
Revolution; the Hoboken Turtle Club goes back to 1797.
Writing in 1756 that New York was one of the most social
places on the continent, William Smith calls attention to
the fact that "the men collect themselves into weekly
evening clubs."[1] Pre-Revolutionary visitors to America,
moving in the polite society of its then metropolitan centers
of New York, Philadelphia, Boston and Charleston, record
hospitality extended to them at clubs to which hosts took
them to spend a convivial evening with outstanding fellow
citizens.

Patterned after the clubs of England, American meetings
were held at taverns or at the homes of club members. The
evenings were spent much in the same way as at similar
London club meetings. The social feature centered around
an elaborate meal with formal toasts and liberal allowances
of drink.

In his diary, John Adams speaks of visiting in Boston,
in August 1771, at "Cordis's, the British Coffee House in
the front room, towards Long Wharf where the Merchant's
Club has met this twenty years."[2]

The Marquis de Chastellux, when in Boston, in 1780–2,
notes an evening spent at a club:

> This assembly is held every Tuesday in rotation,
> at the Houses of the different members who compose
> it; this was the day for Mr. Russel, an honest mer-
> chant, who gave us an excellent reception. The laws of
> the club are not straitening, the number of dishes
> for supper alone are limited, and there must be only

two of meat, for supper is not the American repast.
Vegetables, pies, and especially good wine, are not
spared. The hour of assembly is after tea, when the
company play at cards, converse and read the public
papers, and sit down to table between nine and ten.
The supper was as free as if there had been no strangers; songs were given at table . . .[3]

Perhaps it illustrates both the urbanity as well as the
travelled experience of the great Jewish merchants of
Colonial Newport, that at least as early as 1761 they should
have organized and maintained a social club of much the
same character as those of the English and Boston merchants. November 25, 1761, this club adopted a set of
rules, which apparently were amended a fortnight later by
the addition of a fourteenth, as follows:

First: — The club to be held every Wednesday
evening during the winter season. The members to
be nine in number; and by the majority of votes a
chairman to be elected to serve one month only.

Second: — After one month, or four club nights,
a new chairman to be elected in the manner aforesaid.

Third: — No person to be admitted as a member
of said club without approbation of the members.

Fourth: — Each of the members shall have liberty
to invite his friends to the club, well understood, one
at a time only.

Fifth: — The hours of club to be from 5 to 10, in
the manner following: From 5 to 8 each member is
at liberty to divert at cards, and in order to avoid the
name of a gaming club, the following restrictions
shall be strictly observed, viz: That no member shall
presume or offer to play for more than twenty shillings at whist, picquet or any other game besides his

club; on proof of gaming for any more, the member or members so offending shall pay the value of four bottles good wine for the use and benefit of the ensuing club night.

Sixth: — At eight of the clock the supper (if ready) to be brought in. At ten the club to be adjusted and paid, and no cards or any other game shall be allowed after supper.

Seventh: — After supper if any of the members have any motion to make relating to the club he must wait till the Chairman has just drank some loyal toast.

Eighth: — That none of the members shall (hold?) during (a club meeting?) conversation relating to Synagogue affairs, on the forfeit of the value of four bottles good wine for the use as aforesaid.

Ninth: — If any of the members should behave unruly, curse, swear or offer to fight, the chairman shall lay such fine as he sees fit, not exceeding, for each offence, four bottles good wine for the use aforesaid.

Tenth: — If any of the members happen to be sick or absent, by acquainting Mr. Myer with the same, shall be exempt from paying anything towards the club, but if no notice given as aforesaid, shall pay his quota of the supper only.

Eleventh: — If any of the members does not meet at club nights, and can't offer sufficient reason for so doing, the chairman with the members shall determine if he or they are to pay the proportion of the whole club, or the quota of supper only.

Twelfth: — If any of the members neglect coming to club three nights successively without being sick or absent, shall be deemed unwilling, consequently his name shall be erased from the list, not to be admitted during the season without the consent of the chairman and all the members.

Thirteenth: — Every member, after signing the articles, and not willing afterwards to conform to the same, his or their names shall be erased out of the list, and no more to be admitted during the season.

In witness whereof the members of said club have signed their respective names the day and year above written.

MOSES LOPEZ   MOSES LEVY
ISAAC POLOCK   ISSACHAR POLOCK
JACOB ISAACS   NAPH'T HART, JR.
ABR'M SARZEDAS   JACOB RODS. RIVERA
NAP'T. HART.

Fourteenth: — At a club held the 16th day of December 1761, it is resolved and agreed by the chairman and the majority of all the members that these articles be inserted amongst the rules of said club, viz:

That in case the chairman is not at the club, the secretary, for the time being, shall take his place, and the same obedience shall be paid him as if the chairman was present, and to be invested with equal authority. As also the said secretary is hereby empowered to nominate with the concurrence of the members then present, a secretary to supply his place for the time being; and that every month a secretary shall be elected in the same manner and form as the chairman is elected.

'VERA COPPIA'.[4]

There is in all this an intriguing glimpse of the social life of this Newport Jewish community, of the stately whist, the elaborate meal and the formal toasts with formidable potions of wines gathered on their ships' voyages from the famous vineyards of distant lands. In those days,

202 JEWISH PIONEERS AND PATRIOTS

when the after-dinner speaker was unknown and when the meal was an impressive succession of elaborate courses, a "loyal toast" was a post-prandial ceremony of solemnity, proposed by the chairman and drunk in full bumpers by the standing assembly. The toast to the King was not uncommonly followed by that to "The Prince of Wales and the Rest of the Royal Family," and then by one to "The Visitors," and then by others until the company disbanded in a mellowed glow of good fellowship.

A club of nine seems a small number; but inasmuch as it has been recorded that, in 1760, including women and children, the Jewish population of Newport numbered fifty-eight,[5] even though this number is challenged as an understatement, it is evident that the club must have contained a fair proportion of its adult Jewish males. Conspicuous by its absence is the name of Aaron Lopez. At this date, even though not yet recognized as Newport's greatest Jewish merchant, Lopez had been for nine years a resident of Newport and had already won an important position as merchant and shipowner. The name of his brother, Moses, heads the list as the name of his future father-in-law adorns its end. It cannot be that a man of Aaron Lopez's social grace and public spirit refused to join his brethren in such a pleasing enterprise. Perhaps, as we can only speculate on the omission, the explanation is that when the signatures were obtained Aaron was absent from Newport on one of his frequent business trips. The roll naming these nine club members comprises the social and commercial leadership of the small Jewish community and is, in many respects, as typical of our early American Jewish settlers as might have been selected. The nine represented families which had emigrated from at least four different countries, Spain, Portugal, Poland and England. Jews and their families had come to this little New England seaport at its very beginning, attracted by the declaration of tolerance and liberty embodied in 1641 in the famous program for the orderly government of the Narragansett region.

> Further ordered by the authority of this Present Court that none be accounted a Delinquent for Doctrine: Provided it be not directly repugnant to the Government or Lawes established.

The following year this policy was permanently reaffirmed.

> It is ordered that that Law of the Last Court made concerning Libtie of Conscience in point of Doctrine is perpetuated.[6]

The energy and boldness of this little group of Jews had greatly contributed towards making Newport an important center of trade, until more ships were sailing from that port than from old New York. They were active merchants, ship owners, importers of the products of Europe, of the neighboring colonies as well as those of the West Indies, manufacturers, and shopkeepers, all at the same time. Rivera, whose fleet sailed to all Atlantic ports where trade flourished, established the first spermaceti candle factory in Rhode Island. Isaacs, successively active as shopkeeper, ship builder, insurance broker, invented a method of converting salt water into fresh water which through Thomas Jefferson he unsuccessfully sought to sell to the government. At the time of Washington's visit to Newport in 1790 he presented him with a bottle of this water, extracted from ocean water, so free from saline matter as to answer for all common and culinary purposes.

Most of the groups were members of St. John's Lodge

of Masons and had been founders and supporters of Newport's famous Redwood Library. In all directions they
were active in varied aspects of Newport's commercial and
social life.

Their chief communal interest, however, centered around
the synagogue. These nine men not only took turns in
succeeding each other in the high offices of that institution,
but most of them were numbered amongst its founders who
had brought from Boston the famous Colonial architect,
Peter Harrison, to build the beautiful synagogue which is
still one of Newport's most prized ornaments. It is not to be
wondered at that, in the interest of peace and good fellowship during club meetings, discussion of controversial synagogue topics was taboo. They thus escaped the danger of
having heated arguments interfere with the enjoyment and
the flavor of the fourth bottle forfeited by some incautious
member.

Today, almost three centuries later, death has not separated them. Many of that worthy nine lie buried in the
celebrated old Newport Jewish burying ground still lovely
in the center of the modern city. They are those of whom
the poet Longfellow wrote:

How strange it seems! These Hebrew in their
          graves
     Close by the street of this fair seaport town,
Silent besides the never silent waves,
     At rest in all this moving up and down!

Gone are the living, but the dead remain
     And not neglected; for a hand unseen,
Scattering its bounty, like a summer rain
     Still keeps their graves and their
          remembrance green.

Were a second chapter of club life among American Jews to be written, it would present a far different aspect from this picture of the gatherings of this little Newport community. Lusty immigrant youths from Germany, scattered through our many growing cities of post Civil War America, more than a century later, would be the club members. It would not tell of staid and formal imitations of an English institution, nor would it be the transportation from their homeland of the drinking or singing clubs of Germany, nor even of its *Turn Verein.* It would portray the evolution of indigenous and spontaneous comings together which an immigrant people fashioned to their own needs.

After some of the German Jewish immigrants had achieved sufficient prosperity to have some leisure to seek the pleasures of social life, they were faced with an anomalous situation. Most of them, still young unmarried men and women, lived in our large cities with no homes of their own. Where there were families, these were large and none so well off that the family home had spare room suitable for social affairs. Fashionable society of that day in America entertained in spacious mansions which the social leaders had built as the symbols of success and wealth. For the great urban middle classes, sociables, suppers and parish entertainments in the church vestries were the center of social life. There were few halls or meeting places available to the general public for social gatherings.

For these Jews their synagogues were places for the serious practice of religion, in connection with which schools for their children and charitable organizations might function; but, unlike the churches, there were no places within their jurisdiction for social life. Therefore, the young people, and the heads of the families as well, joined together in

establishing social clubs. At the beginning, these were very
simple, until they became sufficiently prosperous to build
quarters of their own. There the young people had space
for meetings, dances and music, with rooms where their
elders could foregather for cards, sewing, or gossip. Such
clubs became the social centers for their members and often
played a dominating role in the society of many a community. There parties were given, weddings celebrated and
the more prosperous entertained guests at private functions;
while amateur theatricals, club balls, poker games, musicals,
dances and athletic facilities provided a busy round of
activities. There, too, charity boards transacted business.
Sometimes even synagogue trustees met there, and all Jewish
communal activities radiated from its rooms, so that it
may conservatively be said that the influence of such clubs
touched every corner of Jewish city life of the day.

18

"THE CAMPBELLS ARE COMING"

CAMPBELLS and Taylors at any gathering of family clans have a right to boast long and loudly of the distinguished records which their families have achieved through many generations since early colonial days. Proudly they trace their ancestors to early English and Scotch settlers. Probably most of them have never heard of Campernelli or the Campernals, or ever given a thought to the old synagogue in Newport or to the pious Jews who lie buried in its graveyard. Yet here is a tale to tell — a tale which shows why many a Campbell and many a Taylor, and their allied families, should know of old Mordecai and the Campernals.

In 1642 the Portuguese Jews, settled in Brazil, had been so successful in introducing the cultivation and manufacture of sugar that they decided they could afford a professional rabbi to be their spiritual leader and direct the education of their children. They sent to their friends and relatives in Amsterdam to select a rabbi for them. The choice fell upon a learned youth, Isaac da Fonseca Aboab, who had already achieved a position of distinction in that Dutch community. Rabbi Aboab accepted the call and immediately left for Pernambuco. Thus, although he returned after a few years to Holland, he became America's earliest rabbi, and was probably the first Jewish author who lived in the western hemisphere.

Accompanying him from Amsterdam to Brazil came his young friend, Mordecai Campanelli.[1] When, in 1654, the Dutch surrendered Brazil back to the Portuguese, Mordecai sought a new home. Attracted by the prospects of religious freedom promised by those who were settling in Newport, Rhode Island, he was amongst the earliest of those whom that liberality attracted there.[2]

He quickly became one of the outstanding members of Newport's Jewish community. Mordecai Campanal, as he then called himself, was in 1677 one of the two Jews who bought the plot of land for its famous cemetery dedicated to the use of the "Jews and their Nation, Society or Friends." Although vehemently and convincingly controverted, it was long the tradition that in his Newport house, in 1658, a masonic meeting was held in North America for the first time. The late N. H. Gould, a local historian, reported an ancient record to the effect: "Wee mett att y House off Mordecai Campunall and affter Synagog Wee gave Abm Moses the degrees of Macourie."[3] But there can be no doubt that the services of the Jewish congregation before the days of a synagogue were held in his house.

In 1678 he visited the Barbados to induce members of his family and other Jews to join the settlement at Newport. Evidently he was successful, for it is recorded that Mordecai Campernell returned from the Barbados for New England, April 1, 1679, in the ketch Swallow,[4] and by 1685 we find settled in Newport a goodly group of additional Campernal families, David, Daniel and Abraham.[5] When, in 1685, Major Dyre brought his famous suit to enforce the seizure of their goods as aliens against "fforeigne Jews" of Newport, of the nine defendants four were Campernals. Their success in that famous litigation definitely resulted in civil equality for Jewish settlers in Rhode Island and established a broad interpretation of liberal religious toleration for the colony. In 1698 (October 5th), still another David Campanell, described as a mariner, arrived in Newport in the sloop *Speedwell* from New York. Whether he was related to the other David is unknown.

The little group of Campernals seems to have prospered and definitely to have become an integral and important part of Newport, beginning to spread out into the neighboring communities. Before 1700 some of these Campanalls moved to Boston; for on September 9, 1695, one John Head and Judith Campanall there filed marriage intentions. In the following year, April 1, 1696, a Daniel Campenall and Elizabeth Shelton married there.[6] Some twenty-five years later we find that another David Campanell, evidently a man of adventurous disposition, left Newport to seek his fortune in Boston. Perhaps the good fortune of this Judith and Daniel had attracted his attention to the opportunities offered in that growing town, and David hoped that another Campanell might find welcome there. He was so insignificant and he came so unheralded, that there is no record available to fix the date when he arrived in Boston. Where he lived there, we know not. We cannot even say what was his trade. Perhaps he was only a sailor seeking a home port. Was he just a trader who found, to his sorrow, that the pious Puritan fathers were quite able to hold their own in a trade? It may be suspected he was a journeyman mechanic looking for a larger opportunity than Newport afforded. We deduce from later history that he was old enough to have left a family behind, in Newport, waiting the success of his efforts to find a new home.

Evidently few opportunities offered themselves to this Boston visitor and he had few acquaintances and no influential friends; for on June 15, 1726, the selectmen of the town sent Mr. Eneas Slater to warn him "to depart the town of Boston as the law directs."[7]

In early days in New England communities no one might be an inhabitant without a vote of the town, because the right of inhabitancy carried with it privileges there to acquire land, to use the town common for pasturage and the right to call upon the town for support in case of misfortune. To protect the town, it was the law that no inhabitant should, without official sanction, receive or entertain strangers who were indiscriminatingly classed as "vagabonds and wandering persons remoueing from one Collonie to another to the disatisfaction and burthen of the places where they come as dayly experience showeth." Thus, as early as 1647, there was a regulation:

> It is ordered that no inhabitant shall entertaine man or woman from any towne or countrye as a sojourner or inmate with an intent to remain here, butt shall give notice thereof to the Selectmen of the towne for their approbation within 8 dayes after their cominge to the towne upon penalty of twenty shillings.

When advised of the presence of a stranger, the selectmen issued a formal order, to be served by a town constable upon the visitor, commanding him to depart within a time specified. In 1692 the Massachusetts Bay Colony Act required the "warning out" to be given within three months of the person's arrival in the town, otherwise he gained a settlement. In 1700 the warning out period was extended to a year. This continued until the Settlement Act of 1793 abolished the practice. This was what happened to David Campanell. He was warned out by the Town Fathers of Boston. Whether he was looked upon as a vagabond or merely as a wandering person from another "Collonie," it is evident that no one was willing to take a chance of a twenty shilling fine to befriend him.

Thus David Campanell, described as "a Jew from Rhode Island," was forced to leave the inhospitable community of Boston and continue his wanderings. Evidently unwilling to turn back to Newport, he continued his travels north and east up the Massachusetts shore beyond Salem, over the Newburyport Turnpike, until he reached the town of Ipswich, that lovely village, with its wide-spreading salt-marshes and rich lands, snuggled to the banks of a pleasant tidal river which cuts deep in from the sandy beaches of the Annisquam shore, protected by the bold granite Cape Ann from the buffeting of the ocean. What an inviting prospect it must have presented to this unwanted stranger as he made his way those early New England summer days!

Originally settled as an outpost by John Winthrop and twelve companions from Boston, and known as Agawam, it had been renamed in 1634, by resolution of the "Court of Assistants of the Massachusetts," after old Ipswich in England "in acknowledgement of the great honor and kindness done to our people, who took shipping there." With an influx of settlers of solid English stock, the settlement had grown slowly for almost a hundred years when, that day, David Campanell arrived there. It was a farming community with a little fishing on the side, a typical Essex County village, with a touch of Saltonstall aristocracy and an intellectual hierarchy led by the Reverend Niemiah Ward, but consisting for the most part of a solid, hard-headed, independent yeomanry. Perhaps some wandering Campanell had already discovered there a friendly haven before the adventurous David turned his footsteps in its direction. It may be that some twenty-five years earlier, this very David himself had journeyed to this district. For in the first book of marriages in the neighboring town of Rowley, February 3, 1702, there is a record of a marriage between a David Campanell and Elizabeth Doak of Ipswich.[8] Had this Yankee Elizabeth returned with that David to his Jewish Newport, there to bear him children, and now, after all these years, were they returning, wife, husband and children, back to the land of her ancestors?

Obviously David Campanell found Ipswich to his liking, for soon he established a home there to which to bring his family. He became known as a man skilled in weaving and as a successful farmer. A son, David Junior, was baptized on May 19, 1728, in the local parish church. David Junior was of an age when we suspect a lady may have influenced his conversion. Perhaps it was only that preliminary step, so often repeating itself in the history of ambitious Jews, to attain material success by losing their Jewish identity in a community where, in spite of all kinds of opportunities loudly calling for men, prejudice shuts doors to Jews. Be that as it may, the original David continued true to the religious traditions of the family. Four years later, in 1732, David Campanell, the elder, died and was buried in the village churchyard. A special notation was entered on the town records that he was a "a Jew."

In 1734, after David Junior's Christianity had stood a seven years' test, or perhaps after he had fulfilled the biblical tradition of seven years' service, at the Ipswich church, he married Hannah Newmarch, the second daughter of Zaccheus Newmarch, a well-to-do local farmer.

Ipswich was a town which took its politics very seriously. Each year its inhabitants faithfully assembled at a spring town meeting to discuss town affairs and proceeded, in hotly contested elections, to select distinguished citizens to fill a long list of public offices — town moderator, representative to Great and General Court, fence viewers, sealers of leather, surveyors of highways, perambulators to walk the town boundaries, and special committees to deal with emergency issues. In the May meeting of 1736, David Junior was chosen hog reeve, the official charged with the duty of overseeing and regulating the raising of pigs in the town. He so served for this and the following year and then apparently retired to private life.

At the time of his marriage, David was described as a laborer. Later on, on the death of Zaccheus Newmarch, he acquired farming land in his wife's right and at that time had other property of his own which he cultivated as a farmer. By her he had two children, Hannah and William. The latter served with other Ipswich youths as a soldier during the French and Indian War.

Ipswich was a rebel stronghold, when the Revolution broke out, and undertook early in the conflict to muster soldiers for the Continental Army. May 14, 1777, the town voted a bounty of sixteen pounds "to each able bodyed soldier that shall inlist into the Continental army to serve to the tenth day of January next." In the following January it voted further, "that if any of the above soldiers shall inlist for three years or during the war he shall be entitled to forty shillings more making eighteen pounds in the whole."[9] William Campernell became one of the town's Revolutionary soldiers, serving with its other young men in the Continental army. After the war, William was awarded for these services a pension from the federal government which continued until his death.

He carried on the family trade of weaver for many years in Ipswich, where he lived in a distinguished homestead bought from Thomas Pierce, the town crier.[10] William married three times and left a numerous family well entrenched throughout the Ipswich district.

The town records of Ipswich show four or five generations of Campanels.[11] Good, industrious folk, perhaps a little shrewder in horse trading, a little more adventurous, with every now and again a strain of unexpected delicate good looks showing up in the offspring of plain-looking parents, but otherwise with nothing to distinguish them from their neighbors, these descendants of the adventurous David grew into an ever expanding family circle. On the whole, they formed a rather vigorous group, too busy with the practical affairs of everyday life to bother with their genealogy, and indeed a little indifferent to ordinary book-learning, especially spelling. So it came about that the family name in many branches came to have different spellings: Campernall, Campanell, Campanal, Campnell, Campel, or Campbell indiscriminately, just as the parish clerk or the tax collector chose to record it.

After the Revolution when, as an aftermath of war, the pinch of hard times made itself felt, Ipswich families spread out into the new land opening up to the northeast in the New Hampshire territory, or even farther beyond into the Massachusetts territory to the north, which was later to

Ipswich July 8 the 1779

Col Isaac Smith Sir pay William Camprall
for Ty shillings a month in specey at the sti____
tated price for Six months he being ingaged
in the Six months servey   William Dodge per order
                              of the Town Comeity

I Except to pay the within order
                              Isaac Smith

July 4 Recd of Barnabas Dodge two
three shillings & 6d which with what I have
Recd of Col Smith is in full of this Order
                              William Campernell

William Campernells Receipt 1779

12-7-
9-16-6
2-3-6

William Campernell's Receipt for Six Months' Pay as Soldier of the Revolution

become the State of Maine. Free land, well wooded, fed by many streams, with an abundance of both fish and game, and many a pleasant valley with wide stretches of good pasture, offered a lure to frugal, hard-working, thrifty farmers, far from tax-gatherers or bill collectors whom they had found too numerous around their old homesteads!

In those days, after the Revolution, no one was too great or too poor to take a flutter in speculating in land. Even George Washington is said to have yielded to this temptation. Everyone expected that the land which he took up as a squatter would yield him an immediate fortune. If the profit failed to materialize as quickly as was hoped, they still, somehow, merely postponed the realization of dreams, and a man counted upon his holdings as the foundation of great family estates for future generations.

So, on to New Hampshire, beyond into Maine, onward, onward, pushed the trek of these Campanals, sharing in the clearing of virgin soil, cutting down forests, building new towns which never grew into the metropolises of which they dreamed.[12] Plowing, planting, slaving at humble daily toil, and always, in spite of all past disillusionments, pushing on in the expectation that in the next turn of the road Utopia at last would be found.

An outstanding instance of such hopeful expectations was the Hannah Campanel (1756–1842), daughter of William of Ipswich, who married Richard Taylor, a shoemaker and a Revolutionary soldier of a not undistinguished war record. He was originally from North Hampton, of the fifth generation from Anthony Taylor, one of the founders of Hampton. After his marriage, Richard and his wife Hannah first settled at Effingham, New Hampshire, and when that new little village seemed to grow too slowly, they moved on to a still more distant outpost, Newfield, Maine. There they lived and reared a numerous family which today is scattered through the country as far as the Pacific Coast. Many a Taylor in that distinguished New England family traces back his ancestry to this Richard and Hannah.[13]

Thus, into many a New England village, Campanels came and went — just plain, everday folk — never suspected of Jewish antecedents, indeed, perhaps themselves ignorant of it, probably considered, if ever a thought was given the subject, as goodly, shrewd, hardheaded, thrifty Scotch. So often did similarity of name breed confusion, that shortly after Campanels arrived in a village, we find Campbells flourishing and thereafter look in vain for Campanels. Often, too, we find Campbell and Campanel graves sharing the same family burial lots.

Many a good New England family may thus, if they are inclined to genealogy, trace their hardy Scotch pioneer ancestry to these early Campernels.

> The Campbells are comin' o-ho, o-ho,
> The Campbells are comin' o-ho, o-ho,
> The Campbells are comin' to bonnie Lochlevan,
> The Campbells are comin' o-ho, o-ho!

19

ESTHER'S ADVENTURES IN QUEBEC

IN 1738 Quebec was already a growing town of more than four thousand inhabitants. It had long wholly recovered from the days when, only a struggling outpost founded on the site of the Indian village of Stradaconé, it had been captured and held by the English. In 1690, when the attack on it directed from New England under Sir William Phipps had been repulsed, it proudly boasted that never again would it be taken by an enemy. Vauban, the great French engineer, had completely rebuilt its fortification and it had become the outstanding challenge of French North America to Yankee New England and the British colonies to the south.

From its site on a high promontory overlooking the St. Lawrence, with its cathedral, college and governor's palace towering over the one story houses lining the steep streets which led from its busy water front to the upper city, it was an impressive sight as it was first beheld by a traveller of that day from a vessel rounding the Island of Orleans in the bend of the river.

When the youth, Jacques La Fargue, standing in the bow of the good ship *St. Michel* from LaRochelle, on an early September day of 1738, first caught sight of Quebec as the little vessel tacked against current and tide, back and forth across the river, it was not surprising that he thrilled with anticipations of adventure in so beautiful a new world. But when the vessel had made the shore and the time came when he was free to look around, he soon found that, after all, it was for a lively lad but a dull port of a frontier land. Priests and nuns dominated the life of the town. More than a thousand rough Indian traders, with their comings and goings at this season of the year and their rushing of preparations for the winter's trapping, were the center of the busy life of every street. Indians, even from afar, attending the missions and studying the ways of Christianity, outnumbered those who came to the town to drink the white man's firewater. The number of government officials seemed astonishing for so small a town, until it was remembered that this was the center from which was governed all the vast territory to which the French laid claim in North America.

The Governor, the Marquis de Beauharnois, occupied the great palace in the upper city which served both for his residence and for offices of government. Fully conscious of his great responsibility as ruler of a vast domain, he governed ably and with conscious vigilance that his Church and his country should ever aggressively extend their influence and territorial claims to the west, and to the south, where his pioneers and their English enemies waged that constant warfare which finally broke into the open conflict known as the French and Indian War. There also was the Intendant Hocquart, whose high office united the duties and powers of mayor, chief of police, judge, minister of public works and executive director, an efficient official and a remarkable man with a keen interest in everything and in everybody in Quebec.

The youthful Jacques, once his day's work in the loading of the vessel ceased, found himself at loose ends. Especially over Sunday time hung heavy on his hands when, from morning until night, the people were expected to attend the services which the priests seemed to be continually conducting at the many altars with which the town was so liberally provided. Perhaps it was his failure to join his fellow sailors at these services which first brought him to the notice of the authorities. At any rate, it was not very long before he was haled before the town officials and then, as the ancient records note, "quite accidently" his secret was discovered. First, that he was not the handsome, careless, young lad who had nonchalantly swaggered around the town, but a young girl, Esther Brandeau, masquerading as a man under the name of Jacques La Fargue; and, worse still, a Jewess! A Jewess in the pious Catholic citadel of the godly Bishop Laval of reverend memory, where never yet had an unbelieving Jew set foot!

This was so serious a matter that it was immediately brought before the governor and the intendant to take in hand, lest the girl corrupt the morals of the community. So they earnestly and piously pondered the problem, consulting their associates, both lay and ecclesiastical, that in their united wisdom a decision might be arrived at pleasing to both God and man. Was it a crime in Quebec for a woman to apparel herself as a man and call herself by a masculine name? No law, no official regulation covering the situation, was to be found in their books. The young woman had conducted herself so discreetly that the police could not put their finger on any offense with which she might be charged.

At last the intendant turned to the lawyers for advice and guidance. After further thumbing their books and studying the statutes, the brilliant idea of applying the principles of the *Code Noir* to Esther was suggested. How, asked the governor, could that be? Does not the *Code Noir* regulate Negro slavery and apply only to our island possessions? How can that *Code* help us here in Canada? Besides, Esther is a Jewess, not a Negro slave. Then it was pointed out that the king, as an adjunct to the regulation of Negro slavery, had commanded that, to maintain the discipline of the Catholic Church, the Edict of 1615 banishing Jews from France should be extended to his *Isles de l'Amérique* and it was enjoined upon all officers to chase the Jews out of his islands. Although only Martinique, Guadeloupe and St. Christopher were especially named, yet, in 1722, the law had been stretched to include the territory of Louisiana; so why should it not now be applied to Canada as well? Was not Quebec equally entitled to protection against Jews? This, at least, seemed to offer some ground on which they might proceed. Therefore Esther, the Jewess, should be compelled to depart. But how, and when? As gallant French gentlemen they could not just take a charming young girl, even if she were a Jewess, and turn her out of the town where she most assuredly would be a victim of Indian cruelty. But depart she must; and until they solved the problem of ways and means, theirs was the duty to protect their pious community from so corrupting a contact. Now that she was on their hands and the whole town knew her secret, the young woman must no longer be left at large and they must proceed in orderly and legal fashion. So first the intendant ordered her arrested. As there was no place in Quebec in which to imprison a woman, they placed

her in the General Hospital, under the close surveillance of
the Sisters of Charity. Next she must be brought forward
for examination before his Honor, the *Commissaire de la
Marine, Chargé à Québec de la Police des Gens de Mer*.
Before that magistrate, with due formality, under pompous
questioning, with apparent humility, the girl told her story.

She was twenty years old, daughter of David Brandeau,
a Jew, trader, of St. Esprit, near Bayonne. Five years
before, her father and mother had placed her on a Dutch
vessel to take her to Amsterdam to an aunt and a brother.
The vessel was wrecked on the bar of Bayonne, but she
was rescued and brought safely to shore with one of the
crew. She then went to live with a Christian widow at
nearby Biarritz. She found life dull in a small French village,
so Esther decided to run away. Realizing that she lived
in a man's world, Esther determined to overcome, or to
escape, the handicap of her sex, and dressing herself as a
boy she started for Bordeaux. There she shipped, under
the name of Pierre Alansiette, on a vessel destined for
Nantes. After reaching Nantes she deserted and went to
Rennes where she worked for a tailor for six months. When
that no longer proved interesting, she travelled to Clissoy,
where she was employed by the Recollets as a servant.
After three months in the convent she ran away to St.
Malo, where she worked for a baker. Next she went to
Vitre, where she had a situation with an ex-captain of
infantry. Back she wandered to Nantes. On her way there
she was arrested as a thief and confined in prison at Noisel,
but after twenty-four hours it was found that a mistake
had been made and she was set free. So, finding that even
the life of a wandering adventurer was not all her dreams
had fancied, Esther made up her mind that the new world,

of which she had been hearing so much, was probably the Utopia she sought and decided to look up an opportunity to go to America. Accordingly she made her way to the busy port of La Rochelle where she assumed the name of Jacques La Fargue and managed to get passage on the vessel *St. Michel* bound for Quebec.

Asked why she had concealed her sex during five years, she explained that after her shipwreck, after she had lived with the widow at Bayonne, "she thereupon resolved not to return to her father and mother in order that she might enjoy the same liberty as the Christians."

This is the story as Esther told it, solemnly transcribed by officials as a *procès-verbal* and duly and officially subscribed by her. On the face of it there were many improbabilities in the tale and it seems likely that her manner of telling it did not convince her listeners of its accuracy and truthfulness. Fantastic on its face, from a lively young woman, not too serious and delightfully vague, we can readily imagine the side remarks which showed she was not taking the affair or the officials with that solemnity to which they were accustomed and that she herself was rather enjoying her part as the center of so much attention from these punctilious French officials.

It is not difficult to picture Esther, with her tongue in her cheek, thus enjoying herself as she spun out this yarn, embellishing it beyond the dry legal summary which has come down to us from the ancient archives. At any rate, when it was all properly recorded and authenticated, Intendant Hocquart thought this was too puzzling a case for the Quebec authorities to assume the responsibility of handling. He caused it to be embodied in a formal report which he sent to the French minister for the colonies at

Paris with a request that the Quebec Government might be instructed what to do. Does it not indicate that even the intendant himself was not wholly immune from the feminine wiles of Esther when he adds to this official communication: "Since her arrival here at Quebec she has been quite discrete in her conduct. She seems anxious to become a convert to Catholicism but dreads the arrival of her relatives"?

As a cautious official, he was taking no chances; so, at the same time, he instituted an independent investigation to be made in France to check the girl's story through a M. de Pellisier, an official of Bayonne, to whom he appealed for the fullest information and a prompt report.

Evidently Esther was now resolved to get what enjoyment she could out of her visit. She soon got tired playing the game of being converted into a good Catholic and threw it over. Then she kept changing the story of her adventures, until she had everyone upset guessing which of the conflicting versions of her narratives, if any of them at all, was to be believed. Then she began teasing the good Sisters of Charity at the hospital, until they were so distraught that they insisted the government should find other accommodations for her. As her new quarters failed to suit the young lady, Esther insisted upon picking and choosing and changing her place of abode, living at her ease, until she had made so many changes that half the town had been her host. Yet, through all the disturbance she caused, Esther displayed an uncanny art in dealing with men. Even the dour old Intendant Hocquart could not find it in his heart to say she was bad. Now wilful and demanding, now yielding and clinging, at times gentle and soft, then witty and keen with sharp-tongued satire, clear-eyed, with a wisdom which astonished her hearers mixed with childishness, she used all the charms of her sex and played with official Quebec like a cat with a mouse.

At last the long awaited report was received from the intendant's investigator. This proved to be upsetting. David Brandeau admitted to being the father of twelve children, four dead and buried — and he could show their graves — the other eight all present and accounted for without a missing Esther amongst them. Perhaps, like a wise Jew of his day, David knew that it was not healthy for any Jew to be an object of too close an interest from French officialdom and that his safest course was to put himself out of the picture and to trust to Esther's resourcefulness to take care of herself. Or was he actuated by the Christian superstition to avoid the unlucky 13 in his family circle?

In the meantime, the French colonial minister had passed the problem back to the Quebec authorities, writing, under date of April 21, 1739, that he did not believe Esther's story:

> I do not think that one ought to believe the entire story of Esther Brandeau who came to Canada last year on board the ship *St. Michel* in the disguise of a boy, saying she is a Jewess. Be that as it may, I approve your action in placing her in the Quebec General Hospital, and would be greatly pleased to hear that she had become a convert to our faith. You should deal with her in accordance with her own conduct in the colony and with the information which the Sieur de Pelissier, the Ordinator of Bayonne, will convey to you.

There was not much consolation for the worried intendant in such an official avoidance of responsibility. He again wrote to His Excellency, the French Minister for the Colonies, to hurry further instructions:

M. Pelissier, whom I had informed as to the adventures of Esther Brandeau, a young Jewess who came to this country last year, writes to say that she may be the illegitimate child of David Brandeau of Bayonne who told him that he had still eight children at home and that four were dead. I have again questioned the girl, in order to get at the truth ... She is so flighty that she has been unable to settle down at the General Hospital or at any of the several private houses where I had her placed. The turnkey of the prison is the last who had her in charge and has given her a home. Her conduct has not been absolutely bad, but her character is fickle and she is at one time docile and at another rebellious under the instructions kindly given her by zealous ecclesiastics. Nothing is left me but to send her back. Sieur Lafergue, master of the vessel *Le Comte de Matignon*, is to take charge of her and deliver her over to M. de Bélamy.

Now this course of conduct once decided upon, there still remained a question of finance. Who was to pay the expenses of getting Esther out of Quebec back to France? This was indeed a delicate problem of colonial administration. Finally, there being no precedent by which a decision could be arrived at, as the Quebec authorities, the colonial office, and the home government were equally unwilling to assume the burden, the difficulty was put before the king, Louis XV himself, for solution. He, with regal liberality, avoided deciding so complicated an issue between the contending departments by undertaking personally to defray the expense.

The colonial minister thereupon pronounced his benediction on this happy untangling of the problem and wrote to Intendant Hocquart:

You have done well to return the woman, Esther Brandeau, to France. From her own story it was quite clear that you would be obliged to do it.

So Esther returned to France as the king's guest!

With this, the written chapter of Esther's adventures in Quebec closes. History is silent as to her further fate. May we not feel sure that a woman of her adventurous spirit and sense of humor went gaily through life, and that, when the time came in her old age to entertain her grand-children with tales of the days of her youth, a bright-eyed old lady fondly smiled as she described the far distant Quebec and told how a little Jewish girl had returned from far away America to France as the king's guest?

20

LADY REBECCA

Johnson of Bath

Sir Henry Johnson, 1st Bart. G.C.B., b. 1 Jan. 1748, a general in the army, Colonel 5th regiment of foot, and governor of Ross Castle, commanded at the battle of New Ross, 5 June 1798, and was created a baronet 1 Dec. 1818. He m. in 1782 Rebecca, dau. of David Franks, of Philadelphia, and by her (who d. March, 1823) had issue,

1. Henry Allen (Sir), 2nd bart.
2. George Pigot, Capt. 81st foot, d. in Spain 1812.

Arms Per pale sa. and az., on a saltier arg., between three towers, or, fired ppr., one in chief and two in fesse, and two tilting spears saltierwise in base of the second, five cocks of the first. *Crest* — a tower arg.; on the battlement a cock ppr. *Supporters* — Dexter, a grenadier (28th regt.), habited and accoutred and arms ordered ppr.; sinister, a light infantry man (same regt.), habited and accoutred, and arms trailled ppr., supporting with his exterior hand a flag-staff also ppr., therefrom flowing a banner gu., inscribed 'New Ross,' in letters of gold. *Mottoes* — above the crest, 'Vicisti et Vivimus.' Below the shield, 'Nunquam non paratus'.

Burke's *Peerage*

IF IN a happier day a golfer paused on the links over-looking the City of Bath, he looked upon a panorama of gentle green Cotswold hills through which the river Avon wound its slow way around a quiet country town. The graceful crescents of aristocratic Georgian houses, the stately parades, the wide squares with dignified public buildings are so redolent of its great tradition and the nostalgia of the gallant days of Beau Nash, that no imagination is too dull to visualize these half deserted streets resounding

again with their long vanished fashionable throngs intent
on eighteenth-century gaieties. Bath to all English speaking
people must ever be the picture of pleasure, frivolity, gay
fashion and gouty living of the England of the days of the
country squires which Fielding, Smollett, Sheridan, Frances
Burney and Oliver Goldsmith, as well as Thackeray and
Dickens of a later generation, made a part of our common
Anglo-Saxon heritage. As the old ballad goes:

> Of all the gay places the world can afford,
> By gentle and simple for pastime ador'd
> Fine balls and fine concerts, fine buildings
>   and springs,
> Fine walks, and fine views, and a thousand
>   fine things,
> Not to mention the sweet situation and air,
> What place, my dear mother, with Bath can
>   compare?

One fall day, as the eighteenth century was drawing to a
close and Bath was still in the heyday of its glory, a group
of elderly dowagers occupied a corner of the great pump
salon. In spite of the ancient rules, promulgated by Beau
Nash, that lies and scandal be shunned by all company,
they were engaged in that most universal of indoor sports,
gossiping about their friends and neighbors, and particularly
about the absent Lady Rebecca Johnson.

"They say she's a Jewess," said Lady Barclay, "and the
Colonel married her when he was off in the Colonies fighting
the Indians at some frontier outpost I believe they call
Philadelphia."

"Was it the east India or the West Indies?" asked the
rich widow, Lady Grundy.

Lady Rebecca Johnson

"Oh America, my dear," explained the General's wife.

"It's the way she carries herself; it's not that she's beautiful. Fine feathers, you know —," continued Lady Barclay.

"Nonsense." said the Duchess. "I say she is beautiful. Ask any young beau and you will hear what the men think."

"It's the things she says, so unexpected-like and puzzling, that makes them all laugh; that's what brings them around her wherever she goes, though for the life of me I never can see what's amusing," interrupted the stout Lady Dunce.

"Aye, beauty and wit," added the Duchess, "is a hard combination to beat."

"Jewish impudence, I call it," whispers Lady Candor to her neighbor, Lady Barclay.

"She dances divinely," sighed the gouty lady from Wales.

"At her age too! She must be all of fifty," added Lady Temple.

"The way she has with the young men, she doesn't give the young girls a chance," injected the Bishop's wife, "and as for her dressing, do you think —"

The Duchess silenced that pontifical lady with a finality which closed the session: "She's still the toast of the season and, bless her kind heart, gay spirits, wit and lovely manners, she's my friend."

In the days of her matronly maturity Rebecca cut as great a figure in the fashionable society of Bath as she had when she reigned the belle of the pre-Revolutionary Philadelphia of her youth.

Born in 1760, the fourth of five children of David Franks, Lady Rebecca Johnson came from a distinguished Jewish family which at her birth was in the third American generation. The family has been traced to Aaron Franks of Germany, who became an influential member of the London Jewish community towards the end of the seventeenth century. Her father, David Franks, was recognized as one of Philadelphia's outstanding wealthy merchants and moved in the city's most exclusive social circles. In 1748 he was a member of the Pennsylvania Assembly. In 1765 he was one of the eighty-four Philadelphia merchants signing the non-importation agreement. He had acted as a British governmental agent in the French and Indian War and, when the Revolution broke out, he still continued this connection as "agent to the contractors for victualling the troops of the King of Great Britain."

Revolutionary Philadelphia, as the seat of the Continental Congress, was then not only politically the heart of the colonies but its leading social capital with a brilliant and gay life in which, in spite of war, the patriotic Whigs and the Tory magnates still continued to vie in friendly rivalry for social supremacy. In 1778, General Howe captured Philadelphia and established his headquarters there. The Continental Congress was compelled to seek refuge at York, General Washington was driven to the heartbreaking winter of Valley Forge, while the handsome and polished young English officers attached to General Howe's army added a lively and colorful element to the social life of the city.

Such was the Philadelphia in which Rebecca Franks reigned as acknowledged belle, renowned for beauty, grace and wit. True, Miss Betty Shippen might dispute with her the claim of the town's most beautiful girl; but Rebecca had no rival as the social favorite of the day. Young and old alike paid her court. Indeed, it is said that old General

Howe himself was no infrequent visitor at her home and that "there were rare doings at David Franks' when General Howe would tie his horse at the door and go in to call on the young ladies." Especially it was reported he enjoyed a good laugh at Miss Rebecca's spirited sallies.

With all this Rebecca appears as a sweet young girl with brains and a turn for quick brilliant repartee which lent a piquant charm to her natural beauty. Indeed, her witticisms were constantly being repeated for the edification of those who were not fortunate enough to have been present when they were uttered. Some of them were even recorded in the chronicles of the day lest they be lost to future generations.

Preserved in the archives of the Maryland Historical Society, one of her girlish letters of this period to her friend, Anne Harrison of Wye Island, Maryland, has been so frequently quoted in all accounts of Colonial social life that it has become an American classic.

Dear Nancy.— You may see the above is not my writing; a very smart beau, I assure you, wrote it, but not being acquainted with your disposition was afraid to go on.

I expected ere this to have had an answer to the letter I wrote by Betty Tilghman. What is your excuse. I hope 'tis want of opportunity and not inclination.

You can have no idea of the life of continued amusement I live in. I can scarce have a moment to myself. I have stole this while everybody is retired to dress for dinner. I am but just come from under Mr. J. Black's hands and most elegantly am I dressed for a ball this evening at Smith's where we have one every Thursday. You would not know the room 'tis so much improv'd.

I wish to Heaven you were going with us this evening to judge for yourself. I spent Tuesday evening at Sir Wm Howes where we had a concert and Dance. I asked his leave to send you a Handkerchief to show the fashions. He very politely gave me permission to send anything you wanted, tho' I told him you were a Delegate's Lady. I want to get a pair of Buckles for your Brother Joe.

If I can't, tell him to be in the fashion he must get a pair of Harness one. The Dress is more ridiculous and pretty than anything that ever I saw — great quantity of different coloured feathers on the head at a time besides a thousand other things. The Hair dress'd very high in the shape Miss Vining's was the night we returned from Smiths — the Hat we found in your Mother's Closet wou'd be of a proper size. I have an afternoon cap with one wing — tho' I assure you I go less in the fashion than most of the Ladies — no being dress'd without a hoop. B. Bond makes her first appearance tonight at the rooms.

No loss for partners, even I am engaged to seven different gentlemen for you must know 'tis a fix'd rule never to dance but two dances at a time with the same person. Oh how I wish Mr. P. wou'd let you come in for a week or two — tell him I'll answer for your being let to return. I know you are as fond of a gay life as myself — you'd have an opportunity of rakeing as much as you choose either at Plays, Balls Concerts or Assemblys. I've been but 3 evenings alone since we mov'd to town. I begin now to be almost tired. Tell Mrs. Harrison she has got a gentleman in her house, who promises me not to let a single thing in it be hurt and I'm sure he'll keep his word — the family she left in it still remain. I had a long conversation about you the other evening with John Saunders. He is just the same as when you knew him — two or three more of your old acquaint-

ances are in town such as Prideaux & Jock DeLancy
they often ask after you. Is Mrs. White with you.
I long to hear all that concerns you. Do pray try to
get an opportunity. The clock is now striking four,
and Moses is just going out to dinner — quite the
Congress hours. Moses wrote to your Mother about
her house six weeks ago. Did she get the letter. All
your Philadelphia friends well and desire their
loves — Mine to all in Maryland.

When you see the Miss Tilghmans, tell them I
never hear a new song or piece of music, that I dont
wish them to have it. I must go finish dressing as
I'm engaged out to Tea.

God bless you.
R. F.

Thursday
Feby 26, '78.

I send some of the most fashionable Ribbon and
Gauze have tried to get Joe's Buckles in all the best
shops, but in vain. B. Redman is here and sends
her love.

In 1778, Sir William Howe relinquished the command of
the British Army in America to Sir Henry Clinton and
returned to England. His officers in Philadelphia, under
the leadership of Major André, resolved to stage, as a
parting compliment, a series of entertainments which should
outdo anything ever witnessed in the country. Copying a
recent London success, they planned a great pageant, a
Meschianza (Italian medley), beginning with a grand
regatta, then a series of tableaux followed by a procession
through especially erected triumphal arches, and ending with
a grand ball.

Rebecca, chosen one of the two "Queens of Beauty," was
the outstanding figure of the gorgeous fête. History has

recorded her appearance as the quintessence of the luxurious fashion of the day. Eighteen years old, of fine figure, clothed in a white silk gown trimmed with black, with a white sash edged with black, hers was "a polonaise dress, which formed a flowing robe and was open in front to the waist. The sash, six inches wide, was filled with spangles; also the veil, which was edged with silver lace." The head dress was towering, filled with a profusion of pearls and jewels.

It was not long after this that the British evacuated Philadelphia, making New York their headquarters, and General Washington and the Continental Congress again returned. At first there was an attempt by the Whig ladies to ostracize from society the Tory ladies who had taken part in the *Meschianza*, but it was soon found to be impossible, and Rebecca again resumed her social leadership. Coming from this period is the story that Lieutenant-Colonel Jack Stewart of Maryland, who served in the Continental Army, jealous of the late social successes of the red-coated British officers, dressed himself in a scarlet coat to attend an assembly. When he met Miss Franks, he asked her to notice his attire, attempting to twit her on the attentions she had accepted from the British officers:

"I have adopted your color, my princess, the better to secure a kind reception; deign to smile on a true knight." Turning to her friends Rebecca remarked:

"How the ass glories in the lion's skin!"

In 1780 her Tory father, David Franks, decided to leave Philadelphia with his family and remove to New York. It is said that the Executive Council of Pennsylvania, in issuing the pass to permit this, intimated that compulsory measures would be adopted if he did not avail himself of its use.

After the brilliance of Philadelphia the life of New York seemed to Rebecca to lack the social graces to which she was accustomed. A letter which she wrote to her sister, Abigail, then the wife of Andrew Hamilton, Esquire, of the Woodlands, was preserved by being intercepted and placed in their files by the American Commissary of Prisoners. It is so incisive a picture of the society of the day and sheds so much light on the life she led that, although somewhat lengthy, it is here reproduced almost in extenso.

Flatbush, Saturday 10 o'clk. August 10th 1781

My Dear Abby,

The night before last I receiv'd yr letter — by Comfort — I wish I had been in town to have an-swer'd it, and sent the things out; but I fancy ere I could have receiv'd yrs he must have left E(lizabeth) Town; and a few days ago I got yrs and the checkers — all of which I thank you and them for. If I have time this morning I'll answer them and the girls' letters. You will think I have taken up my abode for the Summer at M^{rs} V(an) Horn's, but this day I return to the disagreeable hot town — much against my will, and the inclinations of this family— but I cannot bear Papa's being so much alone — nor will he be persuaded to quit it — tho' I am sure he can have no business to keep him. Two nights he staid with us, which is all I've seen of him since I left home. I am quite angry with him. I have wrote you several times within these two weeks — you can have no cause to complain, without it is of being too often troubled with my nonsense. Those you mention'd sending by P(olly) R(edman) have not yet come to hand. The ham is safe — the crackers havn't as yet made their appearance. I fear they never will, tho' I heard they were safe on S(taten) Island. I fancy the person to whose care they were sent thought them too good to part with. The person who sent them and the ham, I beg you'll give my sincere thanks to.

You ask a description of the Miss V(an) Horn that was with me — Cornelia — she is in disposition as fine a girl as ever you saw — a great deal of good humour and good sense. Her person is too large for a beauty, in my opinion, and yet I am not partial to a little woman; her complection, eyes and teeth are very good, and a great quantity of light brown hair (Entre nous, the girls of New York excell us Philadelphians in that particular and in their forms). A sweet countenance and agreeable smile. Her feet, as you desire, I'll say nothing about — they are V(an) Horn's and what you'd call Willings. But her sister Kitty is the belle of the family I think, tho' some give the preference to Betsy. You'll ask how many thousand there are, only five. Kitty's form is much in the stile of our admir'd Mrs Galloway, but rather taller and larger — her complection very fine, and the finest hair I ever saw. Her teeth are beginning to decay, which is the case of most N(ew) Y(ork) girls after eighteen: and a great deal of elegance of manner. By the by, few New York ladies know how to entertain company in their own houses unless they introduce card tables except this family, (who are remarkable for their good sense and ease). I don't know a woman or girl that can chat above half an hour, and that on the form of a cap, the colour of a ribbon or the set of a hoop-stay or jupon. I will do our ladies, that is Philadelphians, the justice to say they have more cleverness in the turn of an eye than the N(ew) Y(ork) girls have in their whole composition. With what ease, have I seen a Chew, a Penn, Oswald, Allen, and a thousand others entertain a large circle of both sexes, and the conversation without the aid of cards not flag or seem the least strain'd or stupid. Here, or more properly speaking

in N(ew) Y(ork), you enter the room with a formal
set curtesy and after the how do's, 't is a fine, or a bad
day, and those trifling nothings are finish'd, all's a
dead calm 'till the cards are introduced, when you see
pleasure dancing in the eyes of all the matrons and
they seem to gain new life. The misses, if they have a
favourite swain, frequently decline playing for the
pleasure of making love — for to all appearances
'tis the ladies and not the gentlemen, that shew a
preference nowadays. 'Tis here, I fancy, always leap
year. For my part that am used to quite another
mode of behaviour, I cannot help shewing my surprise, perhaps they call it ignorance, when I see a
lady single out her pet to lean almost in his arms at
an Assembly or play-house, (which I give my honour
I have too often seen both in married and single),
and to hear a lady confess a partiality for a man who
perhaps she has not seen three times. Well, I declare
such a gentleman is a delightful creature, and I could
love him for my husband — or I could marry such or
such a person; and scandal says most who have been
married, the advances have first come from the ladie's
side, or she has got a male friend to introduce him
and puff her off. 'Tis really the case, and with me
they lose half their charms — and I fancy there wou'd
be more marriage was another mode adopted; but
they've made the men so saucy that I sincerely believe
the lowest Ensign thinks 'tis but ask, and have — a
red coat and smart epaulette is sufficient to secure a
female heart.

I was oblig'd to cut just as I finished the *Heart*.
General Robertson, Commodore Affleck and Major
Murray made their appearance, and as I was writing
in the parlour quite *en deshabille*, I was obliged to
make the best of my (way) out. I am glad of it as it
broke my ill-natured train of ideas. I am quite
ashamed of it. There is too much truth to have it

known, but if it should be known I'll throw the blame
on you, as 'twas owing to the question you ask'd of
this family. Remember, I again say, they are excepted in every particular. I shall send a pattern of
the newest bonnet — there is no crown, but gauze
raised on wire, and quite pinched to a sugar loaf at
top — the lighter the trimming the more fashionable,
and all quilling. Two more beaux — Captain Affleck
and a Mr Biddulph — the first frightful, the other
very genteel and clever. Lord! if this letter is seen I
shall be killed. If it is, I must fly to you for protection.
You may imagine what an indifferent I am to continue writing and beaux in the room. But so it is — I
am not what I was. . . .

And now my dear Abby I am going to tell you a
piece of news that you'll dislike as much as I do.
What think you of Moses* coming out with a cockade!
He writes to Papa and me 'tis his serious resolve, and
we must not be surprised if we see him this Summer.
The idea of entering an Ensign at his time of life
distresses (me) more than anything I've met with
since I left you. All the comfort I have is that his
uncle M. will not allow him. I have not had an opportunity of asking Papa's opinion of it, as I received
the letters since I've been here; but I am certain he
must disapprove of it as much as I do. Was he ten or
twelve years younger I should not have the smallest
objection — but 'tis too late for him to enter into
such a life — and after the indulgence he's ever been
used to he'll never brook being commanded from post
to pillar by every brat of boy who may chance to be
longer in the service. Tomorrow I shall write to him
and make use of every argument I am mistress of to
dissuade him from so mad a project, which I hope

---

* Their brother.

will arrive in time to prevent it, for if he once enters
I would be the first to oppose his quitting it — as I
ever lov'd a steady character. The danger of the war
I have in a measure reconciled myself to. 'Tis only
his age I object to and the dis-agreeable idea of his
being sent the Lord knows where. If he does enter,
which I hope to God he may not, I wish he may join
the 17ᵗʰ, or else get into the Dragoons — the latter
I think he'll prefer on account of his lameness. He
has not I believe wrote to you by this oppor'ty —
aunt Franks and aunt Richa I believe have. . . .

Nanny Van Horn and self employed yesterday
morning in trying to dress a rag baby in the fashion,
but could not succeed. It shall however go, as 'twill
in some degree give you an idea of the fashion as to
the Jacket and pinning on of the handkerchief. Yours
you say reaches to the arm. I know it, but it must
be pinned up to the top of the shoulder and quite
under the arm, as you would a girl's Vandyke. The
fuller it sets the handsomer 'tis thought. Nobody
ever sets a handkerchief out in the neck — and a
gauze handkerchief is always worn double, and the
largest that can be got. 'Tis pinned round the throat
as Mʳˢ Penn always did, and made to set out before
like a chitterling of a man's shirt. The ladies here
always wear either a pin or broach as the men do.
But what put it in your head both the aprons was for
B. B. I am sure I mention'd one was for you. I shall
send her something by the first oppurtunity for her
remaining half dollar and Miss V. I wish I cou'd have
been in town to have sent them by Comfort. I have
wrote you so long a letter that you must make the
girls take a share of it, as I have not time to write
them now, and there is nothing new to tell them.
What I alluded to the Monday afternoon's was the
Militia Day. Tell P(eggy) C(hew) I beg she'll ac-

cept the spangles and thread. 'Tis the only return
I can make for the pleasure I receive from her very
entertaining letters. Tell Mrs Bond I hadn't a line
by this packet from Phene, nor does Moses for a
wonder mention him. She may rely on any letters
coming to us being forwarded to her or him by the
first safe opport'y. I very much doubt your having
patience to get thro' this scrawl.— I have not, therefore shall not attempt reading it over.

Yesterday the Grenadiers had a race at the Flat-
lands, and in the afternoon this house swarm'd with
beaux and some very smart ones. How the girls
wou'd have envy'd me cou'd they have peep'd and
seen how I was surrounded and yet I shou'd have
(felt) as happy if not much more to have spent the
afternoon with the Thursday Party at the Woodlands.
I am happy to hear you're out there, as the town must
be dreadfull this hot summer. N(ew) Y(ork) is bad
enough tho' I do not think 'tis as warm as Philadelphia. The negro boy is not arrived, the last I heard
from there, they, or rather he, was on the look out for
a good one. I begin to have the fidgets 'tis so long
since I've heard — not a line since the 10th of last
month. Y(ou)r health in punch. The girls join with
me in begging to be remember'd, particularly to
Mrs Harleston and her mother. I hope you'll visit
them. Do — if 'tis only on Harleston's account whose
memory I ever shall respect. I have spent happier
days with him than I fear I ever shall experience
again. If you tell Billy H(amilton) I say so, he'll swear
I still retain a remainder of my former *penchant*, but
assure him 'tis only a pure and lively friendship. Letters this moment from you and P(eggy) C(hew) and
one from Mrs Arnold — I must stop to read them.
'Tis dated the 5th, and the one from P. C. the 4th. I
thank you both, and let this letter for once satisfy

cept the spangles and thread. 'Tis the only return
I can make for the pleasure I receive from her very
entertaining letters. Tell Mrs Bond I hadn't a line
by this packet from Phene, nor does Moses for a
wonder mention him. She may rely on any letters
coming to us being forwarded to her or him by the
first safe opport'y. I very much doubt your having
patience to get thro' this scrawl.— I have not, therefore shall not attempt reading it over.

her and you. Tell B B her apron cost a dollar, of course I have half a dollar remaining. To Nancy Coxe and all my Carolina acquaintance I beg my best love and respects. I shall as soon as I go to town this evening, send M^rs A(rnol)d's letter. I have not seen or heard of her these two months. Her name is as little mentioned as her husband's. Mrs Robert Morris and daughters drank tea here this week. Neither of the girls are married or going to. I fancy Major B. don't wish to marry a whole family, which would be the case there. I should love to see Jem Postell — if you see him, tell him so. I don't pity Gurney. Tell Billy I oftner think of him than I fear he does of me, Mrs. Armstrong, &c. Well, this is sufficiently long — love to every body.

I have not had one Magazine sent me since I came here. The other books if possible you shall have. Josy S(wift) looks as handsome as ever, and stutters as usual. Tell P(eggy) C(hew) I give her leave to read all I write if she'll take the trouble. I am happy here, tell her 'tis only for a visit — I wish to be with you.

Yours,

R. F.

At the age of 22, Rebecca married, in New York, Lieutenant-Colonel Henry Johnson, an officer in the British army. The newspaper of the day, the *New York Gazette and Weekly Mercury* of Monday, January 28, 1782, carried the news of the event:

Last Thursday evening was married at her father's house in the Broad-Way, Miss Franks, youngest

daughter of David Franks, Esq. to Henry Johnston
(*sic*) Esq., nephew to General Walsh and Lieut.
Colonel to the XVII Regiment foot.

She returned with him to England to make their home
in Bath.

In contrast with the hectic wartime days of fast moving
business and politics to which she had been accustomed,
she now retired to the comfortable domestic life befitting a
young married lady of the eighteenth century.

She had two sons, Henry Allen, who succeeded as the
second baronet, and George Pigot. Both of them later
were officers in the army. George, captain of a British
infantry regiment, was killed in the Peninsular campaign
of 1812.

As his duty called, Colonel Johnson saw active army
service, now here, now there, until he was sent to Ireland
as Inspector-General of recruiting. There he was promoted
to be Governor of Ross Castle. As Major-General he was
in command at the battle of New Ross during the Irish
uprisings of '98, where he won a much praised victory. By
1809, when he retired from the army, he had become a
General. He was created a baronet in 1818.

As the years passed, Lady Rebecca, no longer the jolly
beauty of keen sarcasms and clever quips with heart intent
on beaux, ribbons and dances, became a stately lady, distinguished by her grace, urbanity and hospitality, who
quite naturally assumed leadership in the social life of Bath.

She had the happiness of seeing her oldest son marry an
American, Elizabeth Philipse, daughter of that most aris-
tocratic of New York Dutch families — the Philipses of
Philipseburg.

One of her old Philadelphia friends who visited her in Bath in 1810 wrote home that she had found her still charming and beautiful, but "rather inclining to embonpoint," and still stimulating and cheerful company.

In 1816 General Winfield Scott, then a young soldier of twenty-nine, fresh from triumphs won in the war of 1812, was sent abroad on a diplomatic mission by a grateful American government. He came to England armed with a letter of introduction to the great Lady Rebecca. Eagerly he journeyed to Bath to present it that he might meet the lady whose brilliance, beauty and wit was still in his day a Philadelphia tradition. In stilted mid-Victorian style he has told his adventure in the third person:

> She had become from bad health prematurely old — a very near approach to a ghost, but with eyes still bright, and other remains of her former self.
>
> She had been rolled out in an easy chair to receive him [Scott]. On presentation, he was transfixed by her eager, but kindly gaze. "Is this the young rebel?" were her first words. "My dear, it is your countryman!" said Sir Henry, fearing that Scott might take offense. "Yes, it is" she quickly added, "the young rebel; and you have taken the liberty to beat his Majesty's troops." Scott, by a pleasant word or two, parried the impeachment as well as he could; but the lady followed up the accusation, with specific references, which surprised not a little. Scott soon found himself seated by her side, with a hand clasped in both of hers — cold and clammy, as in the article of death. Taking a sudden turn, she exclaimed, with emphasis: "I have gloried in my rebel countrymen!" Then pointing to Heaven, with both hands, she added, in a most affecting tone: "Would to God I, too, had been a patriot." A gentle remonstrance was

interposed by the husband, who had been carried away by sympathy up to this moment. Turning now to him, she said, with earnestness of truth: "I do not, I have never regretted my marriage. No woman was ever blessed with a kinder, a better husband; but I ought to have been a patriot before marriage." Hers were the only dry eyes of the party.

The *Gentleman's Magazine* for March 1823, in its obituaries of notables, carried the following:

> Somersetshire — In Bath, 63, Rebecca, wife of Gen. Sir Henry Johnson, G.C.B.— dau. of David Franks, esq. and sister to John Franks, esq. of Isleworth. By her husband she had two sons, one killed while gallantly fighting in the Peninsula, and the other is now Knight of the Military Order of William, etc., etc.

21

MEDFORD'S JEWISH STREET

THAT Newport should have named one of its principal
streets after the first Jewish rabbi settled there may
not be surprising considering how early and how important
were its pioneer Jewish settlers. We pass up and down
Touro Street and view Newport's old synagogue and the
old Jewish burying ground with hardly a thought of the
street's name. But why should Medford have a Touro
Avenue? Was it merely a borrowing from Newport, or is
there a story?

The ancient Massachusetts town of Medford today is
no more than a northern suburb of metropolitan Boston.
Situated on the Mystic River, seven miles from Boston,
founded in 1630 by a settler from Salem, it was in Colonial
days an important seaport where vessels were not only
built but carried on a large foreign commerce. While it
never attained the ancient distinction of the ports of Boston,
Newport or New York as a center of commercial activity,
it was a factor in the Colonial West India trade. As early
as 1715–1720, due to its peculiarly good water, distilleries
began to flourish there. The fame of its rum manufactured
from West India molasses still persists in the traditions of
"Medford rum." Schooners of the largest tonnage sailed
up and down the river to the distillery wharves which lined
the shore. The town had shown a steady growth from less
than a thousand at the time of the Revolution to almost

1800 by 1830. The temperance wave which swept through the country in 1830 dealt a fatal blow to this industry, from which the town never fully recovered.

The Touros were an ancient Dutch Jewish family who had settled in Curaçao as early as 1650. Isaac Touro, at the age of 20, came to Newport in 1758 and became the first rabbi of its first synagogue.

During the American Revolution the Jews of Newport espoused the American cause; so, when the British captured that city, the Jews were compelled to flee. Rabbi Isaac Touro, with his wife Reyna and his two sons Judah and Abraham, fled to Jamaica where he died in 1783. Moses Michael Hays, the eminent Boston merchant, Isaac Touro's brother-in-law, brought the widowed mother and her two boys back to Boston where they grew up as members of his household.

At the age of twenty-three Abraham was sent as a super-cargo on a trading voyage to the Mediterranean. Then, after four years of further commercial training, he migrated to New Orleans, then still a French possession, where he built up a large and successful business and became one of America's leading merchants. After amassing a fortune he returned to Boston, where he made his home with his sister Rebecca and continued his business activities. He had a shipyard in Medford where he built his own vessels and soon became recognized as one of Massachusetts' leading citizens.

That Abraham Touro was a loyal Jew is evidenced by a curious incident entered upon the town records of Boston. The first entry in its twenty-first book, dated 1816, reads:

Mr. Abraham Touro applied to the Town Clerk & requested that his religious profession might be recorded on the Town's books — & that he belonged to a Synagogue of the Jews.

Nor is this all. When, after having been closed for fifty years, the Newport synagogue was reopened in 1850, the city recalled that

the synagogue, the street on which it is situated, as also the burying grounds, are kept in elegant order, from the proceeds of a legacy by the late Abraham Touro, now amounting to fifteen thousand dollars, and to the liberality of the well known Judah Touro of New Orleans.

By his will Abraham Touro bequeathed ten thousand dollars

to the Legislature of the State of Rhode Island, for the purpose of supporting the Jewish Synagogue in that state, in special trust to be appropriated to that object, in such manner as the said legislature together with the municipal authority of the Town of Newport may from time to time direct and appoint.

In 1823, by act of its General Assembly, the State of Rhode Island passed appropriate legislation to accept the legacy. To insure the faithful discharge of its trust, a law was passed providing that neither the city council of Newport, nor any other, should in any manner "interfere with or restrain the full free exercise of the Jewish religion in said synagogue by any individual of that faith residing in Newport." The General Treasurer of the State of Rhode Island, the Mayor of the City of Newport, and three persons elected by the Congregation Jeshuat Israel, were by this legislation vested with the authority and duty of safeguarding the synagogue.

Thus the State of Rhode Island, in contrast with what we have seen in less happy lands, has the unique distinction of serving as the protector and guardian of a synagogue.[1]

When, thirty-two years later, his brother Judah Touro of New Orleans died and left ten thousand dollars "to endow the ministry" of the Jewish synagogue of Newport, the City of Newport received the fund and is perhaps the only American city which officially pays part of the salary of a rabbi to officiate in the local synagogue. So state and city unite in thus preserving the old Newport synagogue as an enduring example of the ideal of religious and racial equality in our common Americanism.

In the days of which we write the suburban town of Medford was not only the center of the rum trade, but was known also as the center of a choice and aristocratic society. Governor Brooks, the famous Magoun family and other good old Colonial leaders, had elegant homesteads where they lived in state and entertained in a way which added a second fame to the town. Governor Brooks was Medford's most distinguished citizen. Native of the town (1752), he had served at the battle of Lexington and Concord, at the siege of Boston and throughout the Revolution, attaining the rank of Lieutenant-Colonel in the 8th Massachusetts Regiment. He had then held public office until, in 1816, he was elected Governor of Massachusetts. He died in 1825. Abraham Touro, as a close friend of Governor Brooks, was attracted to Medford and built there a splendid summer home — a great, white, circular structure which was one of the landmarks of the district.

On October 25, 1822, at the early age of 48, Abraham Touro died in Boston as a result of an accident.

Now his death gave rise to a strange Medford tradition. The story was repeated from mouth to mouth until it became history:

> When General LaFayette reached Massachusetts, Mr. Touro offered him his noble horse for his entrance into Boston. On the day of that triumphal entry, Mr. Touro was standing in his chaise to catch his first sight of the illustrious visitor, when a sudden start of his horse threw him from his place and broke his leg. The fracture was a very bad one and the patient grew worse daily. The physicians and surgeons did all they could, and finally assured him that nothing but amputation could save his life. With a Jew's traditionary prejudice against that operation, he firmly answered thus: "No! I will never go into heaven with one leg."

Inasmuch as Lafayette did not return to America until two years after Touro's death, no other comment seems necessary.

The newspaper of the day reports his death in its dry routine way:

> While viewing the military parade on the 3d inst. in a chaise, his horse was frightened by the fire of the artillery and became unmanageable, and Mr. T. in leaping from the chaise fractured his leg so seriously, that notwithstanding the best surgical assistance, a mortification ensued and terminated his life.

Recently there have come to light some further details from a local Medford historian:

> Mr. Dudley Hall told me in 1853 (that) Mr. Touro lent his own horse to a military friend to ride on the parade — and his friend sent his own horse to Mr.

Touro, to use in place of his own — after breakfast
he concluded to drive the horse into Boston, and
drove over to Mr. Hall, to ride with him. Mr. H. did
not wish to go that day, but Mr. Touro urged him,
and finally told him he did not like to go alone with
so spirited a horse as he had, when Mr. H. got into
the Chaise, and rode into Boston, and then left him
(at) head of Elm Street, and went into State Street.
Mr. Touro then drove up to the Common, where
the accident happened. B. L. S(wan) says Mr.
Touro was standing up in his Chaise to look over
the heads of the Crowd, and see the Troops, when at
12, a Cannon was fired — his horse started, and
turned around when he fell out — his leg was broken
below the knee.

His old mansion in South Street disappeared years ago,
but the fame of its beauty was long Medford's pride.

How and why Medford came to name this street after its
first Jewish resident we know not. However, his name is
not alone perpetuated in this unimportant street. He also
lives in the annals of American art, for his portrait is one of
the distinguished paintings of Gilbert Stuart and presents
him as a very attractive and charming young man.

Abraham Touro was the earliest of our great American
Jewish philanthropists.[2] Not only had he been generous
during his lifetime but, besides his bequest for the Newport
synagogue, he gave $5,000 to the City of Newport for re-
pairing and preserving the street leading from the Burying
Ground to Main Street. He left $10,000 to Shearith Israel
of New York. In a broad charity that knew no bounds of
creed, a bequest of $10,000 to the Massachusetts General
Hospital marked him as the institution's greatest benefactor
of that day. Other non-sectarian legacies were $5,000 to the

Abraham Touro's House

Boston Female Asylum, $5,000 to the Asylum of Indigent
Boys, and $5,000 to the Boston Humane Society.

His brother, Judah Touro, who did not return to Boston
but continued as a conspicuous merchant in New Orleans
until his death in 1854, is better known, because of his greater
riches, as the Great Jewish Philanthropist. Every needy
cause turned to him for help and seldom left empty-handed.
We have alluded to his generosity which in 1822 rescued the
New Orleans Unitarian Church. In New Orleans he founded
the first free public library, erected an infirmary, and
built a synagogue for its Jews. When in 1840 it seemed
that, for lack of funds, the building of the Bunker Hill
monument would have to be abandoned or postponed,
Judah Touro came forward with a donation of $10,000 to
prevent such failure. In 1843, when the monument was
dedicated, the local poet of the occasion celebrated this
timely generosity:

> Amos[3] and Judah — venerated names
>   Patriarch and prophet, press their equal
>   claims,
> Like generous coursers, running neck and neck
>   Each aids the work by giving it a check,
> Christian and Jew, they carry out one plan,
>   For though of different faiths, each in heart
>   a man.

Judah Touro's will, famous in its day as an unparalleled
example of a charity which knew no limitations of creed or
space, distributed his huge fortune in a manner in which no
other possessor of a large fortune up to that time had done.
To New Orleans was left $80,000 to establish an almshouse
besides gifts of $5,000 each to its Society for the Relief of
Orphans, St. Armas Asylum for the Relief of Destitute

Females and Children, New Orleans Female Orphan Asylum, St. Mary's Catholic Boys Asylum, Milne Asylum, Firemans' Charitable Association, Seaman's Home, and enough to found a Hebrew Hospital for New Orleans.

To the City of Newport he bequeathed $10,000 that the famous old Norse Stone Mill might be preserved as a public monument, and $3,000 to its Redwood Library. In addition to generous provisions to the New Orleans and Newport synagogues, every American synagogue then in existence received a gift of from $2,000 to $5,000. To the work of Moses Montefiore in Palestine he left $50,000[4] in addition to providing $10,000 for the North American Relief Society for the Indigent Jews in Jerusalem. Jewish philanthropies throughout our country were also handsomely remembered, while of Boston's Christian institutions he bequeathed $10,000 to the Massachusetts Female Hospital, $5,000 to the Asylum of Orphan Boys in Boston and $500 to the Female Orphan Asylum.

In accordance with wishes expressed in their respective wills, both these brothers, the first of America's Jewish philanthropists, lie in the beautiful cemetery outside the Newport Synagogue.

Abraham Touro's tombstone records his virtues:

> Deeply lamented by his afflicted relatives
> and innumerable friends,

> Distinguished and esteemed in those virtues
> and good qualities which exalt the
> character of man.

22

A 'FORTY-NINER

"All men are usurpers somewhat in their way,
  But the high and the lowly acknowledged his sway,
  And even the children would pause in their play
  With greetings for Emperor Norton."
            Emperor Norton I — Fred Emerson Brooks.

ALMOST as soon as it had happened, no dwelling place
of man was too remote to learn the news that gold had
been discovered in California. The world needed no wire-
less to hear that. As from the dawn of history, Argonauts
swarmed from every quarter of the globe, drawn irresistibly
by the magnetic lure of gold, to follow a course to the en-
chanted shores of a new Colchis. Over land, over sea, around
the stormy Horn, across the plague-infested Panama Isth-
mus, traversing wide arid western plains and climbing steep
mountains, from the north, south, west and east mad hordes
of gold-crazed fortune-hunters poured towards the straggling
Spanish villages which had been California before this discovery.

November 23, 1849, the little Hamburg schooner, *Fran-
zeska*, from Rio, was ending a long, slow voyage as she
approached the Golden Gate and sailed through its bay
towards sprawling San Francisco. Her seven passengers
were at last reaching the goal of their dreams as its strange
panorama unfolded itself.

Joshua Abraham Norton, one of these seven, was a Jew
born in London, tall and well built, of gentlemanly appear-

ance, thirty years of age, who had already sought his fortune far from his native land. In South Africa, with his father, a pioneer farmer and trader who had settled there in 1820, he had already met with both adventure and some of the ups and downs of fortune. The father, John Norton, had been one of the founders of Algoa Bay, now Port Elizabeth. Joshua had left Algoa Bay to seek a wider field of adventure in California.

The San Francisco which he first beheld that winter day of '49 had already outgrown the insignificant cluster of Mexican huts which had been the original settlement of Yerba Buena Cove, known to American whalers as a convenient port in which to replenish their supply of water. A small town of a few hundred in July, by September it numbered its thousands, and by this November day an irresistible influx of newcomers was stretching its boundaries not only along the foreshore into the sand dunes but into the surrounding hillsides. A crowded, conglomerate, expanding frontier outpost, it was visibly an unplanned city of wooden shacks, canvas tents, a maze of rickety lean-tos, old adobe huts and new brick buildings, placed, regardless of neighbors, wherever space afforded. Vessels had been run ashore, abandoned by gold-crazed crews and left to rot. Indiscriminately crowding each other were stores, tents, saloons, hotels, warehouses, brothels, huts, boarding houses where men slept thirty or forty to a room, and gambling halls which ran twenty-four hours a day. There had been, as yet, no time to build streets. The roads were still little more than quagmires through which a constant stream of caravans passed in and out of town. Back and forth to the mines they hustled night and day. The sides of these roads were overrun with merchandise. The town hummed with the blare of raucous music, the roar of whiskey madness, the hustle of busy traders and the steady bang of carpenters' hammers building new shelters into which impatient owners moved without waiting completion. Over all was feverish impatience.

The people pouring in from every end of the earth were of all sorts and conditions: miners from all the mines of the world, merchants, cutthroats, ministers, gamblers, staid bankers, musicians, unruly sailors, patent medicine quacks, dandies, hoodlums, thieves, fortune tellers, card sharpers, steady mechanics, clerks, farmers, those who had never lived outside a city, dissipated ruffians and evangelists — soldiers of fortune all. Truly a glorious, ridiculous, mad, polyglot horde from all races and ranks, the vicious and the respectable, all youthful and alive, untrammelled by any past, all buoyed up by the spirit of adventure and the lure of gold, self-confident conquerors of a new land, ready to stake their all on a chance with Dame Fortune.

San Francisco was in a constant state of excitement as each day brought its new crop of rumors from some mine to start a mad rush to another unknown camp. The return of successful miners with gold was a daily event around which the life of the city gyrated. Their gold dust furnished new fodder for the dissipations of Montgomery Street or for the pockets of the more staid, where they served as fresh funds for speculations in real estate and trade.

Business was a gamble. Profits or losses were enormous. No one could foresee the market from day to day. The arrival of a ship with an unexpected cargo changed values overnight. Shipments selected without any regard to California needs arrived from distant ports: stoves never to be used, ladies' garments beyond the need of the few women of the town, razors for men who did not shave, enough chewing tobacco to keep San Francisco supplied for sixty-five years, anything usual or unusual which distant merchants guessed might produce extraordinary profits. The expense of doing business was enormous. Cartage of goods across the city often cost more than the transportation from Boston or New York to San Francisco. Daily public auctions were held of miner's supplies, building materials, food, clothing, tools, house lots, mining claims or anything anyone wanted to turn into cash. As ships came and went the market alternated between plethora and scarcity. One day a commodity might be selling at 50c and on the next for $10. As has been said: "Of the things actually and seriously needed in California there might at one moment come twenty times too much and shortly thereafter there might be nothing at all of the kind needed discoverable in the market."[1] It was the ideal opportunity for a shrewd, bold trader when business was a thing of quick decisions, big deals, easy money, slapdash methods and quick turns, where fortunes were made or lost on a hunch or a guess.

Into this vortex of commercial chaos Norton plunged with avidity. It was just the kind of market for which his training and character fitted him. Contemporaries described him as having remarkable native shrewdness, a quick and clear mind, accurate business judgment and a high standard of personal and financial integrity. He began to buy and sell both on his own account and as a broker and commission agent for others. He dealt in all sorts of commodities. He speculated in town lots, mines and real estate. Tradition claims his realty holdings to have been so extensive that he himself did not know the location of all he owned. Indeed, the early records show him the owner of much property of astonishing value. His business quickly assumed such size-able proportions that he was recognized as an important factor in the commercial life of the city. He quickly made and lost several fortunes.[2]

In the center of the business district, on Montgomery Street, he erected a large barn-like store, across the whole front of which ran a sign "J. A. Norton, Merchant." By 1853 his fortune was estimated as between a quarter and a half million dollars. That was the zenith of his commercial career.

As 1853 drew to a close, San Francisco had another of its series of disastrous fires. Not as great a holocaust as that of '49, when a million dollars of property was burned, or that of '50, when the losses reached seven millions, still its wake left widespread wreck and ruin. To Norton it brought absolute disaster. Not only did he lose his fortune, but it caused him such a serious mental upset that ever thereafter he was hopelessly deranged.

For the five ensuing years he disappeared from San Francisco. For that period his history is a blank. In 1859 he reappeared on the scene, a pathetic, broken man, though still a stocky picturesque figure, impressive, with stately manner, a harmless mental derelict.

Perhaps it was the suggestion of some joker with a per-verted sense of humor, or perhaps only the delusions of his now disordered mind, but Norton, claiming that an act of the Legislature had created him Emperor of the United States, issued a formal proclamation (September 17, 1859) to astonished San Francisco:

> At the peremptory request and desire of a large majority of the citizens of these United States, I,

Joshua Norton, formerly of Algoa Bay, Cape of Good Hope, and now for the past nine years and ten months of San Francisco, California, declare and proclaim myself Emperor of these U. S., and in virtue of the authority thereby in me vested, do hereby order and direct the representatives of the different States of the Union to assemble in Musical Hall, of this city, on the 1st day of February next, then and there to make such alterations in the existing laws of the Union as may ameliorate the evils under which the country is laboring, and thereby cause confidence to exist, both at home and abroad, in our stability and integrity.

NORTON I,

Emperor of the United States.

17th Sept., 1859

At first he was only another of a motley company of mountebanks who paraded the San Francisco streets and cadged a livelihood from an amused public who saw diversion in the antics of "Old Rosey," "Robert Macaire," "George Washington Coombs," "Money King," "Gutter-Snipe," and a horde of lesser eccentrics. But soon he made a distinct place for himself in the city life and the "Emperor" ascended his throne and held sway over his loyal subjects of San Francisco. His innate gentlemanly bearing, his stately and calm dignity and punctilious etiquette, his facility in expressing sensible sentiments on public questions, the harmless, pompous seriousness with which he took himself and his responsibility to the public, appealed both to the crude sense of humor of young San Francisco and to the generous benevolence of the serious community. His formal sonorous proclamations sounded learned and regal to ears accustomed to hell-roaring slang. His gracious courtliness was in appealing contrast to the rude hurly-burly of the day, while his harmless foibles tickled popular fancy. But above all, his gentle kindliness to all, and especially to children, and his solicitous interest in the public welfare won for him from the public an outward homage and a protecting financial guardianship.

His costume was a glory to behold. He dressed the part in a coat of navy blue, cut in military style, with prominent brass buttons and huge gold-plated epaulettes. His shoes were notorious for their size and usual state of shabbiness. Ordinarily he wore a small blue cap trimmed with gold braid, but upon formal occasions he appeared in a beaver decorated with a rosette and bright plumes. A flower in his lapel and a multi-colored silk handkerchief dangling from his breast pocket, completed his outfit. Commonly he carried a gold-headed cane which was superseded, when business of importance demanded, by a massive sword, the gift of an admiring blacksmith.

When replacements were necessary, it became a public duty to see that his wardrobe was replenished. Nor did the Emperor himself have to call attention to his needs. There was always some loyal subject eager to take that duty upon himself and there was sure to be a prompt response to the royal requisitions:

Know ye whom it may concern that I, Norton I, Emperor, *Dei gratia*, of the United States and Protector of Mexico, have heard serious complaints from our adherents and all that our imperial wardrobe is a national disgrace, and even His Majesty the King of Spain has had his sympathy excited so far as to offer us a suit of clothing, which we have a delicacy in accepting. Therefore we warn those whose duty it is to attend to these affairs that their scalps are in danger if our said need is unheeded.

He became a welcome butt for the newspaper wags of the day and they used him for write-ups to fill empty local columns until they built him into a city institution. As the generation which had known him as plain Joshua A. Norton, merchant, gave place to a generation of newcomers, he became the symbol of the golden days of the forty-niners. Fantastic legends and intriguing romances were invented, repeated and exaggerated until doubts were even raised whether there was not some basis in truth for his regal status. A fancied resemblance to Napoleon III furnished gossip that he was the son of that unfortunate monarch. Some even seriously spoke of his being a natural son of King William IV by a Scotch Jewess.

Early in his career, disturbed by the troubles in neighboring Mexico, he had taken the affairs of that nation under his care by assuming the added title of "Protector of Mexico." But after the Maximilian fiasco, he announced "it was impossible to protect such an unsettled nation," and dropped that responsibility.

His empire once established, he proceeded to reign as he thought fitting. Although he felt himself entitled to a palace where he could hold court and entertain fellow potentates, his actual quarters were humble. He lived at the Eureka Lodging House (Hotel) on Sacramento Street as a guest of the Occidental Lodge F. & A. M. of which he had been a charter member. He spent his time strutting pompously

STEAMER DAY IN SAN FRANCISCO.

Norton is the sixth figure to the left of the lamp-post

The "Emperor's" Currency

through the city, with his two dogs, Bummer and Lazarus, at his heels, which themselves also soon became public characters. Daily, as he sauntered down the principal streets, greeting friends and acquaintances, he stopped to debate the news and affairs of city, state and nation, on which he was unusually well informed and which he discussed sensibly. When hungry, he dined almost anywhere at will, at any hotel, restaurant or saloon he selected, for he had the freedom of all such places and had only to give his orders to be served as an honored guest.

He was a constant attendant at synagogues, churches, Sunday schools, libraries, school graduations and public meetings, to all of which he was freely admitted and which he often took occasion to address. He was a welcome visitor to theatres, to concerts and to lecture halls. He rode street cars free. Tributes of cigars were a matter of course. Shops supplied him gratis with whatever his modest demands deigned to require. Once the city council voted him an outfit at the expense of the city. The public loyally played its part.

Whenever he was in need of money, he drew a check upon whatever bank he chose and, according to established custom, his checks were always honored. It was of no moment that the Emperor never had money in the bank. It must be added that the Emperor never abused this privilege and his drawings were modest. At other times the Emperor supplied his financial needs by taxing his subjects; always, however, giving them a receipt in the form of his Imperial scrip. Such scrip for small amounts, issued by "the Imperial Government of Norton I," under "Our Royal hand and seal," was often conspicuously posted on store windows to advertise

Imperial patronage. Copies are still to be found in many an archive of early California memorabilia.

The Emperor's "Proclamations" made an unique appeal to contemporary San Franciscans who welcomed them with good-natured amusement. They were given wide publicity by the local press. Today, together with the popular cartoons of the Emperor, many of them drawn by that well-known early California artist, Edward E. Jump, these proclamations form an interesting incident in the history of early California journalism. They reflect local popular interest and reactions, not only to local events, but to the greater national and international happenings of the day. The municipal authorities received his commendation or blame as their acts were approved or disapproved. They proclaimed that the Civil War had been terminated through his good offices and he undertook to direct reconstruction. In European affairs he claimed to have brought peace between the French and Germans in the Franco-Prussian War. All American political activities were his immediate concern.

NORTON, *Dei gratia*, EMPEROR OF THE UNITED STATES AND PROTECTOR OF MEXICO: Being anxious that the physicians should continue unabated in their zeal for the total obliteration of the small pox, do hereby command the City authorities, in all places where the disease has been or may continue, to make compensation in honor or money to all physicians who may make the most effective cures in case of small pox.

NORTON I

Oakland, Feb. 15, 1869.

WE, NORTON I, EMPEROR OF THE UNITED STATES AND PROTECTOR OF MEXICO, do hereby protest against any action of Congress depreciating National Bonds as a disgrace to the Nation; being convinced that our integrity is OUR ONLY SALVATION, and all foreigners whom it may concern are hereby advised of our determination.

NORTON I

Oakland, Feb. 15, 1869.

WHEREAS the action of the United States Senate in the Belknap affair proves the total depravity of the present system and Constitution of the United States, being unable to punish crime, now, therefore, WE, NORTON I, *Dei gratia*, EMPEROR, in order to save the nation from utter ruin and disgrace, do hereby abolish the entire WASHINGTON SYSTEM, and declare the laws of NORTON I paramount, for the present.

NORTON I

Oakland, Aug. 9, 1876.

It was considered the height of accomplishment for some prankish wag to issue burlesque telegrams and proclamations under the Emperor's name.

We, Norton I, do hereby decree that the office of President, Vice-President, and Speaker of the House of Representatives of the United States are, from and after this date, abolished.

We further decree that the Senate of the United States elect a prominent Democrat as their presiding officer, to act as President until the next election, and to reconstruct the Cabinet according to our wishes hereafter to be declared.

Done at our palace this 21st day of December, A. D., 1862.

NORTON I

Owing to the unsettled questions between His Majesty Maximilian I, El Duque de Gwino, The Tycoon, the King of the Mosquitos, the King of the Cannibal Islands, etc., the usual display of bunting on foreign shipping and on public buildings, in commemoration of our 46th birthday, will be omitted.

NORTON I

Emperor of the United States

Feb. 4, 1865.

PROCLAMATION FROM HIS HIGHNESS, NORTON I — Whereas, reliable information has reached us to the effect that our neighboring sovereign, the reigning Queen of the Friendly Islands, is desirous of annexing her dominions to the United States, and herself to our royal person, and whereas, it is our pleasure to acquiesce in all means of civilization and population, now therefore we, Norton I, *Dei gratia*, Emperor of the United States and Protector of Mexico, do order and direct, first, that Oakland shall be the coast termination of the Central Pacific Railroad; secondly, that a suspension bridge be constructed from the improvements lately ordered by our royal decree at Oakland Point, to Yerba Buena, from thence to the mountain range of Saucilleto and from thence to the Farallones, to be of sufficient strength and size for a railroad; and thirdly, the Central Pacific Railroad Company are charged with the carrying out of this work, for purposes that will hereafter appear. Whereof fail not under pain of death.

Given under our hand this 18th day of August, A. D. 1869, and in the 17th year of our reign, in our present Capitol, the City of Oakland.

NORTON I

Norton stepped into the pages of English literature when Robert Louis Stevenson, in *The Wrecker*, describing the bizarre San Francisco of his day, wrote of Emperor Norton calling to collect an arrearage of taxes:

> In what other city would a harmless madman who supposed himself emperor of the two Americas have been so fostered and encouraged? Where else would even the people of the streets have respected the poor soul's illusions? Where else would bankers and merchants have received his visits, cashed his cheques and submitted to his small assessments? Where else would he have been suffered to attend and address the exhibition days of schools and colleges? Where else, in God's green earth, could he have taken his pick of restaurants, ransacked the bill of fare and departed scantless? They tell me he was even an exacting patron, threatening to withdraw his custom when dissatisfied; and I can believe it, for his face wore an expression distinctly gastronomical . . . His majesty entered the office — a portly, rather flabby man, with the face of a gentleman, rendered unspeakably pathetic and absurd by the great sabre at his side and the peacock feather in his hat.

On the evening of January 8, 1880, at the age of 61, while walking on California Street, the Emperor dropped dead. He had reigned for twenty-three years. His funeral was a public event. His body lay in state. It is said thirty thousand people of all classes paid respect to his mortal remains. No other scene or time was ever so perfectly set for such a career. Around his memory is the nostalgia of the crude simplicity of the gold-rush pioneer days of youthful, tolerant, sentimental, exuberant San Francisco. Tradition has made of him an amusing and unique local institution. His story is the spontaneous response of the everyday man recognizing in this demented gentleman an altruistic love for his fellow man. A smile and a tear. The Emperor was dead. There was no successor. The metropolis of the west had grown to maturity.

> Ave! Emperor, Morituri,
>   We salute thy dateless dyne;
> Self-appointing, self-anointing,
>   First and last of all thy line!
>
> Never Monarch spread more golden
>   Glamour o'er a golden age
> Than thy proud imperial presence
>   Poured on our unlordly stage.[3]

23

THE HILTON-SELIGMAN AFFAIR

IN THE few pages dealing with Jews, a popular history of society in America, published a few years ago, explains the prevalence of anti-Semitism in the following statement:

> The present anti-Semitism of society — as expressed in visiting lists, club memberships and personal attitudes — is markedly keener in the United States than in England or France where Rothschilds, for example, seem to find virtually no doors barred against them. It is probably an aspect of their insecurity, that timidity and conventionalism which looms so large in our social picture. But much of it unquestionably arises from waves of successively poorer and less desirable Jewish migration, chiefly from Poland and Russia, which have had a most damaging effect upon the social standing of the Jew in America.[1]

This latter observation is erroneous. There has always been some form of anti-Semitism here, as long as there have been Jews in America. In fact, old traditional prejudices and animosities had immigrated with the first settlers. Even the wide expanses of the western world had proved too small to allow Spanish, English, French and Dutch colonists to dwell in the new hemisphere as peaceable neighbors. Our old records of earlier days breathe prejudice against all strangers when only too often they were unnecessarily tagged as Frenchmen, Irish, or Jews, to show that they were not of the majority.

Prejudice against Jews may be greater today than formerly because there are more people in the United States to share
it and more Jews to feel it, but it is not something new. It
existed almost as an indigenous growth in the early days
when there were only Portuguese, Dutch and Spanish Jews.
It was here, later, for the German Jews when they became
the predominant Jewish element of the country.

When the Jewish minority was small and insignificant,
anti-Semitism was naturally feeble. The best statistics available estimate that, in the United States in 1818, there were
3,000 Jews in a population of 9,500,000, barely 4/1000 of 1%
of the inhabitants. By 1877 the number of Jews had increased to 229,087 in a population of 43,661,963, that is
52/100 of 1%.

The earliest colonists, themselves victims of persecution
who had come to America that they might enjoy religious
freedom, conceived of that freedom as a monopoly for their
own particular form of belief. Most of the colonies offered
no welcome to "Jews, Infidels and Turks," or even to dissenters of any sort. Inasmuch as neither "Infidels" nor
"Turks" presented themselves to join the settlements, and
as Quakers had a refuge in Pennsylvania, Catholics in Maryland and dissenters in Rhode Island, Jews alone were equally
unwanted everywhere. Even in liberal Rhode Island, with
its religiously heterogeneous population, the Jews were
looked upon as exotic. Wherever a Jew settled he was
labelled "Jew" and, thus labelled, was marked as a being
apart from the rest of the community. Only by long years
of earnest endeavor did Jews finally win political and economic equality in some of the colonies; although almost
everywhere a bar of social discrimination still stretched
across their path. But, by and large, abstract expressions of

hostility towards the Jews found slight place in American life.

Up to 1877 the Jew was not especially singled out as an object of antipathy. While theoretically the Founders, under the influence of the philosophy of "natural rights," had proclaimed that all men, irrespective of "race, creed, or color," were entitled to equality, in practice the country was "white, Protestant, and native." As the immigrant became a factor in the population, suspicion and hatred of the foreigner infected the country until it assumed an important role in the Know-Nothing politics of the mid-nineteenth century. It was not until 1864, when the Republicans were seeking to re-elect Lincoln, that a great American political party dared to say a word for the newer Americans. Then, for the first time, a platform plank voiced recognition of America's adopted children: "That foreign immigration, which has added so much to the wealth, development of resources and increase of power to this nation — the asylum of the oppressed of all nations — should be fostered and encouraged by a liberal and just policy."

As the post-Civil War boom flattened out and financial and industrial disaster shook the country through the panic of 1873, with an appalling number of business failures and railroad and bank defaults, the people turned to the foreigner for a scapegoat. The Democratic Party platform of 1876, and those of both parties in 1880, called for the exclusion of the Chinese. From that day on the subjects of immigration and of the foreigner in our midst have never been absent from our politics. From the days of Know-Nothingism through the Ku Klux Klan, the A. P. A. and "America First," there has always been an element which kept alive an agitation against some race, religion or group and spread the venom of such antagonisms in the nation's blood stream. All this is only another example of the masses' reaction to social and economic frustrations which, centuries ago, an early Father of the Church, Tertullian, succinctly summarized for his own group: "If the Tiber rose to the walls of the city, if the inundation of the Nile failed to give the fields enough water, if the heavens did not send rain, if an earthquake occurred, if famine threatened, if pestilence raged, the cry resounded: 'Throw the Christians to the lions!' "

In 1877 the country was beginning to recover from its depression. Those who had survived the panic were again moving forward to a new era of prosperity. A new crop of American millionaires was in the making. Society was reorganizing itself before the onslaught of the newly rich. Business, too, was entering the new age of industrialization. Labor was stirring to assert itself. Politically the contested election of Hayes and Tilden was still racking the country. If, as some socialists explain, anti-Semitism is a manifestation of social disorganization arising out of a sense of insecurity, here was the scene all set. For the Jew was beginning to be a visible factor in American business. Young Jews were beginning to attend the colleges and to enter the professions. Already some Jewish merchants had become men of means, with sufficient leisure to seek the amenities and pleasures of life.

Such was the moment, the summer of 1877, when the United States became nationally conscious of anti-Semitism. The spark was the Hilton-Seligman quarrel. In itself the affair was trivial enough and by no means the first of its kind in the country; but the prominence of the people involved, and the ill-judged publicity given the quarrel, aroused so much public attention that, for the first time, the American people was made aware of, and articulate about, Jews. Thus a slight incident, which might otherwise have been one more sporadic manifestation of individual prejudice, became the beginning of anti-Semitism in the United States.

What added drama to this affair was the fact that it centered about Joseph Seligman, then the Jew most in the public eye of the country. Just because he was so well regarded by the general public, prejudice against the Jews was presented as a clear-cut issue.

Joseph Seligman was born in Baiersdorf, Bavaria, in 1819. He came to the United States in 1837 or 1838 and after working at various jobs started in business in a small way in Lancaster, Pennsylvania. He had seven brothers whom, as he prospered, he brought to this country. Later, with the two eldest, he established a small dry goods shop in Alabama. He changed to the clothing business, moving his brothers to New York City. The concern was exceedingly successful, and the family graduated into the banking business. During the Civil War, J. & W. Seligman had established itself as one of the outstanding American banking firms. It maintained foreign branches in Germany, England and France. It is said that, when the Federal Government's credit most needed support in its war financing, the Seligmans succeeded in selling for it $200,000,000 of government bonds to European investors. In 1871 this firm was appointed one of the fiscal agents of the United States to secure the conversion of its wartime loan, the "5–20s," into new 5% bonds. Moreover, Joseph Seligman had been one of the committee of seventy, composed of New York's leading citizens, which rescued the city from the corruption of the Tweed Ring. He had declined the office of Secretary of the Treasury in Grant's cabinet. In 1877 he was at the height of his career. Financially successful, socially recognized, politically powerful, he ranked amongst the nation's great—concededly the country's outstanding Jew.

In 1876, A. T. Stewart of New York was America's greatest merchant. Canny Scotchman, he had built up the biggest dry goods business in the country. His retail establishment on Ninth Street was New York's leading department store and set styles for the whole country. A. T. Stewart & Company's wholesale business, with a Chicago branch, sold to local merchants in every town and hamlet throughout the land. He had accumulated so great a fortune that, when he died (1876), part of his estate was an investment of $2,000,000 in the Grand Union Hotel in Saratoga. His friend, Judge Henry Hilton, was named as his executor and trustee. Hilton had been a local New York politician, connected with the Tweed Ring, who became important only as he succeeded to the control of the Stewart fortune, the greatest of its day in America.

In the seventies, with the prosperity which followed the Civil War notwithstanding the temporary setback of the panic of '73, Saratoga was without a rival the summer social capital of America. There, in all vulgarity, from every point of the compass of expanding America, foregathered for a restless holiday during the vacation months banking magnates, merchant-princes, politicians, society beaux and belles, railroad overlords, mining Croesuses, the sporting fraternity and all the lesser fry who made up that gilded age. The Saratoga trunk had been invented, so that the women might arrive with fifteen or twenty such, packed with dresses from internationally famous dressmakers. Bedecked with jewels, these women in great public dress displays competed in a parade of costumes, changed three and four times a day and none worn twice during the season. The men sported fast horses, spent their afternoons at the race track and their nights gambling at John Morrissey's Casino — a virile, garish life in the full blare of publicity.

The main feature of the city was its monstrous hotels. Those facing directly on the crowded, noisy street, with covered piazzas along their façades, were boasted to be the largest and longest in the world. Each of the principal hotels was capable of housing thousands of guests. Up and down these piazzas, daytime and nighttime, paraded the fashion show in all pomp and vainglory.

The sophisticated and discriminating young Henry James, who saw this Saratoga at its zenith, describes it as the "democratization of elegance," "characteristically American," where money, finery and possessions ruled. He found the beautiful surrounding country unvisited and unknown. Life gyrated around the hotels with their piazzas and ballrooms, the race track, the gambling casinos and a few stretches of road where aristocratic owners raced spans of thoroughbreds.

The very center of this life was A. T. Stewart's Grand Union Hotel. It outdid its rivals in size, in the wild extravagance of its guests and in its bedizened elegance. On June 13, 1877, Joseph Seligman with his family arrived at the Grand Union and applied for accommodations. He had in the past ten years frequently been a guest there. This time, however, the clerk said to him, "Mr. Seligman, I am required to inform you that Mr. Hilton has given instructions that no Israelites shall be permitted in the future to stop at this Hotel." On being questioned, the clerk added as explanation that, because business had not been good the previous season, Judge Hilton had concluded that Christians had not come to the hotel because of the presence of Jewish guests, and had resolved to run the hotel in the future on "a different principle."

Fighting mad, Seligman immediately made an issue of the refusal. He wrote a bitter and sarcastic letter to Hilton, which he allowed to be made public. It made a vicious personal attack on Hilton. His friends took up the quarrel. There were unwise threats of suits under the then recent Civil Rights Laws, and wild talk of boycotts followed by exchanges of charges and countercharges, recriminations and name calling.

The metropolitan newspapers, suffering from the usual midsummer dearth of interesting news, made this quarrel front page news. It headlined:

> A Sensation at Saratoga. New Rules for the Grand Union. No Jews to be Admitted. Mr. Seligman, the Banker, and his Family Sent Away. His letter to Mr. Hilton. Gathering of Mr. Seligman's Friends. An Indignation Meeting to be held.

Hilton added fuel to the flames by interviews and public letters. "I know what has been done and am fully prepared to abide by it." "As the law yet permits a man to use his property as he pleases and I propose exercising that blessed privilege, notwithstanding Moses and all his descendants may object." "Personally I have no particular feeling on the subject, except probably that I don't like this class as a general thing and don't care whether they like me or not. If they do not wish to trade with our house, I will be perfectly satisfied, nay gratified, as I believe we lose much more than we gain by their custom."

The press of the country spread the news and took up the

issue. Boston, Chicago, Cleveland, Baltimore, east, west,
north and south, almost every city newspaper, as well as the
Jewish press, all featured it. Pro and con, letters to editors
were printed and editorial comment was widespread. Even
in little towns, where there were no Jews, the local newspapers published and commented on the controversy. While
on the whole the sentiment was that such an exhibition of
prejudice was un-American and was to be condemned as
bigotry, "a survival of the dark ages," yet it was not all
one-sided.

The Reverend Henry Ward Beecher, outstanding liberal,
then America's leading clergyman, brother of the author of
Uncle Tom's Cabin and the most popular and respected
preacher of his day, made it the subject of a widely publicized
sermon, repeatedly reprinted, until it has become a sort of
American classic.

> Listen, O ye astonished people; where for fifty years
> North and South and East and West have come to-
> gether, and have been instructed, sometimes by
> ministers and sometimes by Morrisseys, and where
> every form of pleasurable vice, every sort of amuse-
> ment, everything that would draw custom, has been
> common — there, in Saratoga, the Corinth of Amer-
> ica, in a hotel designed to accommodate two thousand
> people, it seems society is so developed that it will
> not consent to go unless everybody that comes is fit
> to associate with men who made their money yester-
> day, or a few years ago, selling codfish.[2]

In a word to the Jews he besought them not to be too
much exercised by such a public insult:

> A hero may be annoyed by a mosquito; but to put
> on his whole armor and call on his followers to join

him in making war on an insect would be beneath
his dignity.

From that day on, Beecher became an outspoken and
acknowledged champion of the Jew; and his potent voice
formulated for many ardent followers their attitude towards
Jews. When, in 1887, President Cleveland hesitated to appoint a Jew as the United States Minister to Turkey, the
President afterwards told Oscar Straus that a letter from
Beecher turned the scale. This letter addressed to Cleveland,
and widely circulated in the newspapers, reads in part:

> But I am interested in another quality — the fact
> that he is a Hebrew. The bitter prejudice against
> Jews which obtains in many parts of Europe ought
> not to receive any countenance in America. It is be-
> cause he is a Jew that I would urge the appointment
> as a fit recognition of this remarkable people who
> are becoming large contributors to American prospe-
> rity and whose intelligence, morality, and large
> liberality in all public measures for the welfare of
> society, should receive from the hands of our Govern-
> ment some such recognition.

> Is it not, also, a duty to set forth in this quiet, but
> effectual method, the genius of American government?
> Which has under its fostering care people of all civil-
> ized nations, which treats them without regard to
> civil, religious, or race peculiarities as common
> citizens? . . . . . . Why should we not make a crown-
> ing testimony to the genius of our people by sending
> a Hebrew to Turkey? The ignorance and superstition
> of mediaeval Europe may account for the prejudices
> of that dark age. But how a Christian in our day
> can turn from a Jew I cannot imagine. Christianity
> itself sucked at the bosom of Judaism, our roots are

in the Old Testament. We are Jews ourselves gone to blossom and fruit. Christianity is Judaism in Evolution and it would be strange for the seed to turn against the stock on which it was grown.

Finally wiser counsel prevailed in the controversy between Seligman and Hilton and the parties allowed the quarrel to drop from public attention. But as the world went on in its own old way, the ugly social scar remained. Then, as an aftermath, as though to keep the wound from healing, Austin Corbin, President of the Long Island Railroad and of the Manhattan Beach Company, which were then jointly attempting to develop Coney Island into a fashionable summer resort for New Yorkers, followed Hilton's lead with an announcement:

> We do not like the Jews as a class. There are some well behaved people among them, but as a rule they make themselves offensive to the kind of people who principally patronize our road and hotel, and I am satisfied we should be better off without than with their custom.

The anti-Jewish agitation thereupon was renewed and extended. Immediate Jewish and Christian indignation found expression in a refusal to deal with A. T. Stewart & Company until the wholesale business was ruined, and what Stewart had left as New York's outstanding retail department store was so affected that ultimately it was saved from extinction only by passing into the hands of John Wanamaker.

Today Saratoga's ancient glory has become but a memory of crasser days romanticized in current popular fiction. The Grand Union survives as a landmark of faded splendor in the new Saratoga which the state of New York is creating. Hilton and Seligman, long in their graves, are forgotten, and their quarrel is interred in the crumbling pages of old newspapers. The incident did, however, give the starting point to articulate public expression of American anti-Semitism and an opportunity for the healthy American reaction to such anti-democratic prejudice.

JEWS IN THE ECONOMIC LIFE
OF AMERICA

24

THE GIDEONS[1]

IN 1674, in Boston's first tax list appears the name of Rowland Gideon "Ye Jew," rated at 18 shillings. By 1674 he was so much at home in the activities of that thriving seaport that he appeared before its court, in association with one Barruch (Baruh), to collect from a reluctant debtor a balance of £100 arising out of a tobacco transaction. With an experience which indicated no amateur hand in approaching early colonial courts, not yet dominated by professional lawyers, he naively presented his pleadings, suggesting that in "comitinge my case to the honn[d] court & Gentlemen of the Jurye praing for the prosperity of your Govern[mt]" he would remind them that "God command ou[r] Fathers that the Same Law should bee for the Stranger & Sowjournner — as for the Israellits."

Behind this somewhat meagre incident lies a romantic family history stretching from the fourteen hundreds into living times, covering much of typical Jewish family history as well as possessing the flavor of Jewish wanderings into many lands.

The de Pinas were, in the sixteenth century, one of the prominent Jewish (Marrano) families of Lisbon. In 1599, Paul de Pina set forth from Lisbon to visit Rome where, it was said, he proposed to become a monk. On his way, at Leghorn, he visited a family friend, Elijah Montalto, a famous Jewish polemist, afterwards physician to the Court of France. From this visit Paul turned back to Lisbon a confirmed Jew. Later, with a kinsman, Diego Gomez, he emigrated to Brazil. Thence he moved to Amsterdam, where he joined the synagogue and assumed the Jewish name of Reuel Jessurum. He became an author of distinction. This Reuel Jessurum had a daughter, Sarah, who was the mother of our Rowland Gideon.

The Gideon-Abudiente family, originally from Lisbon, was distinguished for its great culture and had given to the world poets, grammarians and theologians as well as outstanding merchants and leaders in the Jewish communities. Moses Gideon Abudiente, son of a Gideon Abudiente, early in the sixteenth century, when a young lad, was sent by his Marrano family from his native Lisbon to Amsterdam to be educated. Since in the Holland of that day Jews could openly practice their Judaism, which Portugal at that time did not tolerate, the Dutch branch of the Abudiente family consisted of professing Jews. Perhaps as an incident of his education, the youthful Moses Abudiente married the aforementioned Sarah, daughter of the De Pina family. After living for a time in Glückstadt, in Holstein, Moses Gideon Abudiente and his wife settled in Hamburg. There he achieved a reputation, more than local, as a man of learning and author of distinction. He wrote poetry, a Hebrew grammar and theological works, and died in 1688 leaving, amongst his large family, a son, Rehiel (Rehuel) Abudiente, who anglicized his name as Rowland (Roel) Gideon.

In the seventeenth century the European demand for sugar was so great that the sugar trade offered vast possibilities for great fortune. The early Jewish settlers in

Spanish and Portuguese America quickly drifted into the sugar trade as merchants, refiners and planters. Many of the great Jewish merchants eagerly sent the cadets of their family out to America to seek their fortunes there as sugar planters and traders. No record is available to trace how Rowland Gideon came to America, but there can be little doubt that he joined relatives in the Barbados where the Gideon-Abudiente family had already attained some importance.

The Barbados had been settled by Jewish pioneers as early as 1625. They had come not only from Europe but from the earlier American settlements in Brazil, Surinam and Martinique. The considerable commercial importance which the Barbados attained during the seventeenth and eighteenth centuries was, in no small measure, attributable to the activities of its Jewish immigrants. Both as planters and traders Jews were important factors not only in Barbados sugar but also in molasses, tobacco and rum. Their vessels carried on a lively trade with other English settlements in North America as well as with their French, Danish, Spanish and Portuguese neighbors and at the same time had important European connections through their kinsmen.

Thus this Jewish community grew so increasingly prosperous and important that, in 1655, the Barbados government on their petition granted recognition "that behaving themselves civilly and doing nothing to disturb the peace, they shall enjoy the privileges and laws of the Island relating to foreigners and strangers." By 1679 a synagogue had been established and that small and insignificant island became a center of influence amongst the Jews scattered throughout the far flung settlements of our western hemisphere.

Today little of all this remains — hardly the vestige of a Jewish community — and almost no outward signs survive except, perhaps, in the challenged tradition that the name "Jew Street" in the town of Bridgetown commemorates these early merchants and planters.

It is easy to imagine how, as a young unmarried member of an important merchant family, Rowland Gideon was sent to the West Indies as his family's representative. In the prosperous Barbados Jewish community, amongst family and friends, an attractive young man enjoyed a life that was not all work and hardships. Indeed, there is the tradition that, while there, the youthful Rowland so managed to entangle himself in debt that his family thought it wise to transfer him to the little Boston town of 1674. We imagine that Boston, a promising seaport and a growing trade center, with a reputation for austere living, seemingly far off, appeared to offer a safe haven of exile free from temptations for Gideon.

In Boston the only traces of his activities are found in court records. Other than the suit to which attention has already been called, we find that one Joseph Tebo was before the Suffolk County Court in 1674 for stealing from Gideon and one Daniel Barrow "nine pounds in money and two gold rings valued at three pounds," and that, after being found guilty and duly "whipt wth twenty stripes" and fined forty shillings, Tebo was delivered into the custody of Gideon and Barrow. Again in 1674, as co-plaintiff with "Daniel Baruh," Gideon allowed a suit against the wealthy, litigious, Boston Quaker, Nicholas Moulder, to be non-suited for want of prosecution.

The fact that Gideon was associated in these three different transactions with the same person leads to a surmise that the connection between the two was more than casual and that they were probably partners or otherwise somewhat permanently connected together in business. Especially does this receive confirmation in the fact that the name of Baruh, or Barrow, was that adopted by one of the distinguished Jewish families of the Barbados — the Louzada, a family in which the Spanish Dukedom "do Losada y Lousada" was revived in 1848.

Aaron Baruch Louzada was one of the leading Jewish merchants of Bridgetown, while his brother, Moses Barro (Barruh), was one of the Jewish residents of London in the time of Cromwell and an enrolled broker of the city of London. The members of this prominent Jewish family had anglicized their names to Barrow, Burrough or Baruch, and were landowners of considerable importance in Jamaica. While no Daniel Barru or Barrows has been identified in the list of Barbados Jews, it may fairly be assumed that Rowland Gideon's business associate was a youthful member of this family.[2]

In 1679 Rowland was a passenger "in the Ketch *Phoenix* of Antegoa," and in that same year was granted by the British government letters of denization under which he had the right to reside in any English colony. Five years later we find him living with a wife, Bathsheba, on the Island of Nevis.[3] While settled there, he appears to have been one of the victims of the French invasion of that island. Although his plantation suffered from French depredations, he managed to resettle it. Ultimately he was one of the inhabitants of that unhappy island to share in the £103,003 indemnity appropriated in 1711 by the English government to compensate the proprietors and planters of Nevis and St. Christopher for damages suffered at the hands of the French. In the meantime, however, he returned to Barbados where, in 1692, he appears listed as "Roel Gidion" amongst "The Jews' Plantations and Houses."

In 1651 Great Britain passed its famous Navigation Act, excluding its colonies from direct trade with foreign markets. This opened up important opportunities for London Jewish merchants. The important industries of the West Indies, such as that of sugar, were to a large extent in Jewish hands. London then was offering the outstanding opportunity to a Jewish merchant, especially to one with American connections, who could import its colonial products and from London trade with all the European markets. "Under the circumstances," wrote the historian Lucien Wolf, "it is not surprising that the Jewish merchants of London, during the latter half of the seventeenth century, became not only a wealthy and influential class, but a factor of very decided importance and utility in the commercial system of the metropolis."[4] It was, therefore, as if this was the opening made to order for Rowland Gideon, and it can occasion no surprise that we next hear of him as settled in London. In 1694, after the decease of his wife, Bathsheba, he married Esther do Porto of a prominent family of the London Marrano community.

In 1697–8 he received the honor of admission as a liveryman of the Painters' & Stainers' Company and, as a consequence, received the freedom of the City of London and thus, perhaps, became the second Jew to be so honored, the first being his brother Simson Haim Abudiente, in 1689. This was a rather extraordinary distinction for a Jew as, at

An Answer to Benjamin Gillam his pretended Reasons of Appeale from a Judgmt of the County Court of Suffolk obtained against him by Rowland Gideon upon a plaine Bill owned in Court the 27th of July 1685 &c.

The appellant Alegeth that the plt sued by booke and Bill and produced no Bookes and that his Renders as a ground of his weake appeale, for who will blame a man to have two String to his bow; Espetially in time of danger by either of which the debt was manifest, and its as true that the appelle speakes without Booke, In affirming that no Booke was produced to the Court who was not there, though the Booke was.

To the second Reason I answer, that never any thing was In Controuersie Relateing to any Error In the acct. and for no ground for any obligation, So Solemne as the appellant mentions to Rectifie Errors Neither was the Bill demand much Lesse Extorted from the appellant at the time of his Receaving the goods, but about two monnth after. whereas there was time Sufficient to Examine the acct. and had there bene any Reasonable Compliance with the first paimt, of one hundred pound which was to bee In a month after the 5th of November tis Likely no bill had euer bene Demanded, but after two month passed and nothing Receaued and after that, but twenty pound of one hundred, it could not but giue ground of suspition to the plt who then demanded Bill for his paimt, the one on demand the other at Spring, soe then the appellant Signed the first to pay with Convenient Speed (an unusuall terme of time for Such Goods receaued) and now not paid till fiue month after done, In tobacco at 1/8 penie p pound aboue the market, this after the plt had prefered the appellant to giue them first pound to Restore him his goods again The other Bill that was to bee paid at Spring, which might bee concluded the 20th of Aprill hee would not Signed but the 20th of July as appeares the Bill and y haueing him Such dodgeing for the first paimt of that not but fee the same owne and being In debt to others and to keep good hands was forced to take the first opertunity Least the neglect might haue Suspended an fond till march next.

And as to his Supplement to Enforce my Bookes they are Ready as well for this as the Last Court Though now Euidence is a needlesse as an unusuall In the practise of this Court where, as God Command one father that the same Law should bee for the Stranger & Soiourner as for the Jsraellite, I may Expect equall Justice thus Committing my Case to the honrd Court and Gentlemen of the Jurie praying the prosperity of your Gouermt And that you may bee Guided for the decideing Matters, And So Remaine
Yor Honrs Humble Servant
Rowland: Gideon

Rowland Gideon's Signature

Marriage Contract between Rowland Gideon and Esther do Porto, 1694 that date, it was generally held that Jews were ineligible both for admission to these ancient guilds or to the freedom of the City of London. For years he carried on business as a West India merchant. In 1701 he was *Hatan Torah* of the ancient synagogue of London, Bevis Marks, and the following year, 1702, became its treasurer and was so serving the year in which its new synagogue was opened.

In 1713 and 1714 he took an active part in appearing in London before the Commissioners for Trade and Plantations as representative of the sufferers from Nevis in establishing his own and his fellow sufferers' claims against the funds which were then being distributed to compensate them for their French war losses. He died in London on April 5, 1722 and was buried in its old Jewish *Bet Hayim* (cemetery). His grave stone bears the following inscription:

מצבת

קבורת הנביר הישיש הנכבד

בהיר רועיאל אבודיאינטי נל"ע

יום א שני של חול המועד של

פסח יח לחדש ניסן התפב

תנצבה

Sa

Do bemaventurado ROHIEL
ABUDIENTE que fuy DEOS
servido recolher desta para
[sua] Santa Gloria en Domingo
2° dia de Medianos de Pessah
18 Nissan 5482
S B A G D G

Surviving him were four daughters and an only son, Samson (Sampson) Gideon, born in 1699, who inherited from his father's estate the then large fortune of £7901.

Samson also succeeded to his father's business as a West India merchant and was elected to membership in the Painters' & Stainers' Company.

This Samson was a remarkable man. He has been described as of great natural ability, with a high sense of justice and honor, generous, intelligent and of unremitting industry. He had a keen wit, with a happy talent of expressing himself both in writing and conversation. To him is attributed the advice, "Never grant an annuity for her life to an old woman — they wither, but they never die." John Nichols has described him:

> He was a Jew broker, the most considerable of his tribe, the great oracle and leader of what used to be called Jonathan's Coffee-house in Exchange Alley, but has since been dignified, I suppose, by the more appropriate and characteristic name of The Stock Exchange in Threadneedle Street.

As early as 1742 he began to be consulted by the English government about its financing. In 1745 he raised a loan of £1,700,000 for the Crown. In 1749 he advised and carried through the consolidation of the national debt and a reduction of its rate of interest. His services in public finance were rendered without "any gratuity, fee or commission." Indeed, in some quarters Samson Gideon has been given credit for being largely responsible for the financial stability which the government managed to maintain through the troublesome periods of the Jacobite rebellion and the Seven Years' War. As one of the outstanding members of the London Jewish community, Samson Gideon was often regarded as a leader in the Parliamentary struggle to pass the Jews' Naturalization Act of 1753 abolishing Jewish disabilities. His was one of the favorite and outstanding figures portrayed in the contemporary caricatures with which the enemies of the bill attacked its supporters and their Jewish sponsors. He retired from business in 1759 and died of dropsy on October 17, 1762, at the age of 63, leaving the huge fortune of £580,000.[5]

With the growth of wealth, Samson had become socially ambitious and withdrew from the synagogue, although he himself never joined a Christian Church. Samson's wife was Jane Ermell, daughter of Charles Ermell, Esquire, a Christian. They brought up their children as Christians. Although his withdrawal from the synagogue separated him from the London Jewish community, he continued as long as he lived to pay his synagogue dues anonymously. In his will he left a legacy of £1,000 to the Spanish and Portuguese Jewish community of London, provided that he be buried in the Jewish burying ground, and commended his soul "to the gracious and merciful God of Israel."[6]

Like so many self-made men, Samson had his weaknesses. He was dazzled by titles and loved to consort with the great. It is said that he was on terms of intimate friendship with Walpole. Samson appointed the Duke of Devonshire one of his executors and named him residuary legatee should his children die without issue. Samson Gideon's ambition was to found a landed family. He acquired several considerable estates to that end, the most notable of which, Belvedere House in Kent, was described in a contemporary account as follows:

> BELVEDERE HOUSE, this belongs to Samson Gideon, Esq.; is situated on the brow of a hill, near Erith in Kent, and commands a vast extent of a fine country

many miles beyond the Thames, which is about a mile and half distant. This river and navigation add greatly to the beauty of this scene, which exhibits to the eye of the delighted spectator, as pleasing a landskip of the kind as imagination can form. The innumerable ships employed in the immense trade of London, are beheld continually sailing up and down the river. On the other side are prospects not less beautiful, tho' of another kind. This gentleman has very judiciously laid out his grounds, and made many beautiful vistas. The house is but small tho' an addition has been made of a very noble room.

He was anxious to secure a baronetcy and pushed his claim for that reward for his public services in government financing with persistence. While the government refused him that honor,[7] his son, Samson, born in 1745, grandson of our Gideon, was, as a compromise, created a baronet in his fourteenth year (May 21, 1759). This Samson, the younger, was educated at Eton, and in 1766 married the daughter of the Chief Justice of England, Sir John Eardley Wilmot. In 1770 he was elected to Parliament from Cambridge, and in 1789 was raised to the peerage, taking the title of Baron Eardley, his wife's family name. Young Samson's death without male issue ended his father's ambitious plans.

Of the great-grandchildren of Rowland Gideon, daughters of Samson, the eldest, Maria, married Baron Saye & Sele; the second, Viscount Gage; and a third, the Prussian Count von Gersdorff-Hermsdorf. Baron Eardley left only daughters to continue the line.

Amongst the descendants of this early Boston Jew were the twelfth Lord Saye & Sele; Gladstone's Chancellor of

the Exchequer, the Right Hon. H. C. E. Childers; the wife
of a former Duke of Norfolk; Admiral Eardley Wilmot; Sir
Francis Fremantle, present member of Parliament; Lord
Auckland; and an Irish rebel, Erskine Childers, who strangely, as the brother-in-law of Fiske Warren of the present
distinguished Massachusetts Warren family, again brings
a Massachusetts contact into the family cycle.

Lucien Wolf, the eminent historian, has written:[8]

> The memory of the old Abudientes is preserved in
> a very interesting way in the person of the late head
> of the Childers family, Miss Rowlanda Childers,
> to whom, in default of a surviving male heir to
> her father, the family estates at Cantley, county
> York, descended. The name 'Rowlanda' is of course
> an anglicised and feminine form of the Hebrew
> 'Rehuel,' the name of the father of Samson Gideon.
> To this day it may be heard in the old Sephardi
> Synagogue in Bevis Marks, when, during the service
> on the great Fast of Atonement, the name of Samson
> de Rehuel Abudiente is recited in the list of the dead
> on whose behalf the divine mercy is invoked.

25

PIRATES AND TRINKETS

O N A fair spring day of the year 1744, Isaac Mendez of Kingston, Jamaica, as a loyal British subject, swore in His Majesty George II's High Vice-Admiralty Court of the royal colony of Rhode Island that he had suffered grievous wrong. Upon the Five Books of Moses he swore a most solemn Jewish oath that sixteen hundred and twenty milled pieces of eight, a "gold neck buckle, one wrought three stoned and two plain gold rings, one pair of sissers over laid with silver, and one pair of stoned sleive bottons sed in silver" were his very own proper estate. Humbly he supplicated the Honorable Court that the same may by its "definitive decree and sentence be restored to s^d claimant and that he may be dismist with cost."

So, while continental Europe seethed in a turmoil of war and the Pretender Charles, in the offing with a formidable armament, threatened the peace of England, the Honorable Leonard Lockman, Esquire, His Majesty's Judge, sitting in Newport, proceeded, on Tuesday, May 3, 1744, to make solemn inquiry into the justice of Isaac's claims.

By the middle of the eighteenth century the golden dreams of the Americas pouring riches into Europe from fabulous, inexhaustible mines of gold and silver had faded. In its place England, France, Holland, Portugal and Spain

had come to realize that the riches of America were still
to be won, not by reckless conquistadors, but by planters,
merchants and sailors. Not by hoards of silver, gold and
precious stones, but in cargoes of sugar, tobacco, fish, oil
and furs were fortunes of unmeasured wealth to be garnered
from the vast new domains of the West. In feverish rivalry
fleets poured from every European port, criss-crossing the
Atlantic to America, and hazarding long voyages to the land
of the golden fleece in the far-off West. In that expanding
world feudalism was passing away; the day of the merchant
adventurer and the trader had arrived. As never before
the market place began to dictate national politics and to
dominate diplomatic, military and international policies.

From every colonial port on the Atlantic seaboard frail
sloops and schooners sailed down to the West Indies, on
to South America, to the northern harbors of the French,
English and Dutch settlements, back and forth over the
storm-tossed Atlantic to Europe, endlessly seeking trade
in any and every commodity wherever there was a prospect
of profit.

In those days a voyager on the Spanish main faced more
than the perils of the sea. More than good seamanship was
required to bring safely to port the little vessels to which
the fraternity of hardy traders trusted their fortunes and
their safety. Not only were open hostilities carried over
from the European scene to these waters, but the nations
fought battles for commercial supremacy by unfriendly
laws and arbitrary regulations to shut out rivals from local
colonial trade. Adventure lurked in the offing of every
headland. Any speck on the horizon might be a potential
enemy, for the Caribbean swarmed with privateersmen
commissioned by Spanish, French, English, Colonial, or

Dutch authorities, chartered to seize as prize any vessel of rival nations which they could outsail and outfight.

In this new world of mercantilism the Jews were afforded, by training and by force of necessity, a very real advantage. Families that had been divided and scattered by outbursts of religious fanaticism in the past still retained their connections across national borders. Forced by circumstances to keep their property in "quick assets," they often had the wherewithal to take advantage of opportunities of trade not available to the native merchant. Frequently they knew more languages than the one to which their competitors were usually confined. For generations their very existence had so often depended on taking chances, sizing up situations, and making quick decisions, that these capacities had become almost inbred. So they found, in this American international trade, a congenial sphere for the exercise of their talents. But while the records are replete with their trading activities, their personal adventures emerge but rarely.

Such was the background of his case, as Isaac Mendez came forward to present his plea to the court. Under the law as it then existed, a party was not allowed to testify in his own behalf. But the court was informed that, as Mendez was making a trading voyage in 1743, he was captured by a Spanish vessel and brought prisoner to Cuba. Taken to Havana, he was thrown into the Morro Castle prison. After they had disposed of his ship and its cargo, his captors departed to seek other spoils and little further attention was paid to Mendez. Through friends he was able to arrange for his release and for a passage with a Monsieur Cotrel Lafosse, a French merchant, who was outfitting a vessel for Curaçao. Mendez hoped that, once there, he might buy a ship and outfit a cargo to make up his losses on what the Spaniards had seized.

On April 23, 1744, while the sloop *Fortune* was about to weigh anchor in Havana Harbor, Isaac and "two other Jews," escorted by a "Sarjeant and four soldiers," embarked with their bags and baggage. The captain, having obtained his clearance, set sail that night. Hardly had they gotten under way when, the next morning, two ships were observed approaching them. One of them, the sloop *Revenge*, "a Private man of War," Captain James Allen, Commander, gave chase, soon managed to capture the *Fortune* and put a prize crew aboard. Both ships proceeded northward until they arrived safely at Newport. There Captain Allen, in behalf of his vessel, himself and his crew, promptly filed a libel in the Vice-Admiralty Court of Rhode Island against the sloop *Fortune* and its cargo, to have the same declared forfeited to its captors according to law. It was at this stage of the proceedings that Mendez entered his appearance in court as a claimant of the money and jewelry, alleging that such property should not be adjudged part of the prize to be awarded to the officers and crew of the *Revenge*. He claimed that what a British subject owned, even when found on a captured enemy vessel, is not a lawful prize, but should be returned by its captors to the owner. It was what the lawyers describe as a pretty point of law.

In orderly judicial fashion the trial was opened. Captain James Allen himself deposes:

> On or About the 13th day of April last Past being about four Leagues to the Windward of the Havannah on the Island of Cuba I saw two Sail and gave Chace to them they did not run but as I suppose spoke together I soon came up with them they standing

Stern for Stern with me And upon my Approach
to them and shewing my English Colors they both
fired upon me and at the Second or third Shot by
them fired singly my Gunner was killed and each of
them immediately poured in their Broadsides upon
me I was during the whole Action under English
Colours The Vessel I have now brought in under
Dutch Colours and the other Vessel under French
Colours Whereupon I engaged them and took the
Vessel now brought in and the other escaped.

Then Robert Gibbs, master, and William Higgins,
lieutenant of the *Revenge*, corroborated their captain's tale.
Daniel Pichot, "late master of the sloop called the *Fortune*,"
through an interpreter testified:

He had known the Fortune for two years. She was
owned by Cotel Lafosse of Curracoa from where she
had sailed the previous December for Havana with
"flower Butter Rum Cheese Hams and wine." After
delivery of that cargo she started to return April
23rd, "laden with hides and money — about 6 or
7000 hides and I cant tell how much money, all
which were returns for the Cargo ship'd from Curracoa to Havana."

and that after they had been out about twenty hours from
Havana, when they saw Captain Allen approaching under
English colors, the *Fortune's* French owner and pilot ordered
a fight.

Thomas Bell, pilot of the *Fortune*, told that, when they
first discovered Captain Allen's vessel, "we Prepared to
fight them and fired four Guns at the English Privateer we
being under Dutch Colours and the Privateer under English,
and had all our Powder Chests and everything prepared to
Engage."

John Garey, a Spaniard, described how "we Prepared to fight and fired four or six Guns at the S^d Privateer, before they fired at us, they being under English Colours and we under Dutch."

Then the pilot Bell, obviously animated by some feelings which led him to attempt to settle Mendez's case once for all, retook the witness stand. Truculently he told that he "was merchant and part owner of a vessel of Boston and had been taken a prisoner in the Bay of Hondoras from whence he had been brought to Havana." There he had worked at "six bitts a day in the King's Yard lightoring" a vessel and had "shipped by Cotterel and was in his imploy" at sixteen pieces-of-eight a month, as pilot for a voyage to Curaçao. Then he related the coming of the Jews aboard the *Fortune*. Although he was supposed to have been occupied with efforts to navigate the *Fortune* when she attempted to escape the threatening *Revenge*, he professed to be able to supply all the details:

> Before we was taken I saw the said Mendez and Aaron Touron receive of the people on Board three bags of silver, one bag of five hundred and odd pieces of eight belonged to Mr. Cotterel and the other two belonged to two passengers that were put on shoar after the capture one of 'em was a french man and the other a Spaniard, and also saw eight rings and a gold buckle four pairs of gold buttons and two silver watches, a gold laced Hat and a silver headed cain delivered to the s^d Mendez. The occasion of delivering the said money was the s^d Mendez say^{i}ng he thought one of the Privateers was Capt Hall of Jamaica who belonged to s^d Mendez's father and if it were he promised to secure the s^d money etc. for the gentlemen and that they should be well used.

He added that Mendez and the two other Jews told him
when they first came aboard that

> they had a few Bitts which was the remainder of
> the three bitts a day that were allowed them and
> they said they wished they had an opportunity of
> laying it out in rum and other necessaries.

Then in detail he described the jewelry:

> one a stripd sort of a mourning ring one with a stone
> in it like a Hart with two little green nubs on each
> side the rest were all plain ring . . . a Flourish'd
> wrought buckle and has three nobb at for the stock
> and three tongues.

Further questions brought out that at the critical moments, when they were trying to outsail the *Revenge*, he
had seen all this passing of money and jewelry, of all places
on a ship in the one where you would least expect to find
the pilot — "down in the Hold."

Then a nondescript, Francis Garey, was called and de-
posed that, while on board the *Fortune*, to save them from
capture, he had delivered "three p^r of silver Buckles 20 P^s
of eight and two Lancetts tip^d wth silver" to the Bigest of
the Jews.

> Q^n.   Were any of you ordered down in the Hold and
>   who before the engagm^t wth C. Allen.
> Ans^r I saw Mr. Touro Mr. Delyon and the Dutch
>   boy there and was there myself.

His cross-examination left him even more positive and he
added the detail that he examined the chest which Isaac
brought on board with him the night he embarked and that
"I saw nothing in it untill the next day after it came on
board and then I saw a few shirts in it," and that Mendez

and the two other gentlemen travelling with him had but a single chest.

Captain John Beard of Newport told the Court:

> I have not so personal an acquaintance with the Gent¹ in Court, but I know his father in Jamᵃ wᵗʰ whom I have had a particular acquaintance these 30 years past, and know him to be a man that carries on a considerable trade and has the character of a very honest man and I believe his credit would pass equal to any trading man in Jamᵃ. I know him to trade very largely on the Spanish main and to the South Keys.

Moses Delyon, after being sworn on the Five Books of Moses, was examined. He had been a prisoner with Mendez in Havana and knew of his having been supplied with money by friends; Don Barnado Ladon furnished some 400 pieces-of-eight and Mr. Christopher Cantara about 700 pieces and also a Mr. Castelo an amount unknown to him. This had been arranged through bills of exchange drawn on Isaac's father at Jamaica as well as on the credit of Isaac's own notes. This money had been brought with them on board the Fortune in Isaac's bags. It was to be used when they reached Curaçao to buy a vessel to take them to Jamaica. Of the jewelry he testified that the "wrought buckle wᵗʰ 3 or 4 tongues" was one which Mendez had been given by his father and had worn five years; while of the rings one was given to Isaac "by Mr. Polanko a Spanᵈ lived at Trinidado; and two rings he had in Jamᵃ and one was given him in the More Castle and the other two he bought at the More Castle."

Then Mr. Aaron Touro, likewise sworn as a Jew, who had been a fellow-prisoner of Mendez at Morro Castle for three

and a half months, corroborated the testimony about the
Mendez money and of his having had "a gold neck buckle,
five gold rings, a mumpoz'd ring, a pair of scissors set with
silver and a p^r of sleeve Butt^s set in silver." He knew the
Mendez family from Jamaica. He was with Isaac on six
occasions when he had borrowed money in Havana to take
along to buy a sloop in Curaçao.

There were then produced in Court:

> An oznbrig Bag 17 inch^s long and five inches wide
> A guinea bag 11¾ in^s long and six inch^s wide
> as it lay on the Table.

Under date of May 15, 1744, the record noted that "The
advoca^{ts} on both sides plead to the merits. The Court was
adjourned till 3 O clock P. M."

When court reconvened, Captain Allen's commission was
duly exhibited. Even though the arguments seemed to have
been concluded, Thomas Stodard, "an Inha^t of R^d Island,"
was asked, as an old sea captain who had often been to
Havana, to enlighten the court. He explained that, although
it was always necessary to have permission from the Government or officials to take money on board ship in Havana,
yet it was always possible, "unknown to the Governor," to
get off with your money. Then Danl Pichot, the master of
the *Fortune*, was recalled and added to his former testimony
that he had known Mendez for about two months before he
embarked on his sloop. When he came aboard, he brought
with him two chests and a bed. In Havana, to his knowledge, three French gentlemen had offered Isaac credit to
the value of 3,000 to 4,000 pieces of eight.

This finished the testimony. The court then adjourned to
Friday, May 18th, on which day the learned judge con-

demned the *Fortune* and its cargo to be forfeited as a prize, directed the proceeds to be divided amongst its captors and delivered his Solomon-like judgment on Isaac Mendez's claim as follows:

Having carefully examined the preparatory examinations and given due attantions to the pleas of the advocates on all sides, it appaires very plainly to me that the gold neck buckle one wrought three stoned and tow plain gold rings one pair of sissers over laid with silver and one pair of stoned sleive buttons sed in silver are the proper estate of the aforesy'd Isaac Mendez, and as the sy'd Mendez is a subject of our sovering Lord the King I order and decree that the above mentioned gold neck buckle one wrought three stoned and tew plain gold rings one pair of sissers overlaid with silver and one pair of stoned sleive buttons set in silver be forth with delivered to the sy'd Isaac Mendez

as to the sixteen hundred and twenty milled peices of Eight or Dollars by him also claimed it is with me very doubtful and in order to come to the truth thereof I order and decree that the before mentioned sixteen hundred and twenty milled peices of Eight or Dollars remain in the hands of the Captors they giving security of the sume of Thirty tow hundred and forty peices of Eight or Dollars to the Claiment mr: Isaac Mendez that if he the sy'd Isaac Mendez shal within the space of one year and a day after the date here of produce the orriginal notes and bills of Exchange by him att the Havanna given for monny to him lent for his own risque and property and produce sufficient proff thereof and not only sent by him to purchase goods or merchandizes to be sent to the Havanna or any other place that then the sixteen hundred and twenty peices of Eight or Dollars shal be delivered to the sy'd Isaac Mendez or his assigns

> but in default thereof to be condemned as good and
> Lawful prize for the use of the Captors to be divided
> as they amongst themselfs have agreed

But, alas, when the year and a day had come around
Isaac was far from Newport and probably too much engaged in other gainful activities to bother with the conditions set for the recovery of the pieces of eight. So that on
the dot of the expiration of the year and a day, Captain
James Allen appeared before Judge Lockman and demanded
the cancellation of his bond and the right to divide the
sixteen hundred pieces of eight amongst the brave crew of
the *Revenge*. Upon receiving "Double Costs," the court
graciously allowed the motion.

Thereupon it was entered upon the law books as a principle of English Colonial law, fixed by the precedent of
the case of *Revenge v. Fortune*, that:

> Property of British subjects found on captured vessels
> is not lawful prize and must be returned to its
> owners by captors. Where, however, ownership of
> property has not been sufficiently established, claim-
> ant will be given a year and a day in which to prove
> the same, captors holding the property under bond,
> pending final determination.

26

LET THERE BE LIGHT

ACCUSTOMED as we are today to living in the blaze of electricity, it is hard to realize the gloom and darkness in which for ages our ancestors lived when once night fell. From the days when first the blaze of wood-fires and rush-lights were superseded, through some primitive inventor, by wax candles until the nineteenth century, almost the only improvement in lighting had been in the making of oil-burning lamps.

Although whales had been caught in European waters from very early days, it was not until the middle of the eighteenth century that people came to recognize the superiority of whale oil for lamps and candles over the vegetable oils then commonly used. As this became increasingly apparent, it created a rapidly expanding and profitable market for whale oil and spermaceti candles. Whaling then assumed a new importance in world trade, and the rivalry between the Dutch and the English to capture this market became keener and more far-reaching.

Early voyagers to North America had called attention to the abundance of whales in the western waters. In 1578 Anthony Parckhurst, describing Newfoundland in a letter to Richard Hakluyt, wrote:

> I am informed that there are above 100 saile of Spaniards that are come to take cod (who make all

wet and do drie in when they come home) besides 20
or 30 more that come from Biskaie to kill whale for
traine.

In 1614, off the coast of Maine, Captain John Smith
found whales so plentiful that he turned from the original
object of his voyage to pursue them. Richard Mather,
coming to the Massachusetts Bay Colony in 1635, saw
"mighty whales spewing up water in the air like the smoke
of a chimney of such incredible bigness that I will never
wonder that the body of Jonah could be in the belly of a
whale."

Thus it is natural that the attention of the early settlers
of New England was directed to this source of profitable
enterprise.[1] Indeed, as early as 1688, Secretary Randolph
wrote from Boston to the Lords of Trade in London:

> New Plimouth colony have great profit by whale
> killing. I believe it will be one of our best returns, now
> beaver and peltry fayle us.

While for some time Long Island had the first organized
whale fishing, Connecticut, Rhode Island, and Massachusetts were early close and active rivals for the trade. In
1690 the Massachusetts colony made two shipments (296
barrels) of whale oil to London for the account of the treasury. In Rhode Island the industry was carried on as early
as 1723.

The first manufacturing of sperm candles in this country
was established in Rhode Island some time previous to
1750 by Benjamin Crabb, an Englishman. In that year the
General Court of Massachusetts granted him the monopoly
of making sperm candles "of course sperma Caeti oyle" in
the colony for fourteen years, on the ground that he alone

knew the art and on condition that he teach candle-making to five inhabitants within the next ten years.

Starbuck tells us that "the expense of a manufactory was trifling. The building was of wood, usually about 60 feet by 30 feet, one-half formed with 14 feet posts and used as a work-room, the other half with 8 feet posts and used as a shed. Building and utensils cost about $1,000 and about 600 barrels of head matter would be used each year in such a factory."

When Peter R. Livingston of New York and Robert Jenkins of Rhode Island formed a partnership, in 1766, for manufacturing spermaceti candles, their whole manufacturing outfit was carefully enumerated in the partnership indenture as follows:

```
 1 Large yron screw with a false collar
 2 Long round Barrs 2 guid Barrs and 40 Iron Plates
 1 Brass Box for the screws
   Wooden Press with 4 screws & Plates sufficient
21 doz. candle Molds
 1 Copper mill
 1 smaller mill
50 barskets for Drainers
10 large tubs
 7 sets of working tubs
 6 Troughs & Drainers with sheet lead
 1 large copper
   Sundry small articles
```

The Jews of Newport, who had learned that art in Lisbon, began, as early as 1754 or 1755, to manufacture sperm oil and candles in Rhode Island. By 1760 they had seventeen factories engaged in such activity. These factories were small and their equipment modest.

At first the Newport Jews bought their whale oil from the whalers wherever opportunity offered. Thus in 1756 Henry Lloyd, Aaron Lopez's Boston agent, wrote him that Mr. Quincey had refused his offer of 12/6 a pound for "Sperma ceti" but was willing to accept 13/6 and communicated the information that:

> Mr. Rotch of Nantucket is now here & offers me Head Matter, any quantities I may want at the usual Premio over & above the price of oyl and 2½ per ct. Commissions to be deliver'd at New Port, & will take the oyl from which the Head Matter is extracted in part of pay either at the price of oyl when the Head Matter is deliver'd, or as it shall be when he receives it, which ever you choose at the time of purchase.

Soon some of the Newport Jews had their own whaling vessels fishing all along the Atlantic shore. Tradition has it that Lopez's whalers were the first to seek whales as far off as the Falkland Islands.

Moses Lopez, Aaron Lopez, Jacob Rivera, Joseph de Lucena, Naphtali Hart and their associates carried on an active and large oil and candle trade, sending vessels with their product not only to the other colonies and the West Indies, but to all European markets as well. Newport became the American center for this trade.

The head material of the whale, spermaceti, was, excepting wax, the best material for illuminating-candles. Generally the colonial candles manufactured from it were made six to a pound, but their quality ran by no means uniform. Thus Lopez received a complaint from Jamaica in 1767 that "your spermaceti candles, I am sorry to say, are inferior to any at this markett. I have experience myself and burnt one, which does not answer the Quality. Those I have seen from Boston etc. are very clear, and well prist free from oyle."

The crude whale oil which they refined was made into two grades; the better, a pale yellow, almost white, and the inferior, of a brown color. Many a dispute arose over the grading of oil, and losses from leakage were not unusual.

Whaling, the manufacture of oil for lamps and the making of candles, were amongst the most important American commercial developments of the pre-Revolutionary era. The business was highly speculative, depending very largely on the supply in the market which an incoming vessel found as it reached port after a long voyage. Sometimes a good market was quickly overstocked by arriving vessels adding their competing cargoes before those already on hand could be sold. Sometimes local conditions compelled long and hazardous credits. Indeed, his Captain Wright in 1768 informed Lopez from Savanna Lamarr, Jamaica, "I have been obliged to open two accounts for one box of candles," adding, "They are of the opinion that spt'y candles will be plenty and cheap this later part of the crop; but for my part I see no likehood of it, but the reverse."

Often profit depended on a captain's ability to barter successfully for a cargo of merchandise to market on the return home. Sometimes it was necessary to sail from port to port in search of a market. Much depended on the local agent, much on the captain of the vessel. Sometimes it was wholly chance and luck. Often success or failure was determined by ability to size up long range opportunities at home or abroad. The instability of the market is illustrated when Lopez's Boston agent writes him that oil which had sold for "£146 per Tonn" "this day is fallen to £140" and is daily falling. Thus, also, in 1766 Lopez's English agent at Bristol was advising him that he could get a better price for oil at Newport than in England. The Dutch, English, French, Norwegians, Danes and, in fact, all nations of Europe, were in fierce competition in every market and only too often were backed by government aid by bounties or imposts against rivals. In 1764, Prime Minister Grenville, to encourage the American whale fishery to compete with rival nations in the English markets, abolished bounties paid British fisherman and relieved Americans from all discriminating duties save only an old subsidy of less than one per cent.

European cities were only beginning to install a system of street lighting at night. As late as 1668 the streets of London were lighted by householders who were ordered "to hang out candles duly to the accustomed hour, for the peace and safety of the city." Not until 1716 were lamps substituted and required to be lighted from "six in the evening until eleven." The little New England town of Boston was in advance of many a large European metropolis when it inaugurated street lights in 1773 and had almost 300 lamps to supplement those of its public-spirited citizens.[2]

Oil, with sugar, was one of the commodities which in that day was ready money in the expanding world market. The people everywhere were coming to realize what John Adams explained to William Pitt in negotiating for a trade treaty between Great Britain and the United States (1785), that "the fat of the spermaceti-whale gives the clearest and most beautiful flame of any substance that is known in nature."

In addition to the fight for markets, competition for raw material was equally keen. Rival whaling fleets scoured the Atlantic from Brazil to the Arctic, sailing with hardy crews from dozens of Atlantic ports: Long Island, Newport,

Sales of 30 Boxes of Sperma Ceti Candles Received ⅌ the Sloop London Capt. John Watson from Newport Rhode Island on the proper Acct & Risque of Mr. Aaron Lopez Merchant there viz.

Accounting for a Shipment of Candles to Aaron Lopez, 1765

Amount Sales of 30 Boxes of Spermacæti Candles brought over £ 517. 7. 2½

Charges &c.ª

To Cash paid Cartage from the Wharf .... £. 5.—
To ditto paid Cap.ᵗ Watson's freight of 30 Boxes. 4. 10.—
To Commissions on £ 517. 7. 2½ at 5 ⅌C.............. 25. 17. 4½   30. 12. 4½

N.ᵗ. £ 486. 14. 10

Errors Excepted

Charlestown South Carolina 15.ᵗʰ March 1765.—

Isaac Da Costa

Providence, Nantucket, the Vineyard, Cape Cod, New
Bedford and Boston. As whalers brought their cargoes to
market, merchants of Philadelphia, New York, Boston and
Rhode Island bid competitively against each other for every
catch. Such competition advanced prices of raw materials
so greatly that the manufacturers found themsleves faced
with another serious trade problem. In 1761 nine spermaceti
candle manufacturers, all located in New England, of whom
three were the Jewish firms of Newport, came together and
formulated what is, perhaps, one of the very earliest attempts at monopoly in American commerce.[3] They formed
an association under the name of "The United Company
of Spermaceti Candlers." For a period of seventeen months
they agreed to eliminate competitive buying between them
and to apportion amongst themselves all whales caught in
their territory by purchasing them for joint account. They
then also fixed selling prices. Candles in New England
were to be marketed at prices fixed at not less than 1 s
10½ d sterling per pound with an additional shilling charged
for each box containing 25 pounds.

As was to be expected the agreement did not immediately
put an end to all the abuses it was aimed to prevent. Some
of the members did not play fair; others who had been left
on the outside sought to take advantage of the situation —
fairly or unfairly, but to their own gain. The associates
turned to Rivera as their leader to handle such awkward
situations as arose. It required all his tact and sagacity to
whip the recalcitrants into line or by generous and fair
dealings to induce the outsiders to cooperate, for the mutual
advantage of all, in the attempt to eliminate wasteful and
senseless trade abuses. He was untiring in his attempts to
make the plan workable and successful. It is to the credit

of the Jewish members of the association, Rivera, Aaron Lopez, and Naphtali Hart, that, even though they knew that others had violated the agreement, they were able to affirm a year later that "we can, with trust, assure you that we have not yet procured or given orders for a single barrel, having without the least deviation adhered to the contract."[4]

Evidently, however, the arrangement worked sufficiently satisfactorily so that at its expiration, in 1763, at a meeting in Providence, the plan was continued by dropping two of the minor members and extending it to include a group of Philadelphia manufacturers. The new agreement divided the trade amongst ten in fixed proportions. Of these ten, four were Jews. As an example of trade monopoly the working out of this scheme holds its own in contrast with attempts to control our industry by our later captains of industry. It is worthwhile to present it in extenso.

SPERMACETI CANDLE AGREEMENT

We the Subscribers, Manufacturers of Spermaciti Candles Being met together at Providence in N. E. this 13th Day of April, 1763, have agreed for ourselves and Partners Respectively (notwithstanding any alteration that may happen in our respective Houses within the term herein after mentioned) honorably to adhere and abide By the Following Articles — Viz.

First. That we will and hereby do unite ourselves into one Body for our General and Particular Interest for the full Term of one Year from and after the Date hereof, i. e. until the 13th Day of April, 1764.

Second. That we will not at any time within said Term

By any Means either directly or indirectly By ourselves
or others for us by Present, Promises or otherwise Pay or
engage to Pay or Give for Headmatter more Than ten
Pounds Sterling per tun above the Current Price of Common Merchantable Spermaceeti Body Brown oyl nor
receive any Head-matter at a Greater or Difference. Which
said Price of said Common Oyl shall at all Times be ascertained by the Current Price Given by the Merchants of
Boston for the London Market at the Day the purchaser
receives any Headmatter. But in case There Be No Current
Price Settled at that Day By the Merchants aforesaid then
the next following Current Price by them Given for such
Oyl shall Govern the Price of Said Headmatter.

Third. That from and after the Date hereof and until
the sᵈ 13th day of April, 1764, we will Not by any means,
Directly or indirectly receive or engage Persons Who shall
be our only Buyers or Factors for Headmatter during Said
Term. Viz. Joseph and William Rotch, Sylvanus Macey
and Co, Folger and Gardner, Robert and Jessie Barker,
Obed Macey, Richard Mitchell and Jonathan Burnell, all
of Nantucket, Henry Lloyd of Boston, George Jackson of
Providence, and Benjamin Mason of Newport. And we
will Not By any Means Directly or indirectly Give or allow
our Said Factors More than two and a half per Cent
Consideration as A Commission or otherwise for their
Trouble.

Fourth. That all the Headmatter caught in North
America and Brought into Any Port Thereof after the Date
Hereof and until the Said 13th Day of April, 1764, Shall
Be Considered as one Common Stocke or Dividend, Whether
any of the Vessels are owned by any of us or not to be de-

vided by our Said Factors to Each House of Manufacturers in the following Proportions. Viz.

Nicholas Brown and Co. 20 Barrels out of Every 100 Barrels.

Thomas Robinson and Co.	13 ditto
Isaac Steel and Co.	9 ditto
Aaron Lopez	11 ditto
Moses Lopez	2 ditto
Edward Langdon and Son	4 ditto
Joseph Palmer and Co.	14 ditto
The Philadelphians	7 ditto
Naphtali Hart and Co.	9 ditto
J. Rivera and Co.	11 ditto
	———
	100

And our Said Factors shall be directed under our Hands to divide the Headmatter caught this Year in the above Proportions in the Spring, Summer and Fall seasons, Excepting only that our Said Factors at Nantuckett Be directed to keep in their own Hands about four hundred Bbls of the Fall Headmatter undivided until they Know from Each of our Houses how Much each House has had, in order to make a final Division agreeable to the above Proportion. But in Case Either of us Should Receive any Headmatter From any other Person but only from the Factors aforesaid, Excepting only that seventy Barrels may be received by Naphtali Hart and Co. from Caleb Russell of Dartmouth and thirty barrels by Rivera and Co from Jethro Haddway of Dartmouth which are to be considered as parts of their above Proportions, or should offer a Greater Price or Difference then afores'd for Headmatter: or larger Commissions than afores'd for Factorage: Or should refuse or neglect To

Pay our Said Factors for the Headmatter to their Satisfaction. Then in either of these Four Cases our Said Factors shall Divide the Headmatter which would otherwise have belonged to such Houses (Who shall be deemed to have forfeited their Shares by such dishonorable conduct) among the other Houses in the aforesaid Proportions Near as they Can.

Fifth. That we will not Any of us, Manufacture either in whole or in part any Spermaciti for any other Person, But only For Ourselves respectively.

Sixth. Let our Factors be Directed to Transmit Acctts to Each of our Houses of the Headmatter sent to each House. And of any Breach of these Articles, and in the Month of December next They Shall Send compleat Acctt of all the Headmatter that has been sent to Each House, of all that has come to their knowledge and how it has Been disposed of. They shall also Engage to Give us the Most Early Notice of any attempt to set up any other Spermaceeti Works, Because the Present Manufacturers are More than Sufficient to Manufacture All that is Ever caught in America. They shall Have Copies of These Articles and shall engage under Their Hands to Conform to the Plain Spirit and Entention of em on Their Part.

Seventh. That we will meet again here at Providence the First Tuesday, February Next (provided there has Not in the Mean time Ben any Manifest Breech of These Articles) in order to Continue this Union in such manner as May then be Agreed upon. And we will Then (Each House) deliver to the Chair Man for the Time Being Certificates under Oath or Solemn Affirmation of the Whole Quantity of Headmatter in Gallons received or Secured by Each House, After the Date hereof until each Day of Meeting, and of Whom received.

Eighth. That Messrs John Slocom, P. Rivera, Thom[s] Robinson and M. Brown are hereby appointed to treat with the Said Factors at Newport and Nantuckett, and John Brown to treat with the Said Factor at Providence. And Joseph Palmer to Treat with the said Factor at Boston. And They are All to report their Proceedings with Sd Factors to Nicholas Brown and Co to be Communicated to The Other Manufacturers.

In Witness of our Free Consent to Every of the Foregoing Articles in Their Most Simple, Plain, and Obvious meaning and Declaring upon our Honour, that We will Not in the Least deviate from Either of em unless by Joint Consent; We Hereunto Subscribe our Names this 13th day of April, 1763.

> PALMER AND CO.
> NICHOLAS BROWN AND CO.
> ISAAC STEEL AND COMPY, AND
> RIVERA AND CO
> AARON LOPEZ
> THO ROBINSON AND CO
> NAPH'T HART AND COMP
> MOSES LOPEZ

No records available disclose the results of this agreement.[5] We know from the Lopez account books, and the correspondence of the Newport merchants, that they continued to do a large and important trade in oil and candles down to the time they were forced to abandon Newport upon its capture by the British.

The trade tried to keep the art of candle-making a monopoly and evidently was at least somewhat successful, as

Starbuck says that "the process of manufacture was so carefully kept a secret that it was not until 1772 that the people of Nantucket acquired sufficient knowledge to enable them to carry on the business there," and that was at a period when Nantucket was the home port of an important whaling fleet. Once it learned the secret, Nantucket, at the height of its glory, is said to have established fifteen or more refineries and candleworks.

The importance of the pre-Revolutionary export trade in oil and candles to the United States is indicated by the fact that in 1770 there was exported from America (including Newfoundland, Bahamas and Bermuda) 379,012 pounds of candles valued at £23,688 4/6, 5667 tons of oil valued at £83,012 and 112,971 pounds of whale-bone valued at £19,121. By 1775, a good part of New England's vessels, estimated at over 350, was engaged in the whale fisheries.

When the whaling village of New Bedford was raided by the British, they burned its warehouses and destroyed its vessels until hardly any remnants of its whaling fleet survived. While Newport did not fare so badly physically when it was captured, yet its prolonged occupation by the British troops proved so fatal that it permanently lost its commercial importance.

As a war measure, in 1775, the British Parliament passed a law prohibiting the carrying on of any fishery on any part of the North American coast. Such hostile legislation, the havoc of war, the spread of the use of substitutes, such as tallow candles, in the colonies, all wrought so great an upheaval in the whale-oil industry as almost to bring about its collapse. When peace came, Great Britain imposed a duty on all oil imported from America and adopted steps to encourage its own whale fisheries at the expense of its former colonies. As whaling revived with a later generation, Newport, no longer a center for great Jewish merchants, never attained any importance in the second chapter of the history of oil.

When the time came to write a third chapter for the American history of oil, it was the story of petroleum. There is no outstanding Jewish participation there.

27

UNIFORMS

AS WE sat in the reception room of the hospital and the trim uniformed nurses whisked in and out, the elderly gentleman turned towards me and asked if I had ever heard of how the Red Cross nurses' uniforms came about.

"Florence Nightingale in the Crimean war —" I began, but he interrupted me.

"No," he said, "it has a Russian background, or, perhaps more accurately, there is a Russian Jew in the background. It is a story of America, a tale of Jewish imagination and enterprise here, and a not altogether untypical story of the kind of career many a poor Russian Jewish immigrant has made for himself in the United States, and of a contribution to American life."

And this is the story he told:

When I was a lad in what was then the little town of Poltava in the Ukraine, we Jews had a difficult struggle for a livelihood. I do not believe you have any idea on how little we lived and what a hard struggle it was to exist on the verge of nothing. In 1863, at the age of thirteen, I went to work, just the day after my *Bar Mitzvah*. My chum, Henry Dickstein (who, after he came to America, at the suggestion of his children's schoolteacher, anglicized his name to Dix — Henry A. Dix) went to work on the same day, on his thirteenth birthday, apprenticed to one of our Jewish shopkeepers who ran a village store. Shortly after that I left for America. Henry continued at Poltava. By the time he was thirty-five, by the hardest kind of work and by saving penny by penny, partly with cash and partly on credit, he managed to buy out his employer. At the age of twenty-six he had married and raised a family, and it looked as if he was settled for life to end his days as one of the lucky ones in the Poltava Jewish community.

You know the catastrophe which overwhelmed the Jews of Russia in the eighties. As conditions grew worse and worse, Henry, in 1892, at the age of forty-two, pulled up stakes and came to America. When I met him here, just after the family had landed in New York, they could not speak a word of English and had only a few dollars which they had managed to save from the sale of their Russian property. The very day they landed they began to study the language and it was surprising how quickly they learned. He told me he had made up his mind to become a farmer, so I persuaded him to go down to the Baron de Hirsch colony and agricultural school at Woodbine, New Jersey, to get some training in American farming.

The next I heard he had bought a little farm in that neighborhood and was market-farming. Then one day he told me he had sold his farm — progress was not rapid enough — and, attracted by the clean and cheerful little village of Millville, about twenty miles from Woodbine, he and his wife had decided to capitalize on his experience as a storekeeper in Russia by opening a dry goods store there. They put up a brave struggle to make ends meet, both of them putting in long hours and sparing themselves in no way, but it was no easy task to handle unfamiliar conditions in a strange land.

They supplemented their shopkeeping by peddling through the countryside, selling the rural population "Mother Hubbard" wrappers for everyday wear and "tea gowns" of flowered sateens for Sunday wear. Perhaps you remember those hideous monstrosities of the nineties, devoid of fit, shape or style, shoddy material thrown together in New York sweatshops, with nothing to recommend them but their cheapness? One day, as they were riding around on one of their business trips, Henry looked with distaste on the wares he was trying to sell and asked his wife: "These women who buy these cheap garments surely would like to look better than they now do — why do they wear them?" So they discussed the customers and their wares and came to the conclusion that the only reason there was a market for such poor stuff was that there was nothing better-looking at the price these women could afford, and that, if he and she could produce something which was better-looking and cost no more, women would prefer to buy such garments to make themselves more presentable.

Back they went to their little Millville shop to experiment with his idea. With no knowledge of manufacturing, and no acquaintance with dressmaking or tailoring, husband and wife designed and made their first gowns. They fell far short of what they had planned. They were not good; but they were better than those they had been selling. Then he found a youth who had worked in a Philadelphia dressmaking shop and hired him for $12.00 a week as mechanic and designer. The village girls were hired as operators. Thus they began their manufacturing in a modest way, journeying forth to put to the test the work of their brains and hands. Their garments grew steadily better and before long they were really turning out something which was far ahead of anything else at the price on the market.

From the very first, Dix insisted that every garment should be marked "made by Henry A. Dix" and that it should be simple in style, of good material and carefully stitched. In competition with "job lot" cheap wrappers and house dresses, he emphasized quality —"not how cheap, but how good" his merchandise could be for the price.

In 1896 they remodeled their store into workshop, office and stockroom, where all the family worked to meet the demands of an increasing business. He was opposed to mass production. Even when public recognition of the honest quality of his merchandise created a constantly increasing demand for his goods, and customers, often the largest and most prominent stores of our big cities, came knocking at his doors eager to buy, he refused to expand. He refused to yield to the temptation, as so many manufacturers did in the day of World War I prosperity, of reaching out for the profits of big business. He felt that he did not want to spread out in boom times only to throw faithful workers out of jobs if business slackened. His idea was that a business owed to its workers steady employment throughout the year and that a company which reached out for the very last dollar of trade that it could force could not continue at full speed without serious ups and downs. He resolved that his concern should not grow beyond the point where it could give uninterrupted employment to its workmen in its slackest season under poorest business conditions. Dix would never allow the business to grow at the risk of quality. He insisted his output should never be beyond what he personally could hold up to his standards.

Slowly Dix built, but on a sure foundation, only gradually expanding into the neighboring villages of Bridgeton and Somerville. Finally he had three factories, all rather modest in size, run under his personal direction and working full time through the year, each turning out goods of the same high standard which he had set for his merchandise.

Then came the second development in the business — a switch to the making of uniforms for working girls, so that help in hotels, waitresses in restaurants, maids in a household and saleswomen in shops might have available simple, neat costumes. Up to that time the working girl, while on her job, had made use of any old haphazard second-best dress, so that as a class they presented a drab and motley appearance with an air of dowdiness.

Dix's commonsense made a practical commercial application of what his philosophy had led him to observe as a fundamental trait of human nature — that a trimly uniformed maid will perform her duties more neatly, and that a working girl who, by a tidy appearance makes a favorable impression upon others, will herself feel more self-respecting and, taking more pride in her work, perform her tasks more efficiently. The same Dix standard of quality, taste, workmanship, simplicity and fair prices for the "Dix Uniforms" proved his theory and they became a popular success from coast to coast. A new branch of the women's wear industry was thus created.

From such a start, making uniforms for nurses was a natural advance. Soon no hospital was considered up to date unless its nurses were properly uniformed. In 1917, when the Red Cross adopted a nurse's hospital uniform, it turned to Dix to design it.[1] Then the Dix Red Cross uniform took its place as international insignia, recognized in whatever corner of the earth suffering called for the ministering charity of that noble institution.

During the World War I the United States Government appointed Dix to design and supply nurses' uniforms which could serve both the Red Cross nurses as well as the official army and navy nurses.

In 1922, looking back over his seventy-two years, long years of struggle with never an idle day, Henry Dix, essentially a man of simple tastes now grown rich, faced the problem of the future.

"Money, I have enough of it. Why should I want more? Many years ago I limited the expansion of my business. In 1914 I was a millionaire. What is there I could buy with more money? I like simple life in the country, and I do not need more money for that. But I can do something for these boys and girls who have been true to me and my business for so many years."

So, as that year drew to its close, he turned over his business to his employees. It was all done so unostentatiously that it was some time before the enterprising metropolitan press heard of such an unprecedented reorganization of a nationally famous, big and prosperous business, and were able to satisfy public curiosity with the story of the gift under blazing headlines:

> Man Who Gave Workers $1,000,000 Business calls it merely Justice .... Dix never had a strike in a quarter century of operation. Has made all he wants — declined big price for plants so his employees could have a chance.

Thus Henry Dix, the lad of little Poltava, with contented heart after his years of struggle and toil, turned in his old age to the simple life for which he had ever yearned — to farm and to gather fruits and vegetables raised by the labor of his own hands. His story ends in 1938, at the age of 88; but after him lives the institution he founded and his ideas, so typically American, which transmuted the garment in which our working women toiled into the insignia of self-respecting service.

His had been the vision of the spirit of America which, uniting Plymouth Rock and Ellis Island, created a land of fulfillment, where all the diverse people from every nation of the earth who for centuries have sought our shores shall be fused into a great nation — Americans all.

28

CLOTHING

The most important economic function of the Jews in our day has been in a field very far removed from that of finance. In various branches of industry, they have played an important share in that process — bound up with mass-production and improved distribution — which has wrought in our day a profound sociological change. Time was—and not so very long ago—when the rift between the rich and poor was more profound by far than it is at present and when even the lower middle classes had to content themselves with the ugliest, coarsest and barest necessities of life ... The last generation has witnessed a sociological change unexampled in history. It is the great peaceful revolution of our time, and among the greatest stabilizing forces in the modern world. In assisting to bring this about, rather than in a fictitious financial predominance, lies the real importance of the role of the Jew in modern economic life, and one of his most significant contributions to civilization in recent times.

Cecil Roth
The Jewish Contribution to Civilization

SUGAR and clothing, commonplaces of daily life, will some day be recognized for the part they played in the history of the Jews in America.[1] It has been asserted that the Jews introduced sugar cultivation into the Americas. But even though such a broad claim cannot be substantiated, it must at least be conceded that throughout the seventeenth century the Jews were important if not dominant in sugar cultivation in the New World and in supplying it to the markets of Europe. Originally a luxury available only to the very rich, sugar had by the end of the 17th century begun to be produced in sufficient quantities to be within the reach of the proletariat. Thereby an expanding market was created, and the American colonies prospered because of it. Sugar planting, refining, and trading thus afforded an economic and business foundation for the early settlements of Spanish and Portuguese Jews.

The story of clothing is more easily told for it was part of the economic and social revolution closer to our day, and the stages by which it developed are more clearly marked. Not so long ago all cloth was spun by hand and there was no such thing as a ready-made garment. The rich employed a tailor. The ordinary family was outfitted by the sewing of its women whose efforts might, on special occasions, be supplemented by the work of a seamstress or an itinerant journeyman tailor. Such made-to-order clothing was consequently not only expensive but was planned for long service. Grandfather's suits of clothes were not infrequently considered a respectable part of the inheritance. The poor were clothed in the discarded clothing of the rich. From this situation it is a far cry to the present state of affairs, when a clothing store decorates every Main Street and the garment of the poor does not differ from that of the rich either in type or fashion, and often not even in quality.

In this transformation the American Jew played an important role. The American development of clothing offered the Jews of German origin the same economic opportunities that sugar had offered to the Jews whose ancestors had hailed from Portugal or Spain. This is the story.

Throughout the Middle Ages, Jewish weavers and tailors as well as Jewish traders in textiles and garments existed wherever Jews were permitted to live. As the weavers' and tailors' trade guilds became more powerful and exclusively Christian, they compelled the adoption of repressive regulations by which their Jewish competitors were crowded into the second-hand garment trade and limited in the manufacture of new garments to supplying the small needs of the ghetto. Thereafter the second-hand clothing business and the Jews became intimately associated in the popular mind of Europe; which association was subsequently carried over to America.[1a] It was so deeply rooted that L. Maria Child, reporting on the sights of New York in 1841, observed: "In New York, as elsewhere, the vending of 'old clo'' is a prominent occupation of the Jews." In making this remark, this literary bluestocking overlooked the fact that in her own Boston, as late as 1851, all of the twenty-five exclusively second-hand clothing establishments were strictly "Yankee" and that the like was true of most other American cities. What was true was that the Jews, who by thousands were coming over from Germany to America between the years 1840 and 1860, as well as those who had preceded them during the previous century and a half, had behind them a centuries-long experience in the manufacture of and trade in clothing.

In the meantime a number of factors had been contributing to a revolution in the clothing industry. In the first place there were the French Revolution and the Napoleonic wars. Prior to that European upheaval, a well dressed man wore a long coat of silk, satin or velvet, a waistcoat extending to his knees and often elaborately embroidered, fancy linen, knee-breeches, stockings of silk and buckled shoes. His clothing was thus as colorful and fancy as any woman's. The people of New York followed the Continental fashion[2] and, while Boston and Philadelphia lagged behind fashionable New York, the South, more particularly the rich families of Virginia, often imported their wearing-apparel from abroad and followed the London styles even more ardently.

The French Revolution identified this style of dress with the privileged upper class and the more sober fashion and material which the Third Estate brought into fashion in the nineteenth century — the abandonment of knee-breeches for long trousers and the simplification of shirts and coats — lent themselves to a standardization which opened up opportunities for ready-to-wear garments. At the same time, the mass manufacture of such garments was becoming more widespread because of another series of circumstances.

In Europe the demands of the Napoleonic wars for soldiers' uniforms taught tailors the wholesale production of ready-made soldiers' clothing. When these wars ended, the manufacturers turned their experience to supplying the civilian trade. America had an even longer history of ready-made clothing due to the needs of the new country and the nature of its settlers. As early as 1713–14, Ambrose Vincent called the attention of "merchants, inland traders and others" to a "public vendue or outcry" at the Crown Coffee-House, King Street, Boston, of

> Sundry parcels of men's wearing apparel viz. coats, breeches, hats, shoes and buckles, shirts, neck-cloths and gloves to be put up in small lots for encouragement of the buyers.

After repeating the advertisement a number of times for different dates, he specified a lot as containing: "1 coat, 1 pair breeches, 1 pair shoes, 2 shirts, 1 neck-cloth . . . the gloves in separate lots."[3] In 1765, Jolley Allen offered "men's ready-made cloathing" at his shop near the Draw Bridge, Boston, as imported from London "to be sold by wholesale or retail cheap for cash or short credit."[4] At this time, however, such offerings of clothing appear exceptional and may represent "dumpings in the Colonial market" by English tailors of their misfits.

The real birth of the ready-to-wear clothing industry took place in America a generation or so later, about 1830, and its birthplace seems to have been the whaling center New Bedford, Massachusetts. A whaler, ready to start on a voyage, as its last preparation before sailing, signed on a crew. The sailors then had to be outfitted for a long voyage for varying climates. Often the sailing had to be delayed because of the slow process of making up the sailors' outfits by the local custom tailors. Sooner or later enterprising outfitters were bound to conceive of the idea that such clothing could be made up in advance so as to supply the demand without delay. At first this was wholly a local enterprise, confined to a few small establishments with limited output which produced garments of only the roughest and cheapest quality, the actual work being done by women in their homes.[5] Such manufacturing having proved economically sound, it was expanded to Boston to include the manufacture of clothing of this cheap "slop-shop" grade for slaves and for the Colonial export trade.[6]

This development was accompanied by a tremendous expansion of the market. During the period of the rapid development of the United States, from 1830 to 1860, the system of home manufacture of clothing proved unequal to the needs of the unattached men who flocked to the growing industrial centers and of the pioneers who pushed on to "open up" the West. The result was the creation of an active market in second-hand garments. In fact, in America up to the Civil War the second-hand clothing trade was almost as important as the trade in new garments. The

Boston directory for 1850 shows that, of the one hundred
and eleven clothing stores in the city, twenty-seven dealt
exclusively in second-hand clothing while all the eighty-four
others handled both new and second-hand garments.[7] In his
Economics of Fashion, Nyshom pictures how the second-
hand clothing market developed into a ready-made clothing
trade:

> Having no homes and no wives, sisters or daughters
> in homes to produce clothing for them, a great number
> of men turned to the second-hand stores for replenish-
> ment of their clothing needs. Up to 1830 this demand
> had not been greater than the supply. During the
> 1830's, and more particularly in the 40's, the demand
> grew completely beyond former bounds, so that
> second-hand clothing dealers almost of necessity
> turned to the expedient of having clothing made new
> to be sold ready-made to their customers.

Despite this expansion, however, the clothing industry
remained insignificant in the economic life of the country.
The census of 1830 showed only 3,780 clothiers and 14,988
tailors in a population exceeding 23,000,000. The census of
1840 still shows no classification for clothing among the
manufactured products of the nation.

The next important development in the industry came in
1831 when George Opdyke of New York, who later became
its Mayor, made what was perhaps the first successful
experiment outside of New England with new ready-made
clothing of a better quality. Generally, gentlemen's clothes
in the United States still continued to be made at home or in
custom tailor shops, where the workmen were English,
Irish[8] and German, while native Americans were, usually,

330 JEWISH PIONEERS AND PATRIOTS

the managers and proprietors. It had been found that the great crowds of visitors who passed through the city of New York had little time to wait for measure or to be inconvenienced with a tailor's delays and misfits. Such visitors were excellent prospects for better ready-made clothes. Tailors, therefore, began to keep assortments.[9] Opdyke began to manufacture at his retail store in Hudson Street and to cater to this higher-class trade. Before long he manufactured beyond the needs of the New York market and opened stores in Memphis, New Orleans and Charleston. Thus, it seems, came into being America's first chain of retail stores. Thus, too, the base of the industry was broadened, although during the 1840's the business as a whole was still of no substantial proportions.

It might be well, at this point, to have a look at the clothing which these enterprising manufacturers produced. In 1854, Freedley foresaw in the spread of ready-made clothing "a most important and complete revolution .... in the ancient and respectable occupation of tailoring." But the appearance of the ready-made suit was still a thing of the future. Generally, ready-made manufacturing was confined to coats (top coats), expanding to include vests, pants (pantaloons) or even dress coats. Perhaps the development of the industry can best be traced through typical advertisements of the three decades, 1830, 1840, and 1850. We begin with an early advertisement (1829) of a Boston agent, obviously acting for anonymous custom tailors, selling misfits or garments made up to keep journeymen employed during the dull season. Apparently it is not until 1850 that advertisements feature regular lines of ready-made clothing.

[Dated: 1829]

CHEAP   CASH
COMMISSION   CLOTHIER
STORE
235 Washington Street Boston

(Second Store South of the Marlborough Hotel)
Constantly on hand, every Article constituting a
Gentleman's Wardrobe — viz, Dress Coats, Top
Coats, Frock Coats, Surtouts, Cloaks, Wrappers,
Pantaloons, Vests, Handkerchiefs, Cravats, Stocks,

Collars, Gloves, Hose, Suspenders & &
R. Edward Agent

[Dated: Boston, 1840]

FOR CASH!!   FOR CASH!!
At Chambers   44 Congress Street

The undersigned offers an assortment of Woolen
Goods Such as are to be found among the best selections for

FASHIONABLE WEARING APPAREL!

Which he will make up in the latest and neatest style
for the

AUTUMN AND WINTER

Pilot, Beaver, double milled Surtout, Frock and dress

Coats

BROADCLOTHS!

American, French, German, and English, different
styles of

CASSIMERES

Figured Woolens, Velvet, and Silk Velvet Satine,
figured and plain, and fancy Valencias,

VESTINGS!

At the very lowest market prices, by the piece or
pattern, or made into Garments.

> W. WHITNEY Agent
> 44 Congress Street, upstairs.

[Dated: New York, 1840]

Those mansions of marble, oh say, if thou knowest,
  O'er which the gay standard of Fashion's unfurled,
Where the welcome is warm and the prices are lowest,
  And the clothes are the cheapest and best in the
        world?

If not — fly at once! To Smith Brothers betake you,
  They best can assist you to bear out your plan,
For they either have got or will speedily make you,
  The best suit of clothes ever seen upon man.
    Smith Bros. 122, 138, 140 Fulton St.

[Dated: New York, 1850]

READY MADE CLOTHING

27 Cortlandt Street

Between Western and
  Merchants Hotels   New York

The subscriber offers for sale a very superior stock
of READY MADE CLOTHING AND FURNISHING GOODS
equal, if not superior, to any house in the trade.
CITIZENS AND STRANGERS are respectfully solicited to
call and examine his assortment of

COATS

Black cloth, Dress and Frock Coats, Black and
Colored Sacks, Sack Frocks

Cashmirette and Alpacca Coats, Fine Linens,

Men's Fashions in America, 1831

Sier Sucker and Pongee Coats
Business Coats of every description

PANTS

Black and Colored Cassimeres, Fancy and
White Drilling and India Neukeen Pants

VESTS

Bombazine, Black, and Colored Silk and Satin,
White and Fancy Marseilles Vests

ALSO

Linen and Muslin Shirts, Merino and Silk
Under Shirts and Drawers

GLOVES, HALF HOSE

Linen, Cambric, and Silk Handkerchiefs, &c.
Clothing, made to order in the best style and
sent to any port of the United States
Returning CALIFORNIANS fitted out at short
notice, ready-made or to order
And the goods warranted to give satisfaction

ARMY AND NAVY UNIFORMS

made to order in the best style and according
to the late REGULATIONS

HENRY L. FOSTER
27 Cortlandt Street
NEW YORK

[Dated: New York, 1850]

Remember 76 Fulton Street, Sign of Gen. Taylor —
P. L. Rogers, Wholesale and Retail Clothier,
76 Fulton St. respectfully invites an examination
of his new and elegant style of ready-made
clothing for the fall of 1850 and the Winter of
1850–51.

In the Wholesale Department will be found an
ample stock of well-made and fashionable garments,

calculated to do good service in all sections of the country, and cheaper than ever before offered in this city.

The Retail Department is stocked with an immense variety of overcoats, Sacks, Frocks, Dress Coats, Vests, Pantaloons, &c of every material which fashion sanctions, or economy approves; and the following list will show that the prices are graduated by the very lowest scale of living profits!

OVERCOATS

A most splendid assortment of Drab English Devonshire Kerseys, from..........................	$10.00 to	20.00
Black, Brown and Blue Beavers....	5.00	10.00
Fancy Light Overcoats............	5.00	10.00
Drab, Black and Blue Pilots.......	5.00	15.00
Splendid Dress and Frock Coats....	2.00	6.00

PANTS

Pants of every shade and color.....	2.00	6.00

VESTS

Vests of every style of goods.......	.75	5.00

BOY'S CLOTHING

Sacks and Overcoats..............	2.00	6.00
Jackets.........................	1.50	5.00
Pants...........................	1.25	3.00

Also, a splendid assortment of cloths, Cassimeres, and Vestings constantly on hand and made to order at the shortest notice.

A full suit of Winter Clothing for $5.

A fit guaranteed in all cases, and orders executed in the Custom Department in the most fashionable style and with the utmost promptitude.

P. L. Rogers
No. 76 Fulton St. corner of Gold

The industry was now set for two further advances. The first was the change from a mere retail to a wholesale business. Large scale manufacturing began as a seasonal occupation when Boston merchants, close to the cotton and woolen mills, sent cloth, ready cut for sewing into garments, to the farm districts and fishing villages of New England. There sailors' and farmers' wives and daughters, and sometimes the men as well, used their leisure to supplement their meager earnings by sewing the pieces of cloth into garments.[10] It was said that, by 1860, sixty thousand "females" in New England were employed in sewing.[11] This made Boston the center for the wholesale clothing business, the volume of which was estimated in that year to be worth $15,000,000.[11a]

The second advance was due to the invention of the sewing machine by Elias Howe in 1846[12] and its perfection by Singer in 1851. This improved quality, cheapened cost and speeded manufacture. It had the further effect of changing clothing manufacture from a home to a factory industry. Eased from within and offered expanding opportunities from without, the industry spread to other large cities where the swelling tide of immigration offered cheap labor. By 1860 Boston had dropped to third place in the industry, topped by both New York and Philadelphia and closely followed by Baltimore. Even Cincinnati and Chicago began to be important. These, it is to be noted, were all localities which had attracted German Jewish immigrants, of whom Boston had received comparatively few. In 1856 it was already being pointed out that "one great benefit resulting to the community from the success of the clothing manufacturing is the immense field of employment it has opened to *females* and *immigrants*."[13]

For the first time, the census of 1860 recognized the manufacture of clothing as a national industry. The trade employed 120,539 hands earning upward of $20,000,000 per annum. Freedley reported that, in spite of rumors to the contrary, its wages were high: "females" in the industry were earning from $3 to $7 per week; their pay for piece-work was 75¢ to $1 for making a silk vest, 31¢ to 37¢ for "the commonest pants (which are) thrown together," enabling them to average two pair a day.

Into the general picture described above the German-Jewish immigrants fitted to an amazing extent. In the forties, when the German Jews began to come to this country in considerable numbers, many began their careers by peddling, not only in the eastern cities and countryside, but through the growing towns of the midwest as well. It was a common thing for these peddlers to make long journeys with packs on their backs or, as they became more prosperous, with wagon and team. As they made their longer rounds over country roads, the horse-drawn wagons of these itinerant Jewish peddlers, stocked with an assortment of wares, were welcomed at isolated farms as bringing to the farmer the opportunity to purchase what farms could not produce. They were to many a farm and rural settlement that touch with the markets of the outside world which mail-order houses afford today.

Having laboriously accumulated a little capital the Jews opened general stores or trading posts in the villages or districts through which they had peddled. By the end of the Civil War there was hardly a growing town of the country without a Jewish shopkeeper. Often, as opportunity offered and the communities grew, Jewish shopkeepers developed into merchants or turned to manufacturing. Ultimately there was thus founded a factory or store destined later to figure in America's Big Business.[14]

It was natural for these German-Jewish peddlers and shopkeepers, trained to meet whatever demand made itself felt, to include clothing in the stock of their "general stores" as soon as improvements in manufacturing lowered prices. Where the community was large, they drifted into specializing in clothing. By 1860 some of the more enterprising and successful of these earlier clothing shopkeepers in the larger cities had begun to wholesale and to manufacture. Freedley, in 1854, named Gans, Leberman & Co., and Arnold, Nusbaum & Nirdlinger (Wolf, Arnold & Nirdlinger), both of Philadelphia, in his list of "extensive and respectable clothiers in the United States." Indeed, in an advertisement in 1856, Gans, Leberman & Co. proclaimed itself "The oldest exclusively wholesale clothier in Philadelphia," and announced that its ready-made clothing was "manufactured under the care and superintendence of two of the proprietors who are practical tailors."[15] In 1861, Bishop, in his *History of American Manufacturers*, records two other Jewish firms, Bernheimer Brothers, and William Seligman & Co., in a list of fourteen clothing houses of New York enumerated as amongst the largest in the United States.[16]

During the Civil War the government demand for soldiers' uniforms preëmpted the capacity of this expanding industry;[16a] but as soon as the war ended, civilian demand took up the slack. Wholesale clothing manufacturing grew by leaps and bounds and assumed national proportions. New York became the clothing capital of the country. Manufacturing and wholesaling spread westward. Syracuse, Rochester,[17]

Cincinnati,[18] Cleveland[19] and Chicago[20] became keen competitors for the business, along with its older rivals: Baltimore, Philadelphia and Boston.[20a]

Until late in the eighties, Germans and Irish still continued to predominate among the workmen in the factories. During the twenty years from 1860 to 1880, a constantly increasing number of Jews became proprietors of clothing factories and wholesale as well as retail clothing merchants. Along with this, Jews became skilled clothing workmen, expert foremen and designers.

After the Civil War, conditions in the clothing business thus afforded a particularly attractive field for the very talents which characterized the German Jew. The trade could be quickly learned and did not necessarily require large capital, since mill credits for raw material were liberal. Profits were large and there was a quick turnover, so that energy and hard work earned sure rewards. Ready-made clothing was the lusty "infant industry" of the epoch. It was to that day what automobile manufacturing was to our generation — an industry with wide-open expanding markets, dominated by no business aristocracy and responsive to new ideas. Speeding up production, cutting costs, or other successful experimentation, paid big dividends.

While the trade was highly competitive, it had a national market without fixed prices and a wide spread between the cheapest and the best grades. Then, too, in those early years, clothing styles and material did not change from season to season, so that there were no slow stocks to remain on a manufacturer's hands to be closed out with crippling losses to the beginner or small businessman. Success depended largely on salesmanship; for this was before trademarked or advertised clothing. So large and increasing a proportion of the retail clothing trade in cities and towns drifted into Jewish hands that Jewish manufacturers met no handicaps in selling.[21] Jewish names, which in descendants of a later generation have become famous in Wall Street or distinguished in the arts, sciences and professions, appeared in constantly increasing numbers on signs over imposing establishments which then began to line Broadway, testifying to the importance and success of Jews in the New York market. In 1888, Markens[22] called attention to the fact that, of the 241 clothing manufacturers then located in New York City, 234 were Jews doing an annual business of $55,000,000. Writing of this in the nineties, William C. Browning, one of the patriarchs of the New York clothing trade, says: "In the early days, there was but a single Hebrew in the wholesale business .... now the big wholesale business is largely in the hands of the Jews, as one may see by the bewildering array of signs in Broadway."[23] Other clothing centers only repeated this history.

The next period belonged to the Russian Jews. In the broad general development and expansion of trade and manufacturing which marked the post-Civil War period, Jews had established themselves as important factors in almost all commercial activities. Up to 1882, however, clothing manufacturing was practically the only industry in the United States in which Jewish ownership predominated amongst the employers of labor. When Jews in large numbers began to arrive from Russia in the eighties, and the necessity of finding immediate employment for these refugees was imperative, places were most easily found in the expanding shops and factories controlled by the German Jews. Gradually, Russian Jews displaced the earlier immigrants as clothing workers, so that by 1897, not only in New York but in all clothing centers, three-quarters of the clothing workers were Jews. Figures from the Bureau of Immigration show that, by 1925, 362,642 Jewish immigrants were classified as skilled workmen in the clothing industry.

The progress from the making of ladies' "Mantuas," cloaks, and "mantles" of earlier decades, through the period of the shirtwaist suit days of the gay nineties, to the cloak and suit trade of today, is an industrial romance of the genius and versatility of the Russian Jewish journeymen tailors. After they had learned their trade in the establishments of the German Jews, they opened their own shops in such numbers as to make women's wear their own domain. To them is due the credit for the American women's becoming the best dressed women in the world and for style having been placed within the reach of the slenderest purse.[24]

No industry in our country has been more responsible for changing American social ideas and economic conditions than the Jewish clothing trade. It was amongst the first of American industries to become conscious of "consumer interest." It was the first trade to establish an impartial, independent trade director to adjudicate trade practices and settle industrial disputes. It was a pioneer in banning the use of prison labor and in adopting the use of bargaining agreements between a whole industry's employers and its trade unions.[24a] Necessarily intertwined with this growth of Jewish dominance in the clothing industry are other absorbing chapters of the history of American economics. Such, amongst others, is the development of American trade unionism; both the introduction and later the abolition of the shameful sweatshop; the evolution of factory mass production. Long before the automobile, it invented factory specialization as a contract system which divided manufacturing amongst independent shops devoted to making a single item: coats, trousers or vests.[25] The men's clothing trade was one of the earliest to adopt direct selling, modern advertising and national marketing.[26]

The history of each of these improvements, already embodied in volumes devoted to the social and economic development of America, presents its record of Jewish contributions to present-day American business methods and its industrial systems.

AMERICAN SOLDIERS

29

ASHER POLLOCK, PRIVATE

IN 1776 the British captured Newport, and Rhode Island seemed destined to be a center of military campaigns. As the year 1777 opened, General Washington prepared to strengthen the Continental Army and called upon the Rhode Island General Assembly for two additional battalions of troops. Even before the call, the local Council of War had busily undertaken the task of raising a new levy to replace the soldiers whose enlistments were expiring. The state authorities forthwith recommissioned many of the officers from its two recently disbanded regiments which were retiring from their term of active service in the Jersey campaigns. The task of putting two new battalions into service went on apace.

Colonel Israel Angell, Lieutenant Colonel Jeremiah Olney and Captain William Allen, all experienced officers, were assigned to the Second Battalion and immediately began training new recruits for immediate active service. It seemed to the Continentals possible that a quick aggressive attack on Newport, with the promised help of the French fleet under Count D'Estaing, had a good chance of forcing the British to evacuate the Island.

In response to the call for troops, April 16, 1777, Asher Pollock from Newport enlisted and was assigned to Captain

William Allen's regiment. In the official regimental records he was described as fifty-two years of age, born in London, England, a tallow chandler by trade "size 5 ft. 5 in. hair black, dark complexion." His enlistment was "for the war."

Pollocks were numerous in the Newport Jewish community. By the middle of the eighteenth century they were already well established there. Tradition reports many families of them. Some had come from Poland, some from Austria and others from Hungary. At least six different heads of Pollock families were identified with the synagogue: Zachary, Isacher, Abraham, Isaac, Jacob and Myer. A "Mr. Polak" had conducted services for the congregation before the advent of a professional rabbi. Isaac Pollock had been of that small group of loyal Jews who had brought about the building of the handsome old Newport synagogue. Zachary Pollock had been licensed as a butcher by the town authorities, so as to serve as ritual slaughterer (*shohet*) for his fellow Jews. Myer Pollock was one of Newport's leading merchants, heavily interested in the West India trade and an important factor in the importation of molasses and the manufacture of rum.

The story of one of these Pollocks achieved for the moment some importance, when the great orator, Edmund Burke, arose, May 14, 1781, in the House of Commons to urge Parliament to pass an act to compensate owners for indiscriminate and often unjust seizures and confiscations of private property in St. Eustatius by British military forces enforcing harsh orders. After pointing out that many of these sufferers were Tory friends who had been driven from the rebellious colonies on account of their pro-British sympathies, he proceeded to enforce his point by citing individual cases of such hardship. He said:

Two more Jews had been detected also in a breach of the order for delivering up all their money. Upon one of them were found 900 Johannes. This poor man's case was peculiarly severe; his name was Pollock. He had formerly lived on Rhode Island; and because he had imported tea contrary to the command of the Americans, he was stripped of all he was worth and driven out of the island; his brother shared in his misfortunes, but did not survive them; his death increased the cares of the survivor, as he got an additional family, in his brother's children, to provide for. Another Jew married his sister; and both of them, following the British army, had for their loyalty some lands given them, along with some other American refugees, on Long Island, by Sr. William Howe: they built a kind of fort there to defend themselves; but it was soon after attacked and carried by the Americans, and not a man who defended it escaped either death or captivity; the Jew's brother-in-law fell during the attack; he survived; and had then the family of his deceased brother and brother-in-law, his mother and sister, to support; he settled at St. Eustatius where he maintained his numerous family, and had made some money, when he and his family were once more ruined, by the commanders of a British force, to whose cause he was so attached; and in whose cause he had lost two brothers, and his property twice.

In the summer of 1770 the Newburyport merchant Jonathan Jackson, traveling by boat from Newport to New York, noted among his fellow passengers a Jew by the name of "Ashur Polock" in the company of a "Judaith" family named Hays.[1] The Newport town tax list of 1772 reports "Asher Pollock" taxed at two shillings and records him among those "who left the Island on the breaking of the war and were not registered."[2]

From the day in April of 1777, when Asher enlisted, until the time six years one month and twenty-nine days later, in 1783, when he was discharged from service at the close of the war and awarded "two honorary badges for faithful services," the life of this inconspicuous private is the story of his regiment. The official regimental records which have been preserved for us are hardly more than meager reports of the petty routine of military details. The distribution of shoes, of clothing, of arms and of ammunition; leaves of absence; muster rolls and paymasters' accountings; lists of dead and wounded; and descriptions of physical condition, no matter how faithfully entered upon the records, are after all but thin material out of which to reconstruct the life any soldier in the ranks of the regiment led during the six years of active fighting in which this battalion engaged until, as veterans at the siege of Yorktown, its soldiers saw the end of the war. It is rather from haphazard fragments from private sources that the story must be reconstructed.

So immediate was the need for soldiers at the front in 1777 that training was curtailed. They were short of the proper outfittings for their soldiers. In spite of all this, soldiers could not be kept for local campaigns, but were rushed forward to respond to more urgent calls from spheres of more intense enemy activity. At Peekskill by midsummer, "Col. Angell described his soldiers as being without shoes, and otherwise so poorly clad, that half of them were unfit for any duty, and the regiment had become an object of derision wherever it appeared." In the face of this, they plunged almost immediately into the battles of Brandywine and of Germantown and into the fightings in the Jerseys, so that these Rhode Islanders were well seasoned by actual warfare before they went into winter quarters at Valley Forge, with Washington, for that dreadful and disheartening winter of '77. There cold, starvation, sickness and the lack of food and clothing took a daily appalling toll of victims. The Rhode Island troops shared all the horrors and suffering which have made the name of Valley Forge a sad and tragic byword in American history.

Back in Rhode Island in the spring of 1778, the troops were in encampment at Tiverton as part of General John Sullivan's army, soon again to be engaged against the British in a general offensive designed to force the enemy out of Newport. It was largely a series of Lilliputian local engagements, no one of any great importance, with fluctuating success. By midsummer, when the French fleet arrived off Newport, all was ready for a final test. The attack on Newport appeared to be making some progress when, towards the end of August, over the protest of the American officers, the French fleet sailed off for refitting. The Colonials were indignant. Our Colonel Angell wrote in his diary: "Count DeEstaing, the french admiral . . . left us to-day bound to Boston and I think left us in a most rascally manner." The campaign then flattened out and, on August 31, Colonel Angell found himself and his troops compelled to "retreat off the Island" and before long took up winter quarters at Warren.

The year 1779 was largely spent by the regiment in continuing the Rhode Island campaign. After the evacuation of Newport, in December, they were ordered to Morristown, New Jersey. It was a forced, hard, winter march, a "great part of the way over shoe in mud and some places

up to the men's knees in water." After a season in northern
New Jersey, they were moved to West Point, where they
spent the somewhat quiet summer of 1780, "extreme hott."
By now the regiment had found itself and were disciplined
veterans. Colonel Angell proudly records that summer that
at West Point the brigade was inspected by the Inspector-
General Baron von Steuben and "the Baron was exceedingly pleased with the men, array being in the best order."

As General Washington, after manoeuvring some time
around New York, planned the attack on Cornwallis at
Yorktown, Pollock's regiment received orders to proceed to
Hartford and thence to Philadelphia, where they encamped
a week waiting further instructions. From there they
marched to Elk River, where they were transported by
boat to Little York and then marched on to Yorktown.

A fellow private has told the story of that famous siege
as it must have appeared to Asher and his Rhode Island
companions in the ranks, busy with the daily discharge of
their officer's orders, ignorant of the larger plans of headquarters:

> We encamped within half cannon shot of the
> British and commenced a fortification by digging a
> trench, or rather by each man digging a hole deep
> enough to drop into. When this was accomplished
> we stationed a man to watch the enemy's guns, at
> which every man dropped into his hole. But we soon
> left this ground, and in the night stormed two of the
> fortifications, and dug a trench all around the British
> encampment completely yarding them in. Two
> nights after the storming of the fortifications the
> British undertook to retake them and mustering
> out a small party calling themselves Americans
> came up in the rear of us. They entered the fort with

little difficulty, as there were but few of us in it and very quickly those who were not instantly killed or taken were driven out of it. Four days from that time Lord Cornwallis surrendered.

Officially this second Rhode Island battalion, then under Captain Stephen Olney, is recorded as heading the storming column which took the redoubt of the first fort captured at Yorktown.

In October 1781, after the surrender, the regiment was sent to Saratoga, which they reached after a long and tedious march and which they made their headquarters until the spring of 1783.

For more than six long years, Asher, as a soldier of the Revolution, through all the hardships and deprivations of war, in the routine of camp and on the field of battle, had served his adopted country. On occasions he had been called upon to act as the regimental butcher "on extra service." There are even records showing that he was temporarily lent to "Col. C. Green's Rhode Island Regiment of Foot" for such "extra service." He had come through the war safely and now was approaching the day when, in his fifty-ninth year, he could look forward again to a return to civilian life. But, alas, the Newport he had known was no longer the center of the Jewish life he had left. It was never to recover from the cruel blows of war. The Jews who had done so much for the town were never to return. His was to seek a new home.

Asher was less fortunate than another Pollock — Cusham Polack of Georgia — who, when he retired from his Revolutionary service, received a formal certification from the Georgia delegates in the Continental Congress. This certificate attested of this other Jewish private, "a citizen of the state of Georgia for many years past, (that he) gave early demonstration of his attachment to the American cause, by taking an active part, has been in several engagements against the enemy, when he behaved himself with approbation." It added that he "is entitled to every indulgence usually given by sister states to persons of his description."[3]

Our Asher ended his military career when, without fanfare, he was honorably discharged at Saratoga, New York, June 15, 1783.[4] With his two "honory badges for faithful service," Asher Pollock silently retired to the oblivion of those whose inconspicuous but devoted service in a great cause made our country a land of liberty and freedom.

> He was the winter soldier of Valley Forge;
> Alone at night, alone in the wet snow, ill clad,
> Hungry, frozen, drilling, marching, ever drilling
> Through long drear winter to spring hardships
>   winning.
>
> Again at Yorktown in a wide flung battle line,
> In a rain of bullets charging the enemy,
> American, Jew, answering duty's stern call,
> Unknown man in the ranks, unrememb'd, unsung.
>   Unknown soldier of the Revolution!

30

GENERAL AND GOVERNOR

"But Chrysipphus, Posidonius, Zeno and Boëthus say, that all things are produced by fate. And fate is a connected cause of existing things, or the reason according to which the world is regulated."

Diogenes Laertius Zeno, LXXIV.

IN the year 1938, eighteen hundred veterans of both blue and gray, averaging ninety-four years of age, foregathered in a national celebration of the seventy-fifth anniversary of the Battle of Gettysburg —"the high tide of the Rebellion"— the turning point in the Civil War.

Here we shall tell the tale of one of these soldiers, an immigrant lad, who, by the turn of chance on the eventful days of July, 1863, when history was in the making on that great battlefield, held high command at a crucial point in the battle-line of the Republic. While his life was more spectacular than that of most youths of his time who sought asylum here, it is typical of what Jews, in their loyalty to the land of their adoption, have accomplished in many fields of American adventure.

Edward S. Salomon was born in Schleswig, December 25, 1836, the eldest of eleven children in a family which both on the father's and the mother's sides counted centuries of residence in that province. His father, a merchant, possessed sufficient means to give him an education. Living through the exciting days of '48, young Salomon took a lively interest in military affairs, and military science subsequently became a part of his studies. These were soon finished, and he left home for Hamburg where he entered business.

Like so many ambitious young men of his generation, Salomon surveyed conditions in Germany, after the failure of the Revolution of '48, and decided that the situation was hopeless. In 1853, therefore, he joined the outpouring of German youths which was seeking a more promising future in a land of freedom.

He came to New York, where he found work. His biographers have politely described it as "mercantile pursuits," but the sophisticated may well suspect the phrase to mean such odd jobs as a friendless immigrant lad might manage to pick up. After six months he went west to Chicago. Here he worked first as clerk in a small store in the North Division; later he obtained a position as bookkeeper in a hat and cap store. In 1858 he commenced the study of law and obtained a clerkship with a local justice of the peace. He was admitted to the Bar in 1859.

Immediately he became active in politics. The Republican Party, though comparatively new in American political life, was forging ahead. In Illinois, under the leadership of Abraham Lincoln, it was not only the party of young men, but made a special appeal to one of Salomon's experience and temperament. In 1860, when only twenty-four, he was elected to the Chicago City Council, becoming its youngest member.

At the outbreak of the Civil War, in response to the first call for troops, he joined the Twenty-fourth Illinois Infantry, better known as the Hecker-Jaeger Regiment, and was commissioned a Second Lieutenant. Quickly he won successive promotions to First Lieutenant, Captain and Major. But there was dissension in the regiment, and Salomon resigned.

He left the regiment, however, not the army. For immediately he joined Colonel Hecker in raising a new regiment, the Eighty-second Illinois Infantry, recruited from Chicago's fast growing "foreign elements:" Poles, Hungarians, Jews and Germans, and was commissioned its Lieutenant-Colonel. Originally assigned to the Army of the Potomac, Salomon's regiment took part in various campaigns until, as veterans, it became part of the Great Union Army assembled around Gettysburg.

At the end of June 1863, General Lee, with 70,000 men, flushed with the successes at Fredericksburg and Chancellorsville, sought to relieve the pressure on the South and attempted to stall Grant at Vicksburg by an invasion of Maryland and Pennsylvania. Lee aimed a blow at the heart of the Union. He gambled on the success of a quick thrust to wrest a peace on northern soil.

General Meade, recently placed in command of the army of the Potomac, decided to fight it out with Lee by making his stand at the obscure Pennsylvania town of Gettysburg. He gathered his army of 100,000 in a strong position, on a battlefield shaped like a fishhook of which the shank was Cemetery Ridge.

The two great armies came together on July 1st, and the fighting was fierce. The eleventh corps, of which Colonel Salomon's regiment was a part, bore the brunt of this first day's fight. It was severely punished and beaten back into the town, losing half its effective force. For two days Salomon and his men stood under heavy and constant fire. At times they were engaged in fierce hand-to-hand fighting. Salomon had two horses shot under him and on one occasion escaped capture only by the narrowest of margins. After this hard fighting, during the night of the second day, his men were moved into the graveyard of Cemetery Hill where they lay down among the gravestones. On the fateful July 3rd this spot was to become one of the central points around which the great battle was to rage.

Stationed on the left wing of the Union Army, holding the ridge exposed to shot and shell raining from every direction, his command was the target of the preliminary artillery combat. Then, as Pickett's Division, "in battle array, grand, magnificent and self-possessed," sallied forth on its historic charge, it concentrated its attack beyond the line where Salomon was stationed, so that his command was not directly involved. That gallant onslaught faltered and failed and the battle ended in desultory skirmishes. Lee began his retreat, and victory rested with the Union troops.

In the official report to General Howard of the part taken by his division in the actions of July 2nd and 3rd, General Carl Schurz singled out Colonel Salomon, as one of two officers, for special commendation for his part in that great battle:

> It is my pleasant duty to mention as especially deserving, the names of Lieutenant-Colonel Otto who superintended this operation with great judgment and courage, and of Lieutenant-Colonel Salomon of the 82nd Illinois, who displayed the highest order of coolness and determination under very trying circumstances.

Following Gettysburg, as part of the Twentieth Army Corps, Colonel Salomon and his regiment campaigned under Generals Hooker and Grant in Tennessee in the operations around Chattanooga and in the battles of Lookout Mountain and Missionary Ridge.

Colonel Salomon's next important military activity occurred when, as part of General Sherman's army, his regiment participated in the "March through Georgia." In the fighting before Resaca he successfully led the charge which changed the tide of battle. Through continual skirmishing his division finally advanced to the siege of Atlanta where, on September 4, 1864, he reported:

> To the great gratification of the soldiers, we marched through the conquered city, with colors flying and bands playing, and occupied the works erected by our enemies and from behind which they had sent so many deadly missiles into our ranks.

In concluding his official report to Headquarters of this stage of the campaign, Colonel James B. Robinson, commanding the Third Brigade, took occasion to write:

> I cannot close this report without expressing my high appreciation of, and sincere thanks for the gallantry, ability, and hearty spirit of cooperation displayed by commanders of the regiments of my brigade throughout the period of my command. Their names and regiments, to mention which affords me mingled pride and pleasure, are as follows: ... Colonel E. S. Salomon eighty-second Illinois Volunteers . . . .

From Atlanta, Salomon and his regiment, as part of the Third Brigade, continued on the advance against Savannah. At the end of this successful campaign Colonel Robinson, in his official report, again commended Salomon:

> The immediate command of my brigade during this expedition was intrusted to Lieutenant-Colonel E. S. Salomon of the eighty-second Illinois volunteers who was the senior officer present. I take pleasure in acknowledging the efficiency and zeal with which Lieutenant-Colonel Salomon discharged the duty thus devolving upon him.

The Third Brigade was then transferred to the campaign of the Carolinas, where Salomon, through the months of January to June of 1864, marched through the country fighting with the enemy, wading swamps, building roads, burning houses, cotton and cotton gins of the enemy and living on the country. Hungry and poorly clad, his men had a continuous campaign of forced marches in rain and mud. On one occasion, riding with his staff ahead of his regiment, Salomon unexpectedly butted into a squad of Confederate soldiers who fired upon him and, while his staff was captured, he alone managed to escape.

Again Salomon received a citation at the fight at Bentonville in the report of his commander, Brigadier-General Jackson:

> Lieutenant-Colonel Edward S. Salomon, eighty-second Illinois Volunteers, and Major F. H. Harris, Thirteenth New Jersey Volunteers, and the officers and men of those regiments deserve especial mention for their gallantry in holding an exposed position, on which, in a large measure, depended the fortune of the day.

As this campaign continued through the Carolinas, Salomon was at Raleigh when the glad news of Lee's surrender to Grant arrived and hostilities were ordered suspended. On April 30th the army started home by way of Richmond and Washington. By May 9th they reached Richmond, after a march of one hundred and sixty-two miles in ten days.

From Washington, Lieutenant-Colonel Salomon's last report, May 29, 1865, concludes:

> On the twenty-fourth we participated in the grand review of General Sherman's army before the President and Lieutenant-General Grant and then marched

to our present camp where we are now making preparations to be mustered out of service.

The next day, for six and a half hours, the army of veterans marched along Pennsylvania Avenue in a final review and listened to the farewell address of General Sherman:

> Our work is done, and armed enemies no longer defy us . . . and now . . . we are about to separate, to mingle with the civil world . . . To such as go home, we will only say, that our favored country is so grand, so extensive, so diversified in climate, soil, and productions, that every man may surely find a home and occupation suited to his taste; and none should yield to the natural impotence sure to result from our past life of excitement and adventure.

June 15, 1865, for distinguished gallantry and meritorious service, President Abraham Lincoln[1] appointed Salomon a Brigadier-General of Volunteers "by brevet," upon the recommendation of his commanding officers, Major-General Williams and Brigadier-General Robinson, the latter of whom, in this recommendation to the Secretary of War, summed up Salomon's military service:

> I have the honor to recommend and earnestly request the appointment of Colonel Edward S. Salomon, of the 82nd Regiment, Illinois Volunteers, as Brevet Brigadier-General for gallant and meritorious service.
>
> Colonel Salomon joined this brigade with his regiment at the opening of the campaign against Atlanta in the spring of 1864. During the fighting before Resaca, Georgia, on the 14th and 15th of May, this regiment behaved with great gallantry.
>
> Again, at New Hope, Georgia, on the 25th of the same month, Colonel Salomon led his command with admirable coolness and courage against the enemy.

After having advanced under a severe fire of musketry and artillery more than a mile, he held his line close to the entrenched position of the enemy, without a breastwork, and with a scanty supply of ammunition.

At the battle near Peach Tree Creek, before Atlanta, Georgia, on the 20th of July, 1864, Colonel Salomon performed a most gallant and meritorious part in repulsing the repeated onslaughts made by the enemy. In the face of a furious raking fire, he held his line for four hours, when the enemy withdrew from his front with great loss.

During the siege of Atlanta, Colonel Salomon was ever prominent for his energy, coolness and judgment.

In the fight near Averysboro, North Carolina, on the 16th of March, 1864, Colonel Salomon, as usual, led his regiment into action with great gallantry and skill.

Colonel Salomon has distinguished himself in other engagements besides those which have been mentioned. At Gettysburg and Missionary Ridge his gallantry was conspicuous and challenged the highest admiration.

I consider Colonel Salomon one of the most deserving officers of my acquaintance. His regiment is his highest praise. In point of drill and discipline it is second to none in this corps. Its record will bear safe comparison with any other of the same age in the army.

Colonel Salomon has had a commission as Colonel since April, 1864, but his regiment not containing the requisite number of men he has been unable to get mustered.

Earnestly hoping that his claims will meet your favorable attention. . . .

Salomon received notice of the appointment from the Secretary of War.

War Department, Washington, June 15, 1865

Sir:—You are hereby informed that the President of the United States has appointed you for distinguished gallantry and meritorious service during the war a Brigadier General of Volunteers by Brevet, in the service of the United States, to rank as such from the 13th day of March, one thousand eight hundred and sixty-five. Should the Senate at their next session advise and consent thereto, you will be commissioned accordingly.

Edwin M. Stanton
Secretary of War

To Brev. Brig. Gen.
   Edward S. Salomon,
   U. S. Vols.

As the war closed and his military career ended, General Salomon returned to Chicago. Before long he was elected Clerk of Cook County. In 1868 he was re-elected for a second term of four years. In 1869, as a birthday present, President Grant wired him the appointment as Tenth Governor of Washington Territory. Gladly he accepted this new honor and responsibility and received his commission on March 14, 1870.

Washington Territory, set apart from Oregon only seventeen years earlier, had a population of less than 30,000 inhabitants. It was still almost undeveloped frontier, as the projected trans-continental railroads were still in the building.

Those were the days of the Crédit Mobilier and of the Whiskey Ring as national corrupting influences, and of the Tweed Ring in New York, when the country attained the nadir of moral political standards. Corruption in public service spread its slimy trail throughout the land from the capitol in Washington into every little post-office and district of the United States. The rivalry between ambitious Washington towns for railroad locations was keen and bitter and railroad influence in local politics was open, potent and the source of political turmoil. Everyone in the territory was speculating in land, hoping to gain great wealth in the next happy turn of the wheel of fortune. Territorial affairs were dominated by politicians, only too many of whom were superannuated and broken down political hacks from the East, who had sought a new environment to rehabilitate their fortunes. The territory was a political hotbed of violent partisanship and vote-catching agitation — for statehood, for female suffrage, for a wide variety of public improvements and for all sorts of expenditures of money with attendant struggles for party and personal advantage.

The single message which Governor Salomon addressed to the Legislative Assembly, in October 1871, called attention to the unsatisfactory condition of the territory's finances, to the desirability of establishing an asylum for the insane who had been cared for by private contractors and to the building of further accommodations at the Penitentiary. It asked for the development of a Territorial University and the extension of the public school system. It called for improvements in the administration of the courts and for an exploration of the mineral wealth of the territory.

Unfortunately, Salomon was caught in the whirl of land speculation and became involved in the use of public funds for such purposes. For this he was bitterly attacked by enemies who, to make their criticism more pointed, even alleged that he had appointed Democrats to public office!

Two years of service as governor seemed enough to Salomon and he resigned, retiring from the governorship at the end of a single term. That he had served acceptably was evidenced by the vote of thanks expressed in a resolution of the House of Representatives:

> Resolved that the thanks of this body are due and are hereby tendered to Hon. E. S. Salomon, Governor of Washington Territory, for his prompt attention to the acts of the legislative assembly, and his approval of their measures enacted into laws.

The Pacific Tribune, a leading newspaper of the Northwest, editorially commented on the occasion:

> The acceptance of the Governor's resignation by the President is universally regretted by the people. He was honest, fearless and capable. He mingled freely with the people, identified himself with their interests and generously expended his time and means to bring hither population and to promote our material interests. His official acts are his best records; they have all met the heartiest commendation of our people.
>
> Party behests never made him swerve from official integrity or duty to the whole people. How proudly can he look to this episode of his life. He governed well. He satisfied all, for the welfare of the whole was constantly in his eye; he was true to the position he so happily filled.

Salomon then removed to San Francisco where he resumed his interest and activity in public affairs. He was twice elected to the California legislature, where he was recognized as a leader of the House Republicans and as their ablest speaker. For two terms he also held the office of District Attorney of San Francisco. He assumed an important role in the Loyal Legion, a military order of Union officers, as well as in the Grand Army of the Republic of which he long served as Department Commander for California. He was one of the organizers and, for eight years, commander-in-chief of the Army and Navy League.

In 1898, at the outbreak of the Spanish War, his appointment to the post of Brigadier-General of Volunteers in the Philippines was urged by a large number of prominent veterans. The post, however, eventually went to General Harrison Gray Otis.

At the age of 77, July 18, 1913, Edward S. Salomon died at San Francisco.

31

THE WARRIOR

THIS is the Odyssey of a Russian Jew.

Marco Polo never made a more marvelous journey than that made by the Russian Jewish immigrants who travelled to America in the last quarter of the nineteenth century. In the short space of two months these refugees travelled not only from continent to continent, but traversed centuries of time measured by the contrast between what they had left behind and what they faced on their arrival. Jews who started from some mediaeval, oriental, Russian ghetto, by travelling sixty days came straight from sixteenth-century surroundings — physical, intellectual and moral — to find themselves thrown pell mell into the hustling American nineteenth century. It was more than a change of country, language and customs. The difference between their Russia and the new America was a difference of three centuries of human advancement. The Russian Jewish father and mother, with their family of children, after a lifetime of experiences crowded into a few days, raced, as it were, over these centuries of world changes. As soon as they landed in America the family was faced with the immediate, and all important, necessity of food, clothing and shelter. It was the same fundamental human struggle for bare existence which the original settlers faced when they first landed on our shores.

The rapidity with which these new immigrants and their children adjusted themselves to the new American life is one of the wonder-stories of our country. The celerity of their Americanization was an intellectual phenomenon. No sooner had they landed than the children were in our schools; and he who had been a village artisan or a small country peddler fitted himself into a highly industrialized urban society. The public school system of many an American city educated whole families, not merely in book learning, but in new ideas and standards of life and methods of living. It made Americans of these Jews, children and parents, with a rapidity which surprised even the teachers. The American reaction upon these newcomers was spontaneous. Beards were shaved, *sheitals* disappeared, accents softened in the parent and soon disappeared in the children. Their strength, alertness and restless ambition drove them forward. The children and descendants became stenographers, lawyers, physicians, engineers, merchants, manufacturers, architects, authors, teachers and politicians, until today they walk abreast with the descendants of those who had preceded them by ten generations, everywhere sharing in the patriotic upbuilding and safeguarding of our America. Perhaps the telling of her first experience by a little Russian-Jewish girl presents the picture better than pages of description:[1]

As I read how the patriots planned the Revolution, and the women gave their sons to die in battle, and the heroes led to victory, and the rejoicing people set up the Republic, it dawned on me gradually what was meant by MY COUNTRY. The people all desiring noble things and striving for them together, defying their oppressors, giving their lives for each other —

all this it was that made MY COUNTRY. It was not a thing that I UNDERSTOOD: I could not go home and tell Frieda about it, as I told her other things I learned at school. But I knew one could say "my country" and FEEL it, as one felt "God" or "myself." My teacher, my schoolmates, Miss Dillingham, George Washington himself could not mean more than I when they said "my country," after I had once felt it. For the Country was for all the Citizens, and I WAS A CITIZEN. And when we stood up to sing "America," I shouted the words with all my might. I was in very earnest proclaiming to the world my love for my new-found country.

> I love thy rocks and rills,
> Thy woods and templed hills ...

Such another was Sam Dreben, born, June 1, 1878, of humble Jewish forebears, in the small Russian village of Poltroe. He came to this country in his teens. In a crowded city slum, probably in Philadelphia, he experienced his transformation, from the crude immigrant child sharing the family struggle for a livelihood, into an American youth. We first have a record of him in Philadelphia when, as soon as he reached twenty-one, he enlisted in the United States army. Thereupon began his remarkable career.

He was serving with the 14th U. S. Infantry, under General Lawton, then located in the Philippines. There Dreben first attracted attention. A companion in arms, Pat O'Reilly, tells the dramatic story. Outside of Cavite Viejo the rebel natives had built a long line of intrenchments on the far banks of a creek which wound through rice paddies to Manila Bay. To storm the intrenched position over a fortified bridge down the road came a company of infantry in close formation of columns of four, with bayonets fixed. As they advanced there came a terrible explosion. The captain and eleven men were killed or wounded; the company halted and, thrown into confusion, deployed into a line of skirmishers. One soldier emerged from the smoke still trotting forward towards the bridge. Bullets snapped around him, but he did not notice. Down the road, over the bridge, into the trenches he went as if in a drill on the parade ground. Other troops then began to come, following along in a charge. The natives broke and stampeded. In the trench was found the lone soldier still fighting. When the sergeant demanded of Sam if he thought he was a one-man army, he replied that he had heard the command "Forward!" but nobody said "Stop!"

Then came China and the Boxer Rebellion and the long hike from Tientsin to Peking. After such campaigns back again to the routine of soldiering in an American garrison was sure to prove too dull for Sam.

In 1902, he was discharged at Angel Island, California, with good character, at the end of his first three-years' service. He had had more than the ordinary experience of a United States soldier and it had proved very much to his taste. Consequently, after knocking about for a couple of years, he re-enlisted in 1904. This time, however, he saw only the prosaic peace-time service. Again he was honorably discharged in 1906. Now at the age of 27, after some six years of such military service, "a short, dark, chunky, almost podgy man of self-effacing manner," he must have considered giving up the military career in view of the fact that the promise of romance and extraordinary adventure with which it had started was not materializing. Merely to move from garrison to garrison was not what he looked for in the service. So he set out to seek excitement and adventure.

In 1910, Nicaragua was having one of its periodic revolutions, and the rebels were gathering men and ammunition in the States, shipping them south to the army of General Estrada who was trying to unseat President Zelaya. This appealed to Sam and he was soon holding a commission under General Gabe Conrad. With a group of other American soldiers of fortune he was waging a regular miniature war against the Nicaraguan Government. Nor was it all "chocolate soldier" fighting. There were hand to hand conflicts, rough machine gun work and infantry and cavalry battles. While it all proved a somewhat small affair, contrasted with warfare as Sam later came to know it, it was very real and exciting while it lasted.

In the midst of all this fighting Sam began to acquire more than a local reputation as a resourceful soldier. His reputation grew with each battle until Latin America began to hear exaggerated tales of his wild doings, his soldierly qualities and his happy-go-lucky disposition. One of his fellow American adventurers, Tracy Richardson, has left us a description of the impression Dreben made on him after he had been his companion in three campaigns of the revolutions. He says that Sam was always "kidding," cheerful, carefree and happy, but cool, quick-thinking and of a courage which nothing daunted. "He seemed to take thousands of wild chances with death and emerge by fool, bull luck. But when you knew him, you learned how carefully he planned every detail and how little he left to chance."

After a few months, the rebels marched on to Managua and captured it. General Estrada ousted Zelaya as President and himself took that office. That ended the excitement and the war for the American revolutionists. So with experiences enough to last a lifetime, with his pay in his pocket, there was nothing left for Sam and his companions but to return to the States.

Out of a job, he looked around for another venture. He returned to the United States and there heard that there was a brand new revolution in Honduras, financed by some businessmen in New Orleans. So he packed up his kit and made a beeline for the seat of trouble. He arrived none too soon, for the fighting was well under way when he turned up at the headquarters of General Lee Christmas, in command of the Americans who considered they were running the war.

As soon as Sam reached the scene of operations, General Christmas commissioned him a colonel and put him in charge of a battalion. Most of his army had been railroad employees in the States, now soldiers of fortune with no particular interest in Honduras politics. In fact, the natives themselves were not particularly keen which side won. It was said the Hondurans generally wore two hat bands, one over the other: red for the Federals and green and white for the Revolutionsts, so that they could switch them around as occasion demanded.

Quickly the Revolutionists captured Tegucigalpa, held an election which they carried almost unanimously for their candidate, and another war was over. Dreben was offered a job in the new national army, but he had heard that things were beginning to look interesting in Venezuela and Mexico; he hastened back to the United States so as not to lose the chance for more real fighting.

Back in New Orleans, Sam quickly attached himself to

the payroll of a Venezuelan junta formed to return Castro as President. Just as the expedition was about to leave with its guns and ammunition, the whole scheme blew up and Sam found himself once more at loose ends.

A certain Mexican group then appeared on the scene with overtures for Sam to join a rebel force against Francisco Madero who had just succeeded in ousting Porfirio Diaz as President. With a five-hundred-dollar bonus in his pocket, a commission as colonel in the rebel army on a salary of five hundred dollars (gold) a month and a promise of extra pay for every battle in which he should take part, Sam was shipped to El Paso. From there he easily slipped over the border to join General Inez Salazar in Juarez. Under him the troop advanced to Chihuahua, where they persuaded General Crozco, then Governor of that province, to head the revolt; and the war was on.

In the Battle of Rellano, Dreben and his friend, Tracy Richardson, were in charge of the troops; and, after an intensely hot fight, scored a very real victory over the Federals. Then followed a campaign against Pancho Villa, whom they succeeded in holding in check and driving back. Dreben and Richardson were then transferred to serve under General Campa, whose unreasoning ill-will and active enmity the little group of American officers incurred to such a degree that he ordered them all shot by a firing squad. A firing squad with its prisoners was actually lined up, before wiser counsels prevailed and caused Campa to cancel his hasty orders. The reprieved officers made a beeline back to the army besieging Chihuahua and reached it just in time to join in the final attack which easily captured that town. The Government, recognizing its defeat, was soon in full flight. Another war was over.

Back again in El Paso, Dreben went to work for Pancho
Villa, who was then undertaking to stir up a new Mexican
revolt on his own account, against his old companions in
arms. This service was short, for when the news came that
American forces had landed in Vera Cruz, Sam immediately
volunteered as a guide and scout for the American army.
That expedition, however, was short-lived. American army
activity soon petered out to mere garrison duty and Sam
was again at loose ends.

He returned to El Paso to earn a living in some civilian
occupation. He married and settled down. When his baby
daughter died, Sam was seized by his old unrest. Then
1917 came. A local company was being raised for the World
War I and Sam enlisted with the rank of sergeant. With the
American troops Sam was soon overseas on the battlefields
of France.

With the Thirty-sixth Division, Sergeant Dreben saw real
fighting at St. Étienne, and his Captain dispatched the
news, "Enemy advance on our right repulsed. Sergeant
Dreben has captured three machine guns, three prisoners
and killed fifty of the enemy." Officers who were eye-
witnesses declared that Sam's exploit undoubtedly saved
his company and the French from a surprise flank attack.
He was awarded the French *Medaille Militaire* and *Croix
de Guerre* with palms and won decorations both from Italy
and Belgium in recognition of this splendid work as a
soldier. From the United States he received a Distinguished
Service Cross for extraordinary heroism in action in the
battle of St. Étienne. The citation reads:

He discovered a party of German troops going to
the support of a machine-gun nest situated in a pocket

near where the French and American lines joined.
He called for volunteers and with the aid of about
thirty men rushed the German positions, captured
four machine guns, killed more than forty of the
enemy, captured two and returned to our lines without loss of a man.

After the armistice he returned to El Paso and to peaceful
pursuits, a soldier again only as the gatherings of the American Legion gave him the opportunity to appear with a
chest covered with decorations, to live over again in the
company of his buddies the memories and glories of the past.

Sam's two most cherished possessions throughout his life
were his pride in his Jewish ancestry and his American
citizenship. Kindly and charitable, he was ever ready to
help any poor devil in hard luck and to respond to the call
of any good cause with his purse and his services. Many
are the tales still to be heard in El Paso of his open-handed
generosity.

Like so many of his generation, he found the post-war
America a difficult place in which to make headway. It
was easier for him to face an emeny on a battlefield than to
settle down to the daily grind of a steady job. So, with
many of his fellow soldiers now grown middle-aged, he
drifted, earning a modest living as opportunity offered,
never quite adjusted to civilian life.

His health became a matter of concern. Finally, quite
unexpectedly, after some months of illness, he died in his
doctor's office in Hollywood, California, March 15, 1925.

Immigrant lad, soldier of fortune, picturesque adventurer in Mexican and Central American revolutions, American war hero, Jew and loyal American, in his forty-seventh
year, Sam Dreben closed an eventful career.

444

444444

44444444

In the *El Paso Herald* was written his epitaph:

Here's to Sam Dreben! Jewish immigrant, of old-world peasant stock, a fine upstanding American who loved the United States with a passionate devotion — an honorable man, a loyal friend, a gallant soldier — all honor to his memory, peace to his ashes, eternal happiness to his soul.

And an admiring poet has written:

Now whenever I read articles
That breathe of racial hate,
Or hear arguments that hold his kind to scorn
I always see that photo
With the cap upon his pate
And nose the size of Bugler Dugan's horn.
I see upon his breast
The D. S. C.,
The *Croix de Guerre*, the *Militaire* —
These, too.
And I think, Thank God Almighty
We will always have a few
Like Dreben,
A Jew!

NOTES AND BIBLIOGRAPHY

NOTES TO CHAPTER 1

GEORGE WASHINGTON AND JEWS OF HIS DAY

[1] Rupert Hughes, *George Washington*, N. Y., 1927, I, pp. 400 and 445.

[2] John Corbin, *The Unknown Washington*, N. Y., 1930.

[3] Leon Huhner, "The Jews of Virginia from the Earliest Times to the Close of the Eighteenth Century," in *A. J. H. S.*, XX, p. 85.

[4] H. T. Ezekiel and G. Lichtenstein, *The History of the Jews of Richmond from 1769 to 1917*, Richmond, 1917, pp. 236 ff.

[5] *A. J. H. S.*, XIX, p. 58.

[6] Ibid., XX, p. 90; *Washington's Journal of the Expedition Across the Allegheny Mountains*, J. W. Toner, editor, Albany, 1893, pp. 177, 179, 205.

[7] *A. J. H. S.*, XI, p. 183; XX, p. 91; XXXI, p. 235.

[8] John C. Fitzpatrick, ed., *Writings of George Washington*, Washington, D. C., 1931, vol. II, p. 190.

[9] *A. J. H. S.*, XIX, p. 49.

[10] Ibid., XIX, p. 50; V, pp. 7, 31.

[11] Letter, March 21, 1776, from John Hancock, President, to His Excellency General Washington, Commander in Chief of the Army of the United Colonies, etc., at Cambridge. William Brotherhead, *Book of the Signers*, Philadelphia, 1861, p. 1; Peter Force, Editor, *American Archives*, 4th Series, Washington, 1844, Vol. 5, p. 446.

[12] *A. J. H. S.*, XIX, p. 119; H. S. Morais, *The Jews of Philadelphia*, Philadelphia, 1894, p. 29.

[13] Ibid., V, pp. 32-3.

[14] H. S. Morais, *The Jews of Philadelphia*, Philadelphia, 1894, pp. 11-12.

[15] B. F. Morris, *Christian Life and Character of the Civil Institutions of the United States*, Philadelphia, 1864, p. 459.

[16] No attempt was made here to give a critical text of these letters, the object being to present them in the most readable form.

[17] *A. J. H. S.*, III, pp. 88-94; XII, p. 59n.

NOTES TO CHAPTER 2

THOMAS JEFFERSON AND RELIGIOUS LIBERTY

[1] "I am a Christian in the only sense in which he (Jesus) wished anyone to be; sincerely attached to his doctrines in preference to all others; ascribing to himself every human excellence and believing he never claimed any other."

[2] See note 8.

[3] Letter to John Adams Oct. 13, 1813. H. A. Washington, editor, *Jefferson's Complete Works*, Washington, 1854, vol. 6, p. 220.

[4] "Syllabus of an Estimate of the Merits of the Doctrines of Jesus, compared with those of Others," 1803, in Paul Leicester Ford, editor, *The Writings of Thomas Jefferson*, New York, 1897, vol. VIII, p. 226.

[5] See "America's First Jewish Bookdealer," p. 190, below.

[6] Letter to John Adams, April 8, 1816. A. E. Beigh, editor, *The Writings of Thomas Jefferson*, Washington, 1904, vol. XIV, p. 466.

[7] Mordecai M. Noah, *Travels in England, France, Spain and the Barbary States in the years 1813, 1814 and 1815.* New York and London, 1819, Appendix XXV.

[8] *Jefferson Correspondence*, vol. 6, p. 119.

In a letter to Joseph Marx of Richmond, one of his Jewish friends with whom from time to time he had considerable business dealings, Jefferson wrote:

> Th. Jefferson presents to Mr. Marx his compliments and thanks for the *Transactions of the Paris Sanhedrin*, which he shall read with great interest, and with the regret that he has ever felt at seeing a sect, the parent and basis of all those of Christendom, singled out by all of them for a persecution and oppression which proves that they have profited nothing from the benevolent doctrines of him whom they profess to make the model of their principles and practice.
>
> He salutes Mr. Marx with sentiments of perfect esteem and respect.

Monticello, July 8, 20.

Jefferson Papers, vol. 62, p. 450

In a volume *Selections from the Miscellaneous writings of the late Isaac Harby, Esq.* (Abraham Moise, Charleston, 1829) a letter addressed to Mr. Harby of Charleston is recorded. This letter forcefully presents Jefferson's idea that sectarian influences should be eliminated from public education. To this end he had taken a prominent part in the founding of the University of Virginia. The idea of freedom from unsympathetic religious influence upon Jewish students seeking an education in public institutions was far in advance of his day.

Monticello, January 6, 1826

Sir:

I have to thank you for the copy you have been so kind as to send me of your "Discourse before the Reformed Society of Israelites." I am little acquainted with the liturgy of the Jews, or their mode of worship; but the reformation proposed, and explained in the Discourse, appears entirely reasonable. Nothing is wiser, than that all our institutions should keep pace with the advance of time, and be improved with the improvements of the human mind. I have thought it a cruel addition to the wrongs which that injured sect have suffered, that their youth should be excluded from the instructions in science afforded to all others in our public seminaries, by imposing upon them a course of Theological Reading which their consciences do not permit them to pursue; and in the University lately established there, we have set the example of ceasing to violate the rights of conscience by any injunctions on the different sects respecting their religion.

⁹ "When Mr. Jefferson was going to Paris, one of the Commissioners, for making a Treaty of Peace, he took me into his family; we waited a considerable time at Baltimore for an opportunity to go to Sea (A British Squadron then guarding the Bay of Chesapeak). Congress in the meanwhile received information that a Treaty was already signed and this precluded the necessity of Mr. Jefferson's embarking." From an account of his services written by Colonel Davis Salisbury Franks, *A.J.H.S.*, vol. X, p. 103.

¹⁰ *A.J.H.S.*, vol. XX, p. 161. *The Writings of Albert Gallatin*, Philadelphia, vol. I, p. 206.

¹¹ Paul Leicester Ford, in *The Writings of Thomas Jefferson*, N. Y., 1893, vol. II, pp. 99–103.

¹² "Letter to Miles Kind, Sept. 26, 1814," in H. A. Washington, Editor, *Jefferson's Complete Works*, Washington, 1854, vol. VI, p. 387.

¹³ *The Writings of Thomas Jefferson*, Paul Leicester Ford, Editor, New York, 1892, *Autobiography*, vol. I, p. 62. The Bill itself is printed on page 237 of vol. II and for its history see *A.J.H.S.*, vol. XI, pp. 59–66, and also Reynolds v. U. S. 98 U. S. 145.

In a letter to Madison, December 16, 1786, Jefferson wrote:

The Virginia Act for religious freedom has been received with infinite approbation in Europe, and propagated with enthusiasm. I do not mean by the governments, but by the individuals which compose them. It has been translated into French and Italian, has been sent to most of the Courts of Europe, and has been the best evidence of the falsehoods of these reports which stated us to be an anarchy. It is inserted in the new Encyclopedia, and is appearing in most of the publications respecting America. In fact, it is comfortable to see the standard of reason at length erected, after so many ages during which the human mind has been held in vassalages by Kings, priests and nobles; and it is honorable for us to have produced the first legislature which had the courage to declare that the reason of man may be trusted with the formation of his own opinions." Paul Leicester Ford, *The Writings of Thomas Jefferson*, vol. IV, p. 334.

NOTES TO CHAPTER 3

ABRAHAM LINCOLN AND JEWISH ARMY CHAPLAINS

¹ War Department Training Manual, "The Chaplain," Washington, 1937.
² *A. J. H. S.*, vol. XII, p. 131.
³ Rabbi Voorsanger received the *Croix de Guerre* and was recommended for D. S. M.

⁴ These twelve Rabbis were: Elkan C. Voorsanger, David Tannenbaum, Harry S. Davidowitz, Louis I. Egelson, Lee J. Levinger, Benj. Friedman (succeeding Voorsanger), Jacob Krohngold, Israel Bettan, Harry Richmond, Elias N. Rabinowitz, Solomon B. Freehof, James G. Heller.

BIBLIOGRAPHY

Isaac Markens, Abraham Lincoln and the Jews, New York, 1909.
Lee J. Levinger, A Jewish Chaplain in France, New York, 1921.
Sydney G. Gumpertz, The Jewish Legion of Valor, New York, 1934.
Julian Leavitt, "American Jews in the World War," American Jewish Year Book, vol. 21, pp. 141–155, Philadelphia, 1919.
The American Jewish Committee, The War Record of American Jews, New York, 1919.
Simon Wolf, The American Jew as Patriot, Soldier & Citizen, New York, 1895.
War Department Training Manual, "The Chaplain," Washington, 1937.
U. S. Statutes, Code of the Laws of the United States,
Myer S. Isaacs, "A Jewish Army Chaplain," A. J. H. S., vol. XII, p. 127.

NOTES TO CHAPTER 4

THEODORE ROOSEVELT AND THE RUSSIAN TREATY OF 1832

¹ In October, 1864, Bernard Bernstein, who was born in Russian Poland in 1823, and who emigrated to the United States in 1845 or 1846, owing military duty to Russia, was arrested in that country and imprisoned on a charge of having failed to perform military service. On the sixth day after his arrest he wrote to the Department of State, and the Department, November 29, 1864, instructed the legation at St. Petersburg to take steps to secure his release. He was altogether discharged in March, 1865, in consideration, it was believed, of his American citizenship which he had acquired by naturalization in 1856. His actual imprisonment lasted only several days. The Department of State afterwards declined to make a claim for indemnity.

Bernstein's case formed the subject of a report to Congress. (Message of President Grant, Feb. 8, 1873, H. Ex. Doc. 197, 42d Cong., 3d sess.; Moore's Digest, vol. III, §453, p. 622).

See also: Hearing Before the Committee on Foreign Relations on "Termination of the Treaty of 1832 Between the United States and Russia," Washington, 1911, Appendix I.

² Joint Resolution Providing for the Termination of the Treaty of Eighteen Hundred and Thirty-two Between the United States and Russia.

whereas, The treaty of commerce and navigation between the United States and Russia, concluded on the eighteenth day of December, eighteen hundred and thirty-two, provides in Article XII thereof that it "shall continue in force until the first day of January, in the year of our Lord eighteen hundred and thirty-nine, and if, one year before that day, one of the high contracting parties shall not have announced to the other, by an official notification, its intention to arrest the operation thereof this treaty shall remain obligatory one year beyond that day, and so on until the expiration of the year which shall commence after the date of a similar notification;" and

WHEREAS, On the seventeenth day of December, nineteen hundred and eleven, the President caused to be delivered to the Imperial Russian Government, by the American Ambassador at Saint Petersburg, an official notification on behalf of the Government of the United States, announcing intention to terminate the operation of this treaty upon the expiration of the year commencing on the first of January, nineteen hundred and twelve; and

WHEREAS, Said treaty is no longer responsive in various respects to the political principles and commercial needs of the two countries; and

WHEREAS, The constructions placed thereon by the respective contracting parties differ upon matters of fundamental importance and interest to each: Therefore be it

RESOLVED BY THE SENATE AND HOUSE OF REPRESENTATIVES OF THE UNITED STATES OF AMERICA IN CONGRESS ASSEMBLED, That the notice thus given by the President of the United States to the Government of the Empire of Russia to terminate said treaty in accordance with the terms of the treaty is hereby adopted and ratified.

[3] "In 1905 a Commission known as the Durnovo Commission, composed of high Russian officials and appointed by the Russian Government to suggest new passport statutes, submitted a report in which it stated that as the passport rules 'now in force have proved entirely unsatisfactory in practice, it would seem advisable to abolish them, thus leaving foreign Jews subject only to the rules applicable to foreigners in general.' "
American Jewish Year Book, 1913–14, p. 443.

NOTES TO CHAPTER 5

WAS CHRISTOPHER COLUMBUS A JEW?

[1] Maestre Bernal, physician, who had formerly lived in Tortosa, as a secret Jew who had undergone public penance at Valencia in 1490; Luis de Torres, the interpreter who understood Hebrew, Chaldaic and Arabic; Marco, ship surgeon; Alonzo de la Calle, who bore the name of the Jews' Lane from which he came; and Rodrigo Sanchez of Segovia, a relative of Gabriel Sanchez.

[2] When Columbus set out on his voyage to discover a new passage to the Indies and succeeded only in discovering America, he used as his guide the famous *Perpetual Almanac* of the Spanish Jew, Abraham Zacuto. It was found among the papers of Columbus by his son, Ferdinand Columbus, who issued a life of the great explorer in 1571. There are no annotations in it, but the astronomical data corre-

spond exactly with the calculations of Columbus, who was an expert in the science of navigation. It is now in the Colombina Library at Seville.

[3] Werner Sombart, *The Jew and Modern Capitalism*, New York, 1913, p. 30.

[4] The edict against the Jews was dated March 31, 1492, not as Columbus states.

[5] The letter begins: "As I know that you will have pleasure in the great victory which our Lord hath given me in my voyage, I write you this, by which you shall know that in twenty days I passed over to the Indies with the fleet which the most illustrious King and Queen, our Lords, gave me: where I found very many islands peopled with inhabitants beyond number." *The Spanish Letter of Columbus to Luis de Sant' Angel*, London, 1891, p. 24.

[6] "It is rather in the man's character, as shown by his behaviour and writings, and also by the close association which he had with Jews throughout his life, that one may assert with some confidence that he was either completely Jewish by race, or a half Jew, or, as is still most likely, an offspring from a family of converted Jews which had settled in Genoa and the neighbourhood and intermingled by marriage with local people." Charles Duff, *The Truth About Columbus*, N. Y., 1936, p. 64.

[7] Jacob Wassermann, *Columbus, Don Quixote of the Sea*, Boston, 1930, pp. 150–1.

[8] Henry Vignaud, *The Real Birth Date of Columbus, 1451*, London, 1903, p. ix.

[9] Justin Winsor, *Narrative and Critical History of America*, Boston and New York, 1896, vol. II, p. 1.

[10] Del Olmet: "apart from the declaration of the historians of Genoa regarding the Genoese nationality, there is only the affirmation by Colón himself."

[11] Señor de Madariaga is a strong protagonist for the conclusion that "born in Genoa, Colombo was of Spanish-Jewish origin, bilingual from the first, speaking a popular and uneducated sort of Genoese dialect and brought up by his family in a Spanish atmosphere; therefore a Spanish Jew." He emphasizes that the Spanish equivalent of the name "Colombo" is not the name Columbus ultimately used, "Colón," but the Catalan "Colóm" and that Columbus used the form "Colóm" in a transitional stage to the ultimate "Colón." Among Catalan Jews the family name of Colóm was common. The compromise disguised form of the name Columbus finally adopted, to his mind, indicated a desire to hide a Jewish association. To this Cecil Roth adds: "But it is an extraordinary fact that among Italian Jews the transition from 'Colón' to 'Colombo' and vice versa, which needs so much explanation, was not only possible but invariable. The surname 'Colombo' is even today frequently found in Italy. Sometimes it is simply the Italian translation of the Hebrew name 'Jonah' or Dove — I mean that a man who signed his Hebrew letters 'Colón' was invariably known in the outside world by the name 'Colombo,' which was the easiest approximation that a liquid-voiced Italian could reach. Hence, then, we have the transition between the two forms that Señor de Madariaga is at such pains to discover." Cecil Roth, in *Menorah Journal*, XXVIII, pp. 289–290.

[12] *Colon Español?* Celso Garcia de la Riega, Madrid, 1914.

[13] "Their interpretation of a number of very simple facts is no less astonishing. All that they say about the *Santa Maria*, which Columbus calls the *Galega* because she was built in Galicia, and about the names of Porto Santo, San Salvador, and Trinidad as coming from places so called in Pontevedra, lacks even common sense. The same may be said for their reasons why the name Hispaniola was conferred on Haiti. According to them, Columbus chose this name because he was a Spaniard; otherwise, had he been an Italian or Genoese, he would have christened that isle Italiana or Genovesa!" Henry Vignaud, "Columbus a Spaniard and a Jew," *The American Hist. Rev.*, XVIII, 511.

[14]

S.

S.A.S.

X. M. Y.

Ellmirante (X.p.o. Ferens)

Signifies "Jesus, Mary, Joseph, save me messenger of Christ."

In his *Admiral of the Ocean Sea* (2 vols., Boston, 1942), Professor Samuel E. Morison disdainfully rejects all speculation that Columbus was other than a Genoese Catholic Christian.

He makes short and scornful shift, without any extended discussion, of the possibility of Columbus being a Jew. To his thinking "The usual line of Jew- Columbus is to distort his signature into something of cabalistic significance; another is to point out that his mother's name was Susanna, but besides the chaste Susanna of the Apocrypha there was a Christian martyr, Saint Susanna." He regards the whole issue as "a significant pattern of hypothesis and innuendoes unsupported by anything so vulgar as fact." While Professor Morison concedes that, "as there was much moving about in the Middle Ages, racial snobs and national fanatics may console themselves with the thought that some of the discoverer's remote ancestors may have been Jews or Spaniards or the like," he is sarcastic about "Madariaga's fairy tale of the Enterprise of the Indies being a sort of Zionist movement." He writes *finis* to the controversy with, "I have not attempted to check up on these racial questions, regarding them as impossible to prove or disprove, and probably of less significance than the fact that Columbus and the Queen both had red hair."

[15] "In most cases the triangle, or 'Shield of David,' is combined with the Hebrew S, or *v*, as one of the signs on it. This very S, or *v*, leads to the solution of the strange and mystic signature, which means nothing else but the last confession of the Jews as read from right to left with Hebrew words for each initial — abbreviated it is true — but perfectly acceptable, according to the rabbinical laws, as will be explained further on. And, more, it is meant simultaneously as a *Kaddish* for Colón — or better, as a substitute for a *Kaddish* — the supreme prayer dreamed of continually by all Jews alike, religious or non-religious. Hence the repeated command to his heirs and their heirs to sign exactly like his signature always and perpetually." *Who was 'Columbus'?* Maurice David, New York, 1933, p. 99.

[16] David, pp. 66–67.

[17] Cecil Roth, "Who was Columbus?" *The Menorah Journal*, XXVIII, no. 3, pp. 291–2.

[18] Cf. Cecil Roth, *The Jewish Contribution to Civilization*, Cincinnati, 1940, pp. 76–102.

BIBLIOGRAPHY

WALTER F. McENTIRE, Was Christopher Columbus a Jew? Boston, 1925.

M. KAYSERLING, Christoph Columbus und der Antheil der Juden an den spanischen und portugiesischen Entdeckungen, Berlin, 1894; Revised English translation: Christopher Columbus and the Participations of the Jews in the Spanish and Portuguese Discoveries, New York, 1894.

HENRY VIGNAUD, "Columbus, a Spaniard and a Jew," in *American Historical Review*, XVIII (1913), 505 ff.

CHARLES DUFF, The Truth About Columbus and the Discovery of America, New York, 1936.

MAURICE DAVID, Who was 'Columbus'? New York, 1933.

WASHINGTON IRVING, The Life and Voyage of Christopher Columbus, 3 vols., New York, 1869.

JOHN BOYD THATCHER, Christopher Columbus, New York, 1903.

SALVADOR DE MADARIAGA, Christopher Columbus, London, 1939.

CECIL ROTH, "Who was Columbus?" *The Menorah Journal*, XXVIII (New York, 1940), no. 3, pp. 278–295.

NOTES TO CHAPTER 6

THE MARTYRDOM OF FRANCISCO MALDONADO DE SILVA

[1] "The Green Cross did not merely symbolize, by its color, constancy and eternity, but it was fashioned, as if of freshly cut boughs, to represent living wood, the emblem of the true faith in contradiction to the withered branches that are to be flung into the fire." Rafael Sabatini, *Torquemada and the Spanish Inquisition*, Boston and N. Y., n. d., p. 271.

BIBLIOGRAPHY

Auto de la Fe Celebrado en Lima a 23 de Enero de 1639, Madrid, 1640.

Report by the Holy Office, dated at Lima, May 18, 1636, II, 48 ff.

DON JOSE TORIBIO MEDINA, El Tribunal del Santo Oficio de la Inquisicion en las Prouincias del plata, Santiago de Chile, 1887.

H. C. LEA, The Inquisition in the Spanish Dependencies, New York, 1908, pp. 319–453.

G. A. Kohut, "Jewish Martyrs of the Inquisition in South America," in *A.J.H.S.*, IV, pp. 101–187.

G. A. Kohut, "The Trial of Francisco Maldonado de Silva," *A.J.H.S.*, XI, pp. 163–179.

E. N. Adler, "The Inquisition in Peru," *A.J.H.S.*, XII, pp. 5–31.

NOTES TO CHAPTER 7

JEWS IN THE FRENCH COLONIES

[1] "*A ces causes nous avons dict, declaré, voulu & ordonné: disons, declarons, voulons, ordonnons & nous plaist que tous lesdits Juifs qui se trouveront en cestuy nostre Royaume, pays, terres, & seigneuries de nostre obeyssance, seront tenus sur peine de la vie & de confiscation de tout leurs bien, d'en vuider & se retirer hors d'iceux incontinant, & ce dans le temps & terme d'un mois apres la publication des presentes.*" Lettres Patentes Du Roy, Portant Commandement à touts Juifs & autres faisans professions & exercice de Judaisme, de vuider le Royaume, pays & terres de son obeyssance, à peine de la vie, & de confiscation de leurs biens — Verifiée en Parlement le 18 May 1615.

[2] An official enumeration of 1680 lists 81 Jews, which number had increased to 94 by 1683.

[3] Antoine Biet, *Voyage de la France equinoxiale en l'isle de Cayenne entrepris par les françois en l'année MDCLII*, Paris, 1664, pp. 303–4; F. Dutertre, *Histoire générale des Antilles par les françois*, Paris, 1667, vol. I, pp. 527 ff.

[4] Nellis M. Crouse, *French Pioneers in the West Indies*, N. Y., 1940, pp. 211–3; *A. J. H. S.*, XVIII, pp. 17–18, 18n.

[5] Stewart L. Mims, *Colbert's West India Policy*, New Haven, 1912, pp. 64–5, quoting a manuscript memoir at the *Archives Nationales*.

[6] Samuel Oppenheim, "An early Jewish colony in Western Guiana and its relations to the Jews in Surinam, Cayenne and Tobago," *A. J. H. S.*, XVI, pp. 95–186. See also *A. J. H. S.*, XXIX, pp. 19–20.

[7] The treaty setting forth the conditions granted by M. de la Barre in behalf of the French contained a clause: *Pour ce qui concerne les Juifs qui sont habitués de l'île il leur sera donné toute protection et assistance pour jouir de leurs biens et possession et pour le libre exercice de leur religion et un lieu de l'île qui leur sera assigné par le sieur de la Barre et sous les conditions dont on conviendra apres avoir vu celles accordées par la compagnie ouest-Indes aux dits Juifs.* Archives du Minist. de la Marine, Collect Moreau Saint-Méry-Code de Cayenne, Vol. I, p. 82.

[8] *Revue des Études Juives*, II, 99.

[9] *Peut paroitre trop dur au coeur du roi.*

[10] *D'autres loix tendaient à exclure les François de la Religion protestante . . . L'édit de 1685 menaçait de la mort les juifs qui viendraient s'y établir: tous ces réglemens sont restés sans force, ils ont toujours été enfreints, et l'on trouve dans la Colonie des hommes*

de tous les pays, de toutes les Religions. M.H.D. (Hilliards d'Hauberleuil), *Considérations sur l'état present de la Colonie française de Saint-Dominique*, Paris, 1776, vol. II, p. 52.

BIBLIOGRAPHY

AB. COHEN, "Les Juifs dans les Colonies Française au XVIIIe Siècle," in *Revue des Études Juives*, IV, pp. 127, 236; V, pp. 68, 258.

AB. COHEN, "Les Juifs de la Martinique," *Revue des Études Juives*, II, p. 92.

LEO SHPALL, The Jews in Louisiana, New Orleans, 1936.

JEAN DE MAUPASSANT, Abraham Gradis, Bordeaux, 1917.

MOREAU DE SAINT-MÉRY, Lois et Constitutions des Colonies françaises d'Amérique sous le Vent, Paris, 1787.

ARTHUR D. HART, editor, The Jew in Canada, Toronto & Montreal, 1926.

JEAN BAPTISTE DU TERTRE, Histoire Général des Antilles par les François, Paris, 1667–71.

JEAN BAPTISTE DU TERTRE, Histoire Générale des Isles Christophe. de la Guadeloupe, de la Martinique et autres dans l'Amerique, Paris, 1654.

LÉON BERMAN, Histoire des Juifs de France, Paris, 1937.

SAMUEL OPPENHEIM, "Early Jewish Colony in Western Guiana," in *A. J. H. S.*, XVI, pp. 93–186; see also *A. J. H. S.*, XXXII, pp. 15–20.

NELLIS M. CROUSE, French Pioneers in the West Indies, N. Y., 1940.

NOTES TO CHAPTER 8

COTTON MATHER'S AMBITION

[1] *A. J. H. S.*, XXVI, p. 201, under the title "Cotton Mather and the Jews."

[2] *Three Letters from New England*, London, 1721. Cf. also

> "—— Persecution, Thou Mother of Abominations
> Persecution; Thou Perpetual Fist of Wickedness."
> *Piety & Equity*, Boston, 1717, p. 28.
> "That no man be Persecuted, because he is Conscientiously not of the same Religious Opinions with those that are uppermost."
> *Theopolis Americana*, Boston, 1710.

[3] Cotton Mather, *Goodmen Described*, Boston, 1692.

[4] Cotton Mather, *Malachi*, Boston, 1717, p. 76.

[5] Samuel Mather, M.A., *Life of the Very Reverend and Learned Cotton Mather*, D.D., F.R.S., Boston, 1729, p. 4; see *A. J. H. S.*, XX, p. 65.

[6] "Besides what think you of that Law in the Scripture, Thou shalt not suffer a Witch to Live: Exod. 22.18; which Law you find afterwards more than once executed in Israel? If you would not bee soon tried with Greek and Hebrew, I would here actually perform what I now only profer; That is This: To prove out of the oldest Jewish Rabbins that the Hebrew Word here used in the Original, and out of the oldest Poets, Orators, Historians, that the Greek Word here

used by the Septuagint, signifies one who does preternaturall mischiefs by the Aid of Divels."
"Mather-Calef Paper on Witchcraft," in *Proceedings, Mass. Hist. Soc.*, XLVII, p. 255.

7 "I should surprise you very much if I should proceed hereupon to Demonstrate unto you out of the Talmuds what horrible sorceries were epidemically known and used among the Jews, in those Dayes." Ibid., p. 261.

8 Samuel Mather, *Life of . . . Cotton Mather*, etc., pp. 13–14.

9 Manuscript in the possession of the Massachusetts Historical Society.
"*Biblia Americana* — The First American Attempt at Post-Biblical Jewish History," see L. M. Friedman in *Journal of Jewish Bibliography*, III, nos. 1–2, p. 9.

10 This is taken from a prospectus soliciting subscriptions printed for Cotton Mather. Thomas James Holmes, *Cotton Mather*, Cambridge, 1940, II, p. 732. Mather, in his manuscript, says that his post-biblical Jewish history is taken directly from Basnage's *History of the Jews* which had been made accessible to English readers by Taylor's translation published in London in 1706–8. "What I thus endeavoured has been (mostly) to abridge the noble work of Basnage."

11 *Short History of New England*, Boston, 1694.

12 *Piety and Equity*, Boston, 1717.

13 "Diary of Samuel Sewall," in *Collections, Mass. Hist. Soc.*, Series V, vol. 6, p. 80*, Boston, 1879. See also *A. J. H. S.*, XX, p. 55.

"A modest enquiry into the grounds and occasions of a late pamphlet intituled 'A Memorial of the Present Deplorable State of New England.' "

Ibid., p. 80. Cf. *A. J. H. S.*, XI, p. 79; XX, p. 55.

14 "Diary of Cotton Mather," in *Collections, Mass. Hist. Soc.*, Series VII, vol. VII, p. 64; hereinafter cited as *Diary*.

15 The Faith of the Fathers/or/The Articles of the/True Religion/All of them Exhibited/In the Express Words of the Old Testament/Partly/To confirm those who do profess that Reli/gion of God, and his Messiah/But Chiefly/to Engage the Jewish National unto the Religion of their Patriarchs/And, Bring down the hearts of the Fathers unto/the children, and the Disobedient unto the Wisdom of the Just; and so, to make ready/a People prepared for the Lord.

16 *Diary*, part i, p. 298.

17 The Christian religion "is in reality but the Faith of the Fathers and the religion of the Old Testament from whence the Modern Jews are fallen." See preface to the appendix, "A Relation of the Conversion of a Jew named Shalom Ben Shalomoh," note 14, infra.

18 *Diary*, part i, p. 300.

19 Ibid., p. 302.

20 Ibid., p. 315.

21 Ibid., p. 370.

22 A Relation/of/The Conversion of/a Jew/named Shalom Ben Shalomoh/as himself uttered it, unto a Church/of the Lord Jesus Christ assembled/in Rose-Mary Lane London/September 29, 1699/etc. etc. An appendix to American Tears upon the Ruines of the Greek Churches, Boston, 1701.

²³ June 10, 1700, Sewall wrote "to John Love, Mercht in St. Lawrence Lane London" an order for books and, adding a further list July 1, included: "account ot a Jew lately converted and baptised at the Meeting-house near Ave-Mary-Lane: Four (copies) of them." *Coll. Mass. Hist. Soc.*, Series VI, vol. I, p. 239.

²⁴ *Problema Theologicum.*

²⁵ The Mystery of Israel's Salvation Explained and Applyed, or a Discourse concerning tne General Conversion of the Israelitish Nation, Boston, 1669.

²⁶ *Diary*, part ii, p. 41.

²⁷ Ibid., p. 62.

²⁸ Ibid., p. 219.

²⁹ Ibid., p. 233.

³⁰ Ibid., p. 378.

³¹ "Mather Papers," in *Coll. Mass. Hist. Soc.*, Series IV, vol. VIII, p. 420; see *A. J. H. S.*, XI, p. 80.

³² "November 29, 1717. G. D. I would send my account of the Jewish children at Berlin unto the Master of our grammar schole, with my desire that it be readd publically unto the children in the schole, and that he made suitable Remarks, thereupon unto them."

³³ *Diary*, part ii, p. 494, December 12, 1717.

³⁴ Ibid., p. 469, August 10, 1717.

³⁵ Ibid., p. 500, January 17, 1717/8.

³⁶ "His burthen certainly is almost insupportable, for he would fain have preach'd a Lecture sermon to stir up devout persons to pray for yᵉ conversion of yᵉ Jews." Supposed letter from Rev. Cotton Mather sent anonymously to Judge Sewall, April 13, 1720: *Coll. Mass. Hist. Soc.*, series IV, vol. VIII, p. 217.

³⁷ Lee M. Friedman, "Judah Monis, First Instructor in Hebrew at Harvard University," in *Early American Jews*, Cambridge, 1934.

NOTES TO CHAPTER 9

ARARAT—A CITY OF REFUGE FOR THE JEWS

¹ G. Herbert Cone, "New Matter Relating to Mordecai M. Noah," in *A. J. H. S.*, vol. XI, pp. 130, 132–3.

² In his own account Major Noah writes in the *Buffalo Patriot Extra*: "It was purchased by the friends of Major Noah of New York avowedly to offer it as an asylum for his brethren of the Jewish persuasion."

This would not have been the first American attempt to combine philanthropy towards the Jew with land speculation. In 1819, one W. D. Robinson published an address to "Persons of the Jewish Religion in Europe" calling attention to tracts of land for sale in Mississippi and Missouri territory affording excellent opportunities for agricultural settlement. He invited subscriptions to a fund to assist such emigrants, promising that it would yield large profits to its investors and at the same time win them the eternal gratitude of those assisted. The scheme contemplated that a Jewish emigrant should be sold a tract of land on credit. The prospective settler was to be conveyed free of charge from Europe to New Orleans, thence to the settlement, outfitted and, under instruction and supervision, made into a farmer. Eventually, farmer, investors and the promotors were all to grow prosperous. The scheme seems to have been stillborn.

Charles P. Daly, *The Settlement of the Jews in North America*, New York, 1893, pp. 92–3.

[3] See the account of the stone by Lewis F. Allen in his paper before the Buffalo Historical Society, reprinted in A. B. Makover, *Mordecai M. Noah*, New York, 1917, pp. 60–3.

[4] Isaac Goldberg, *Major Noah — American-Jewish Pioneer*, Philadelphia, 1936, p. 206.

BIBLIOGRAPHY

Lewis F. Allen, "Founding of the City of Ararat on Grand Island by Mordecai M. Noah," in *Buffalo Historical Society Publications*, volume I, Buffalo, 1879.

A. B. Makover, Mordecai M. Noah, New York, 1917.

Isaac Goldberg, Major Noah, Philadelphia, 1936.

Simon Wolf, Selected Addresses and Papers, Cincinnati, 1926, pp. 108–154.

Jewish Encyclopedia, New York, 1906, volume I, Article "Ararat;" volume IX, "Mordecai Manuel Noah."

NOTES TO CHAPTER 10

THE DEDICATION OF MASSACHUSETTS' FIRST SYNAGOGUE

[1] *Boston Mercantile Journal*, September 22, 1840. I am indebted to Mr. S. Broches for this reference.

[2] Some dispute the year from which the congregation should date and believe that it should be 1843. All the original synagogue records (written in German) are lost. In 1907, when children of the founders were still active members of the congregation, *Ohabei Shalom* officially published its by-laws and in the introductory history of the congregation stated:

"In September, 1842, the Jewish residents of Boston . . . . assembled at the house of Peter Spitz (then Fort Hill) to celebrate the New Year Festival, where they held services until February 26, 1843, when a meeting was called and the Congregation *Ohabei Shalom* was formed . . . ."

That the correct date is 1842 is further conclusively demonstrated. For the first time the synagogue was listed by the *Boston Directory* of 1849–50, in "Churches and Ministers in Boston," as "Synagogue of Israelites," "73 Warren" Street, founded "1844." It so continued to be listed through 1853. When the *Directory* of 1854 was published, someone had noticed the error of the date of its founding and it was corrected and continued thereafter to be listed, "1842." 1854 was the first year the congregation had a professional rabbi, Joseph Sachs, and we may surmise that he had seen to the correction.

See also: *Statistics of the Jews of the United States*, Union of American Hebrew Congregations, Philadelphia, 1880, p. 7.

J. J. Lyons & A. DeSola, *A Jewish Calendar for Fifty Years*, Montreal, 1854, p. 149.

[3] I am indebted to Mr. S. Broches for this reference.

[4] "On February 22, 1733, Michael Asher and Isaac Solomon purchased from Joseph Bradford a plot of land on what is now Chambers Street (15 and 17). Here they erected a shop and set aside a part of the lot as a burying-ground for 'the Jewish Nation.' In 1735, Isaac Solomon and his wife Elizabeth sold all their interest in this land to Asher. Asher appears to have fallen upon evil days; at any rate he lost this property the following year. The burying-ground of the Jewish nation was known to be in existence as late as 1750, but all trace of it after that date is lost."
Lee M. Friedman, *Early American Jews*, p. 8.

[5] *The Occident*, vol. IX (October 15, 1851), pp. 380–1.

[6] *Dedication of the New Synagogue of the Congregation Mikveh Israel at Broad and York Streets on September 14, 1909, Elul 29, 5669*, Philadelphia, 1909, pp. 12–13.

[7] *The Occident*, vol. I, p. 407.

[8] M. J. Kohler, "Jewish Life in New York before 1800," in *A. J. H. S.*, vol. III, p. 85.

[9] Theodore Clapp's autobiographical sketches and recollections, in *A. J. H. S.*, vol. XIII, pp. 94 ff., p. 100.

[10] The following set of resolutions was passed by its Board of Trustees:

At a meeting of the Board of Trustees of the Congregation 'Ohabei Shalom' held at their room, on the 31st March, 1852, on motion of Mr. J. Bornstein, seconded by Mr. L. Ondkerk, the following resolutions were unanimously adopted:

"Resolved, That the grateful thanks of the Congregation are due, and are hereby tendered to the Trustees of the Congregation 'B'nai Jeshuran' of New York, for their kindness, in allowing their clergy leave of absence to attend to the consecration of our new Synagogue, and thus depriving themselves, on the Sabbath, of their valuable services.

"Resolved, That we feel ourselves under great obligation to the Trustees of the Congregation 'B'nai Jeshuran' of New York, for the loan of a Sepher Torah kindly sent to us for the same occasion.

"Resolved, That a copy of these resolutions, signed by the President and Secretary of this Board, be forwarded to the Trustees of the Congregation 'B'nai Jeshuran,' and published in the *Asmonean* and *Occident*."

M. Ehrlich, Pres. O. S.

B. Wermser, Secretary
Boston, March 31, 1852

The Occident, vol. X (May 1852), pp. 104–7.

BIBLIOGRAPHY OF CHAPTER 11
ASSER LEVY VAN SWELLEM

LEON HÜHNER, "Asser Levy," in *A. J. H. S.*, VIII, pp. 9–23.

Records of New Amsterdam from 1653 to 1674 Anno Domini, B. Fernow, editor, New York, 1897, Vol. II.

SAMUEL OPPENHEIM, in "Early History of the Jews in New York," *A. J. H. S.*, XVIII, pp. 1–91.

Documents Relating to the Colonial History of the State of New York, E. B. O'Callahan, editor, Albany, 1849–51.

CHARLES P. DALY, The Settlement of the Jews in North America, New York, 1893, pp. 6–58.

SAMUEL OPPENHEIM, "More About Jacob Barsimson," in *A. J. H. S.*, XXIV, pp. 39–52.

Ecclesiastical Records, State of New York, H. Hastings, editor, Albany, 1901, vol. I, pp. 334–6.

NOTES TO CHAPTER 12
MR. HAYS SPEAKS OUT

[1] Published in *The Menorah Journal*, vol. XXVII, p. 77 ff.

[2] C. H. Van Tyne, *The Loyalists in the American Revolution*, New York, 1902, p. 2.

[3] Thomas Paine, *Common Sense*, Philadelphia, 1776, p. 40.

[4] "An Act empowering the Members of the Upper and Lower Houses of Assembly to tender to such of the inhabitants as are hereinafter mentioned a Declaration or Test for Subscription." June, 1776.

[5] *R. I. Archives General Assembly Papers, Revolutionary War, Suspected Persons, 1775–1783*, p. 16. The return day of the subpoena is July 12th, the meeting is dated July 11th.

[6] Ibid., p. 9.

[7] Rabbi Isaac de Abraham Touro, of an ancient Spanish Jewish family, came from Amsterdam in 1758 and became Rabbi of *Jeshuat Israel* at Newport. He left Newport when it was captured by the British, temporarily residing in New York. He died in Jamaica in 1784, aged 44.

[8] Ibid., p. 14.

[9] Ibid., p. 47.

[10] F. B. Dexter, ed., *The Literary Diary of Ezra Stiles*, N. Y., 1901, Vol. I, p. 151.

[11] It was in his household that his nephews, Judah Touro and Abraham Touro, grew up. Of his four daughters two married two brothers, Samuel and Moses Mears Myers, and became residents of Richmond, Va., where they were joined by the other two, the Misses Catherine and Slowey Hays.

In 1798 Hays' name was amongst those voted for as Senator for the County of Suffolk (City of Boston, *Records*, vol. 35, p. 39).

In 1797 he was one of the organizers of Massachusetts' Second Fire Insurance Company, The Massachusetts Mutual Fire Insurance Company, as well as of the Massachusetts Marine Insurance Company in 1799, (*The Insurance Library Ass'n Reports, 1788–1900*, Boston, 1901).

He left what was for the day a large estate, appraised at $82,000. It is interesting to note that amongst his assets, as diverse as lands in Georgia and Rhode Island, shares, bonds and a house in Boston, were "twenty-two Hebrew Books" (*Suffolk County Probate Files*).

[12] G. B. Emerson, ed., *Memoirs of Samuel Joseph May*, Boston, 1874, pp. 15–16.

[13] Robert Treat Paine, Jr., *Works in Verse and Prose*, Boston, 1812, p. 292.

[14] One figure missing.

NOTES TO CHAPTER 13
THE TEN TRIBES LOST AGAIN

[1] Quoted from *The Lost Tribes a Myth*, A. H. Godbey, Durham, 1930, p. 2.

[2] In England the controversy was not without influence. Menasseh ben Israel was received by Oliver Cromwell in Whitehall, in 1655, to discuss the re-admission of the Jews. Although Rabbi Menasseh's mission failed and many years were to pass before the Jews received a legal status in England, a war of books and pamphlets on the subject of the Jews — in which the theory of the Indians and the Ten Tribes played its part — focused the attention of Englishmen on the Jews, their religion and their economic importance. From that time on Jews were permitted, at least anonymously and illegally, to reside unmolested in England until at last, in a more tolerant age, all restrictions were gradually allowed to disappear. (See the works of Roth, Hyamson and Henriques cited below.)

BIBLIOGRAPHY

T. THOROWGOOD, Jewes in America, London, 1650.

T. THOROWGOOD, Jews in America, London, 1660.

H. l'ESTRANGE, Americans No Iewes, London, 1652.

L. WOLF, Menasseh ben Israel's Mission to Oliver Cromwell, London, 1901, pp. xxiv–xxv.

A. H. GODBEY, The Lost Tribes a Myth (contains an interesting bibliography, pp. 711–754), Durham, 1930.

W. ROSENAU, "What Happened to the Ten Tribes?" in *Hebrew Union College Jubilee Volume* (1875–1925), Cincinnati, 1925, pp. 79–88.

DAVID PHILIPSON, "Are There Traces of the Lost Tribes in Ohio?" *A. J. H. S.*, XIII, p. 37 ff.

A. M. HYAMSON, "The Lost Tribes and . . . the Return of the Jews to England," in *J. Q. R.*, XV, p. 640.

CECIL ROTH, History of the Jews in England, London, 1941, pp. 149–172.

———, Menasseh ben Israel, Philadelphia, 1934.

H. S. Q. HENRIQUES, The Return of the Jews to England, London, 1905.

NOTES TO CHAPTER 14
LITERARY AMERICA ADOPTS A JEW

[1] *Essai sur la Régénération Physique, Morale, et Politique des Juifs*, Metz, 1789.

[2] *Dissertation sur Cette Question: Est-il des Moyens de rendre les Juifs plus heureux et plus utiles en France?* Paris, 1788.

[3] *Apologie des Juifs en Réponse à la Question: Est-il des Moyens*, etc., Paris, 1789.

[4] Louis Zangwill, "Richard Cumberland Centenary Memorial Paper," in *J. H. S. E.*, VII, pp. 147–179.

[5] The description of the Jewish maiden is typical. Only Scott does it better. It is said that he knew no Jews and drew his portrait from a description of Rebecca Gratz of Philadelphia by Washington Irving. At any rate, he gave free run to his imagination and did a good job of flamboyant exaggeration:

> "Her form was exquisitely symmetrical, and was shown to advantage by a sort of Eastern dress, which she wore according to the fashion of the females of her nation. Her turban of yellow silk suited well with the darkness of her complexion. The brilliancy of her eyes, the superb arch of her eyebrows, her well-formed aquiline nose, her teeth as white as pearl, and the profusion of her sable tresses which, each arranged in its own little spiral of twisted curls, fell down upon as much of a lovely neck and bosom as a simarre of the richest Persian silk, exhibiting flowers in their natural colours embossed upon a purple ground, permitted to be visible — all these constituted a combination of loveliness, which yielded not to the most beautiful of the maidens who surrounded her. It is true that of the golden and pearl-studded clasps, which closed her vest from the throat to the waist, the three uppermost were left unfastened, on account of the heat, which something enlarged the prospect to which we allude. A diamond necklace, with pendants of inestimable value, were by this means also made more conspicuous. The feather of an ostrich, fastened in her turban, by an agriffe set with brilliants, was another distinction of the beautiful Jewess."
>
> *Ivanhoe*, Chapter 7

[6] Edward D. Coleman, "Plays of Jewish Interest, 1752–1821," in *A. J. H. S.*, XXXIII, pp. 171–198; Evans, 28512–28516.

[7] Lee M. Friedman, "The American Society for Meliorating the Condition of the Jews and Joseph S. C. F. Frey," in *Early American Jews*, Chapter VIII.

[8] ". . . Perhaps the ablest, certainly the most tenacious, race that had ever lived in it (the world) — the race to whom we owed our religion and the purest spiritual stimulus and consolation to be found in all literature — a race in which ability seems as natural and hereditary as the curve of their noses and whose blood, furtively mingling with the bluest bloods in Europe, has quickened them with their own indomitable impulsion." J. R. Lowell, *Democracy*, an address delivered in Birmingham, England, on October 6, 1884.

[9] An animated controversy was carried on in the newspapers of yesterday (*Philadelphia Ledger*, *Boston Post* and others, December 1920–January 1921) over one Moses Simonson, who came in the *Fortune* to Plymouth in 1621 and who was by some identified as this Pilgrim Jew. Moyses P. Simmons, a descendant, indignantly

asserted that his ancestor was of good English stock, a "Symonds, Simonds, Symans," of Devonshire, Dorset, Gloucester, etc., and "with no disrespect to the Jewish People," a stalwart Protestant. The Reverend Paul Sturtevant Howe, Ph.D., joined issue with descendant Moyses, stoutly "satisfied that my ancestor Moses Simonson was a Jew."

[10] This legend is told in *Early American Jews*, by Lee M. Friedman, p. 40.

BIBLIOGRAPHY

OBADIAH OLDPATH (James R. Newhall), Lin, or Jewels of the Third Plantation, Lynn, 1862.

LEWIS & NEWHALL, History of Lynn, Boston, 1865.

COTTON MATHER, Magnalia Christi Americana, Hartford, 1820, Book III, Chapter XXXIII.

First Church of Christ in Lynn, 1636–1932, Lynn, 1932.

MONTAGU F. MODDER, The Jew in the Literature of England, Philadelphia, 1939.

ISRAEL ABRAHAMS, By-Paths in Hebraic Bookland, Philadelphia, 1920.

NOTES TO CHAPTER 15

THE FIRST OLD FARMER'S ALMANAC AND THE JEWS

[1] *Preliminary Check List of American Almanacs, 1639–1800*, Library of Congress, Washington, 1907.

[2] Charles L. Nichols, "Notes on the Almanacs of Massachusetts," *Proceedings of the American Antiquarian Society*, vol. 22 (m. s.), p. 15, at 18.

[3] Ibid., pp. 17 and 18.

[4] For an account of *The Royal George* and its loss, see Commander A. T. Stewart, *H. M. S. Royal George, 1756–1782.* Blue Peter, London, January, 1932.

[5] Cotton Mather's *Biblia Americana* was never published. See "Cotton Mather's Ambition," pp. 95 ff., above.

[6] *The whole genuine and complete works of Flavius Josephus. Also a continuation of the history of the Jews, from Josephus down to the present time*, by George Henry Maynard, L.L.D. . . . New York (incomplete), plates and maps.

NOTES TO CHAPTER 16

AMERICA'S FIRST JEWISH BOOKDEALER

[1] I have borrowed without further acknowledgment from two articles published in *The Colophon*: Charles G. Poore, "Benjamin Gomez — Bookseller," *The Colophon*, Part 8, New York, 1931; and R. W. G. Vail, "A Curtain Call for Benjamin Gomez," *The Colophon*, Part 9, New York, 1932.

[2] *Publications of the Colonial Society of Massachusetts*, Boston, 1905, vol. VII, p. 80.

³ Ibid., 1925, vol. XV, p. lxx.

⁴ Samuel E. Morison, *The Founding of Harvard College*, Cambridge, 1935, p. 266.

⁵ Among which was one small Hebrew Bible inventoried at 6s.

⁶ F. B. Dexter, *Early Private Libraries in New England in a Selection from the Miscellaneous Historical Papers of Fifty Years*, New Haven, 1918.

Thomas Goddard Wright, *Literary Culture in Early New England*, New Haven, 1920, Chapter II.

⁷ Lee M. Friedman, *Early American Jews*, Cambridge, 1934, p. 31.

⁸ *A. J. H. S.*, vol. XXX, nn. 41, 46 & 47. "Isaac Pinto's Prayer Book," in I. Abrahams, *By-Paths in Hebraic Bookland*, Philadelphia, 1920, pp. 171–177.

⁹ For an interesting description and account of this publication see "Early Jewish Literature in America," George A. Kohut, *A. J. H. S.*, vol. III, pp. 118–121, also *A. J. H. S.*, vol. XXX, pp. 57–8, nn. 46, 47.

¹⁰ Lee M. Friedman, *Rabbi Haim Isaac Carigal. His Newport Sermon and His Yale Portrait*, Boston, 1940, pp. 10–14.

¹¹ George Alexander Kohut, "Early Jewish Literature in America, in *A. J. H. S.*, vol. III, pp. 104–5.

¹² *Publications of the Colonial Society of Massachusetts*, vol. XIII, p. 291.

¹³ *Boston News-Letter*, Feb. 6–13, 1715–6.

¹⁴ *Boston News-Letter*, August 20–27, 1716.

¹⁵ "CUTLERY AND STATIONERY.— Just Imported from London and Sold by THOMAS RAND, opposite to the Town Pump in Corn Hill; a large assortment of Stationery and Cutlery Wares, viz. best Writing Paper, Press Boards, large & small, Holman's Ink Powder, best Dutch Quills, Receit and account Books, Slates large and small, Pencils, English & Latin Dictionarys, Lexicons, Most sorts of Latin books, a great Assortment of Histories, Plays, Mariners Compass and Kallenders, Epitomy, Quarter Wagoners, Seaman's Compasses, Scales and Dividers, Case Knives & Forks, Pen-Knives, Jacknives, Ivory Haft, Pocket Butcher's and Shoe Knives, long Stag Cutos, Thimbles, Jews harps, Shears & Scizars, Razors, brass Ink Pots with penknives, Horn ditto, Shoe & Knee Buckles, sleve Buttons, new fashion Breast ditto, Snuff Boxes, Ivory & Horn Combs, Forehead ditto, Ivory Books, Temple and Common Spectacles new fashion Canes, Iron & Ivory head ditto, Whips, Violins & Strings, Wigg Cauls & Ribons, Straps, Hones, & Pipes, raw Silk, Tea Pots & Kittles, gilt Trunks in whole or half Nests, some with brass Locks, Brushes of all Sizes, mops, Wool & Cotton Cards, best white Chappel Needles & Common, Hour Glasses, Children's Toys of all sorts.

Where may be had the French Convert and the Church Primer and Catechism."

Boston Gazette, May 7, 1754.

"STATIONERY.— Just Imported from LONDON in Capt Craige, and to be sold cheap for ready Money by Michael Dennis, at the corner of Scarlett's Wharf. A good assortment of Bibles and Common Prayer-Books of several sizes, West-India Pilots and other Sea Draughts, Mariner's Compasses and Kallenders, Atkinson's and Wilson's Epitome of Navigation, a Complete Assortment of Books for the use of Grammar Schools, Testaments, Psalters, Primmers and Spelling Books, a good variety of Writing Paper, Marble, Blue and Cartridge Paper, Accompt Books large and Small, Brass Compasses, Gunter Scales, Slates in Frames, Pewter and Wood Ink Stands, Ink Powder, Sealing Wax, Wafers, Brass, Bone and Leather Ink Pots, Ivory and Horn Combs, best Dutch Quills, Spectacles of several Sorts, Pocket-Books, Ivory Books, Letter Cases, Cedar and Slate Pencils, Fountain Pens. Seals, Pen Knives, Jack Knives, Buckles, Snuff-Boxes, Scissars, and many other Articles."

Boston Gazette, May 9, 1749.

On July 3, 1794, Berry, Rogers & Berry advertised in the *American Minerva* and *The New York Evening Advertiser,* in addition to a sale of "elegant assortment of superfine lady's and gentlemen's broadcloths," gold and silver epaulets, pistols and "guns with bayonets," silverware, candlesticks, silk stockings imported "in the ship *Sansom* from London." "N. B. a large supply of valuable Books by the last arrivals from London and Dublin." For other and earlier such advertisements see *Mass. His. Soc. Publications,* Vol. X (2nd Series), pp. 540-7.

[16] John Dunton's *Letters from New England,* Prince Society, Boston, 1867, p. 78.

[17] Charles Evans, *American Bibliography,* Chicago, 1903–1934.

[18] Charles K. Bolton, "Circulating Libraries in Boston, 1765–1865," *Publications, Colonial Society of Massachusetts,* vol. XI, p. 196.

[19] *American Minerva,* April 25, 1794.

[20] *The Minerva & Mercantile Evening Advertiser,* May 12, 1797.

[21] There is considerable doubt about this last statement.

[22] *A. J. H. S.,* vol. XXVII, pp. 279–317; *A. J. H. S.,* vol. XVII, p. 197; *A. J. H. S.,* vol. II, p. 141; Charles P. Daly, *Settlement of the Jews in North America,* New York, 1893, p. 30.

[23] Evans, 28022.

[24] Evans, 27555.

[25] See p. 34, above.

[26] Mr. Vail has since identified a twenty-second item: "Burkitt, William. The poor man's help, and young man's guide . . . also Divine Hymns . . . New York: Printed by George Forman for Benjamin Gomez . . . 1795. 204 p., 12 mo. AAS."

[27] *A. J. H. S.,* vol. XXVII, pp. 305–6.

NOTES TO CHAPTER 17

AMERICA'S FIRST JEWISH CLUB

[1] William Smith, *The History of the Province of New York,* London, 1876, p. 271.

[2] John Adams, *Collected Works,* Boston, 1850, p. 290.

[3] Marquis de Chastellux, *Travels in North America in the Years 1780–81–82,* N. Y., 1827, p. 333.

[4] *Newport Historical Magazine,* vol. 4, pp. 58–60.

[5] F. B. Dexter, ed., *The Literary Diary of Ezra Stiles.*

[6] Charles M. Andrews, *Colonial Period of American History,* vol. II, New Haven, 1936, p. 11.

NOTES TO CHAPTER 18

"THE CAMPBELLS ARE COMING"

[1] Max J. Kohler, "The Jews in Newport," *A. J. H. S.*, VI, pp. 62–63.

[2] W. S. Samuel, "Review of the Jewish Colonists in Barbados," in *J. H. S. E.*, XIII, pp. 25–26.

[3] In his *The Beginnings of Freemasonry in America* (New York, 1924), Melvin M. Johnson, Sovereign Grand Commander of the Supreme Council for the Northern Jurisdiction of the United States of America of Masons, quotes Peterson's *History of Rhode Island and Newport* in the past as assigning the introduction of masonry into the United States in 1658 in Rhode Island on the authority of documents now in the possession of N. H. Gould, Esq. The documents being challenged, they were not produced; and the conclusion of M. W. Bro. Thomas A. Doyle, former Grand Master of Masons in Rhode Island, seems inescapable. "I have made many enquiries of the Grand Lodge and others, and do not find that any one has ever seen them; neither do the brethren believe that any proof exists of the truth of Peterson's statement." (pp. 44–47).

[4] *N. E. Historical and Genealogical Record*, VIII, p. 206.

[5] *R. I. Land Evidence*, II, p. 79.

[6] *Report of the Record Commissioners of the City of Boston*, 28, pp. 348–9.

[7] *Report of the Record Commissioners of the City of Boston*, 13 (1885), p. 154.

[8] *Essex Institute Historical Collection*, VI, p. 74; *Rowley Vital Records*, Salem, 1928, p. 262; there is also a record of a marriage of David Campernall to Mary Wilson at Ipswich, March 19, 1711, and of the baptism of a Mary Campernall, daughter of David and Mary, March 30, 1714, *Ipswich Vital Records*, vol. II, p. 89.

[9] *Ipswich Town Records*, IV.

[10] Lee M. Friedman, *Early American Jews*, Cambridge, Mass., 1934, pp. 9 and 10.

[11] *Ipswich Vital Records*, I & II (see last page). Thus, amongst others, are recorded:

MARRIAGES

Campanel
    David Jr. to Hannah Newmarch

                                int. Aug. 24, 1734
    Mary & Thomas Lenter of Wenham

                                int. Apr. 25, 1735
    Ann & William Galloway, Jan. 15, 1761
    David & Mary Wilson

                                int. 19. 3M. 1711
    Sarah & William Robbins, 3d.

                                int. Oct. 31, 1730

Campanell
>Will(ia)m & Mrs. Mina Hurlburt
>
>>int. Jan. 23, 1762
>
>Will(ia)m & Wid. Elizabeth Hodgkins
>
>>Jan. 12, 1765

DEATHS

Campanel

Abigail d. David & Mary	April 13, 1726
David "a Jew"	Oct. 17, 1732
Mary W. David	Feb. 21, 1736

Campanall

Elizabeth unm.	Aug. 14, 1721

Campanell

David lost in Lee's Meadow	Oct. 16, 1739
David	Oct. 21, 1753
Jamima W. (Will(ia)m)	Nov. 1762
——Wid.	Feb. 11, 1774

[12] A David Campernell was placed on the National Pension rolls in 1819 for services in the Revolution as a private in Treats' 21st Infantry, as a resident of Rockingham County. *State Papers, N. H.*, XXX, 1910, p. 210.

[13] Harold Murdock Taylor, *Family History of Anthony Taylor and His Descendants*, Cranston, R. I., 1935, pp. 109–116.

BIBLIOGRAPHY TO CHAPTER 19

ESTHER'S ADVENTURES IN QUEBEC

A. G. Doughty and N. E. Dionne, Quebec Under Two Flags, Quebec, 1903.
Pierre-Georges Roy, La Ville de Quebec sous le Regime Français, Quebec, 1930.
Joseph Marmette, Report on Canadian Archives, 1886.
Arthur D. Hart, The Jew in Canada, Toronto and Montreal, 1926.

BIBLIOGRAPHY TO CHAPTER 20

LADY REBECCA

Publications of the American Jewish Historical Society.
Alexander Graydon, Memoirs of His Own Times, Phila., 1846.
Winfield Scott, Memoirs of Lieut.-General Scott, L.L.D., written by himself, N. Y. ,1864.

HENRY S. MORAIS, The Jews of Philadelphia, Phila., 1894.

H. P. ROSENBACH, The Jews in Philadelphia, Phila., 1883.

Pennsylvania Magazine of History and Biography, vols. III, XVI & XXIII.

SCHARF & WESCOTT, History of Philadelphia.

ELIZABETH F. ELLET, The Women of the American Revolution, Philadelphia, 1900.

LEWIS MELVILLE (L. S. Benjamin), Bath under Beau Nash.

PIERCE EGAN, C. ANSTEY — The New Guide to Bath, London, 1766.

ANNE H. WHARTON, Through Colonial Doorways.

MAX J. KOHLER, Rebecca Franks, New York, 1894.

NOTES TO CHAPTER 21

MEDFORD'S JEWISH STREET

[1] Gutstein, *The Story of the Jews of Newport*, N. Y., 1936, pp. 230–239.

[2] Aaron Hart, "The Primitive Jewish Settlements in America," in the *American Jews' Annual*, 1887, p. 38, answers the question as to the earliest American Jewish philanthropic organization by relating the following:

> In the spring of the year 1820 a Jew who had been a soldier in the American War for Independence was brought in a critical state to the New York City Hospital. He had no friends and no money, but expressed a wish that, being a Jew, some co-religionists might be sent for. John I. Hart and Joseph Davies visited the sufferer and collected some money for him. Soon afterwards he died and about three hundred dollars of the money collected was left. This was the first money with which the Hebrew Benevolent Society of the City of New York was founded. That society was organized on April 8, 1822. . . .

[3] Amos A. Lawrence of Boston (1786–1852).

[4] This $50,000 led to the founding of the Jewish hospital in Jerusalem. The following excerpts from the diaries of Sir Moses and Lady Montefiore edited by Dr. L. Loewe (Chicago, 1890, Vol. II) are of interest.

> Aug. 5, 1854: Mr. Gershon Kursheedt, one of the executors of the late Juda (*sic*) Touro, of New Orleans, arrived to arrange with Sir Moses about the legacy of fifty thousand dollars left at his disposal for the purposes of relieving the poor Israelites in the Holy Land in such manner as Sir Moses should advise. Sir Moses, at the first interview he had with this gentleman, suggested that the money should be employed in building a hospital in Jerusalem. Mr. Kursheedt immediately assented, and Sir Moses gave him the plan and drawing made about a year before, and he said the thing was done. He was most happy, as it settled the principal business he had in England; the co-executors had given him full power to agree to any plan Sir Moses should propose — a letter was prepared by a solicitor to that effect, which Mr. Kursheedt signed. . . . . . . Sir Moses, however, had soon to learn that Mr. Kursheedt had been induced to alter his mind, and had withdrawn the consent he had given to the building of a hospital. . . . .
>
> April 30, 1855. Before leaving England Sir Moses had the satisfaction of receiving a further sum of about £5028 of the Juda Touro legacy already

remitted to him on the 24th of February, and Mr. Kursheedt was now, it appeared, in possession of full power regarding the building of the hospital in Jerusalem . . . . .

July 3rd [Sir Moses writes]: "Mr. Pisani informed me he had received the firman for the building of an hospital!" . . . . .

August 15th. In the presence of a numerous concourse of spectators of various religious denominations, Sir Moses and Lady Montefiore had the satisfaction and happiness to lay the foundation-stone of the proposed hospital, in the presence of Mr. and Mrs. Guedalla, Mr. Gershon Kursheedt, one of the executors of Juda Touro, the American philanthropist, and myself". . .

NOTES TO CHAPTER 22

A 'FORTY-NINER

[1] Josiah Royce, *California*, Boston, 1886, p. 384, quotes a correspondent to the *New York Evening Post*, under date of November, 1849, that bread had risen from twenty-five cents a loaf to fifty cents, the price being for a small loaf not much larger than a breakfast roll.

[2] In 1853, he and an associate attempted to control the rice market. Although previously Norton had conducted such operations successfully, this time, just as they had cornered the market and immense profits were about to be realized, two unexpected shiploads of rice arrived in San Francisco. Prices fell rapidly and huge losses were faced by the syndicate. Complicated litigation ensued, which dragged along in the courts for years. Norton lost heavily. This together with his ruin by the fire of that year were generally considered the cause for his mental breakdown.

[3] Wm. McDevitt, "Ave! Imperator Norton," reprinted in Albert Dressler's *Emperor Norton of the United States*, San Francisco, 1927.

BIBLIOGRAPHY

R. E. COWAN, "Norton I," in *California Historical Society Quarterly*, vol. II, October, 1913.

"Society of California Pioneers," ibid., vol. V, no. 4, December, 1928, pp. 205.

M. W. WOODS, History of Alameda County, pp. 674, 692.

CECIL G. TILTON, William Chapman Ralston, Boston, 1935.

"American Emperor," in *Plain Talk*, May, 1936, Washington, D. C., p. 20.

ALBERT DRESSLER, ed., Emperor Norton of The United States, San Francisco, 1927.

B. E. LLOYD, Lights and Shades in San Francisco, San Francisco, 1876.

JOSIAH ROYCE, California, Boston, 1886.

ALLEN S. LANE, Emperor Norton the Mad Monarch of America, Caldwell, Idaho, 1939.

NOTES TO CHAPTER 23

THE HILTON-SELIGMAN AFFAIR

[1] Dixon Wecter, *The Saga of American Society*, New York, 1937.
[2] Rev. Henry Ward Beecher, "Jew and Gentile," Sunday sermon, June 24, 1877. Reprinted in *An Hour with the American Hebrew*, N. Y., 1879, p. 51; *The Menorah*, March, 1905.

NOTES TO CHAPTER 24

THE GIDEONS

[1] Published originally in *A. J. H. S.*, XXXV, pp. 27–37 under the title, "Rowland Gideon, An Early Boston Jew and his Family."
[2] It is interesting to note that years later Gideon named his eldest daughter "Barah."
[3] Was this a second marriage? In the list of marriages solemnized by rabbis of the Dutch-Portuguese Jewish congregation at Surinam, 1642–1750, we find Reuhel Obidiente and Rahel da Fonseca (*A. J. H. S.*, XVIII, p. 190), but we have not been able to find the record of any marriage to Bathsheba.
[4] Lucien Wolf, *Essays in Jewish History*, London, 1934, p. 132.
[5] A touch of human weakness is revealed in the account of his wealth which he kept in his account books. Striking a balance from time to time, under the heading "which God Preserve," he shows he was worth

£   1,500 in 1719
   40,800 in 1735
   44,000 in 1740
   81,000 in 1745
  156,000 in 1748
  180,000 in 1750
  279,000 in 1755
  285,000 in 1756
  283,000 in 1757, after he had given his daughter £40,000 on her marriage to Lord Gage.
  297,000 in 1759

[6] In addition, he also left £100 to the Portuguese Jew's Hospital and £200 to the "Jew Orphans."
[7] This refusal was communicated to him in a letter from the Duke of Devonshire:

Devonshire-house, June 13, 1757

Sir,
    I have this morning mentioned to his Majesty what you desired about the Baronetage, and acquainted him with the service you had been of in relation to raising the supplies, and particularly how much obliged I thought myself to you, & urged the zeal you had shown on all occasions to serve the public.

The King seemed very well disposed, spoke very handsomely of you, and said he should have no objections himself to oblige you, but was afraid it would make a noise at this time, and therefore desired that I would inform you in the civilest manner, that it was not convenient for him to comply with your request.

I flatter myself you will be persuaded I have done my best to serve you on this occasion; for I do assure you that nothing would have given me greater pleasure than an opportunity of convincing you of the regard with which,

I am, Sir, yours &c.

Devonshire

John Nichols, *Illustrations of the Literary History of the Eighteenth Century*, London, 1831, vol. VI, p. 279.

⁸ Lucien Wolf, ibid., p. 176.

BIBLIOGRAPHY

Lee M. Friedman, "Jews in Massachusetts," in *Early American Jews*, Cambridge, 1934, pp. 5, 153.

Lucien Wolf, "The Family of Gideon Abudiente," in *Essays in Jewish History*, London, 1934, pp. 170–176.

James Picciotto, Sketches in Anglo-Jewish History, London, 1875, pp. 60–64.

Cecil Roth, A History of the Marranos, Philadelphia, 1932, pp. 314–316, 396.

The Jewish Historical Society of England (The Jews' Naturalization Bill, 1753), vol. XI, pp. 208–212.

The Jewish Historical Society of England (The Ancient Burial Ground of the Sephardi Jews), vol. X, pp. 240–241.

John Nichols, Literary Anecdotes of the Eighteenth Century, London, 1812–15, pp. 642 ff.

Calendar of State Papers, Am. & W. I. Series.

Isaac da Costa, Noble Families Among the Sephardic Jews, London, 1936, p. 146.

Public Record Office, C. C. 137/2, No. 112 II.

Wilfred S. Samuel, "Review of the Jewish Colonists in Barbados, 1680," in *J. H. S. E.*, XIII (1934), pp. 36–39.

M. J. Landa, "Kitty Villareal, the DaCostas and Samson Gideon," ibid., pp. 286–288 [cf. X, p. 240].

NOTES TO CHAPTER 26

LET THERE BE LIGHT

¹ From 1731, in writing of the importance of its colonies to Britain, an anonymous pamphleteer says: "The whale fishery produces annually from eleven to thirteen hundred tons of oyl, including what is made in New England . . . in Carolina . . . besides at least forty tons of Whale-Bone." *The Importance of the British Plantations in America to this Kingdom*, Anon., London, 1731.

² "At New York the magistrates occasionally ordered lights 'hung out on a pole' from upper windows of houses 'in the Darke time of the Moon.' This was done by private persons 'without expense to the corporation.' In 1697, 'The Great Inconveniency that Attends this Citty, being a trading place, for want of lights' led the authorities to order lanterns or lights put in the windows nightly, under penalty of a fine for neglect. Within a month, however, they changed this rule and ordered 'A Langthorn & Candle' to be suspended during winter before 'Every Seaventh House in the Severall Wards,' the cost to be defrayed 'in Equall proportions by the Inhabitants of the Said Seaven Houses.' " (Carl Bridenbaugh, *Cities in the Wilderness*, N. Y., 1939, p. 169.)

³ Isaac da Costa was educated for the Rabbinate and came to Charleston from London in 1750. Under date of August 2, 1774, the Rev. Ezra Stiles tells of a visit to him at Newport: "Mr. Acosta, a Jew Huzzan of the Synagogue in Charleston, South Carolina. He is aet 52, born in London and educated under Hochem Rabbi Nieto, there till aet 29, then he came to America and in 1754 instituted a synagogue at Charleston." Stiles' *Diary*, I, p. 453. See also B. A. Elzas, *The Jews of South Carolina*, Phila., 1905.

The sloop *London*, which is referred to in the account, was reported by the South Carolina *Gazette* of November 12, 1764, as having arrived at Charleston November 9, 1764, John Dawson, Master, from Jamaica. On November 26th the newspaper reported that the "sloop may sail or be loaded this week for Jamaica." On December 3rd the sloop had cleared but remained windbound in port until finally cleared December 4th. See illustrations facing pp. 308–9.

⁴   Newport 29th July 1762
Mess. Rᵈ Cranch & Co.
    Gentlemen,
        We were not without hopes that the rational & disinterested Measures you had plann'd and propos'd for the reciprocal Advantage of the sperma ceti manufʳˢ would have had the desired effect; twas entirely with that view that we entered into the contract; but the following Incidents to our no small Mortification, demonstrate, that we are disappointed. We have certain information, that most of the Factors at Nantuckett procur'd all the Head mattʳ, they possibly cou'd, at an advanc'd price, it does not at present appear on whose acctᵗ they have purchas'd, but we have Reason to believe they have no other Method to dispose of it, but to their former employers; we need not acquint you who they are, but this we will Venture to say, it is more than probable, it will be Rec'd at the high price they give, at the disolution of our Articles w'ich at farthest is at no great distance.
        Messr. Robinson & Co. have Rec'd about 50 bbs & Messʳˢ Stelle & Co. between 30 & 40, and as they have inform'd us, the Price is not ascertain'd, we have frankly told them our Opinion, that it is a Manifest Breach of the Articles.
        Mr. Moses Lopez who we always suppos'd was to be equaly concern'd with Mr. Jenkins, we find, is left out of the Question, & is going to Nantucket to purchase on his separate acctᵗ without Limitation.
        The Philadelphians have not thot proper to reply to our Letter on this subject. But Mr. Thoˢ Richardson, who address'd them on Behalf of the Company, writes to Mr. Robinson they had Refus'd to unite us, and we are

well assured had given orders to their Nantucket Factor, to continue purchasing at the market price, but quantity unknown.

Besides the above Hints, you'l please to excuse our once more observing
that Mrss Browns, being allowed the liberty to give to the seller 2½ P cent
more than the Restricted price; has given them the Opportunity of exceeding
every Manufactor who acts upon Principle, from the Benefit of Purchasing
a Single Cask diametrically repugnant both to the letter and spirit of the
Articles which were intended for mutual Benefit; and not to give one manufacture the advantage of the rest.

These circumstances appear to us to have vacated our Articles to all intents
and purposes; and upon the Least reflection you will doubtless view them in
the same light, and as we have the satisfaction to believe Gentlemen, that
you have conducted this whole affair, not only with Probity & honor, but with
the strictest regard to the General Good, tis with reluctance we advice you
for your Government, that we think the articles are absolutely void, and ourselves at liberty to purchase on the best terms we can.

We can with trust assure you, that we have not yet procured or given orders
for a single Barrel having without the least deviation adher'd to the contract,
neither shall we receive a single Barrel this season, if we suffer ourselves to be
any longer Trifled with by a pretended contract, not mutually. . . .

Notwithstanding if such Judicious(?) measures can be concerted, as will
put this affair upon such a basis as to admit of no violation, they shall have
our ready concurences, but we presume it cant be done, witout each Manufacturer has his proportion ascertained.

We are gent Yr M. Obd Sts

> Collins & Rivera
>
> Naph. Hart & Co.
>
> Aaron Lopez

This letter, from the papers of Nicholas Brown, in the John Carter Brown Library of Brown University, is printed in *Jews in New England*, by S. Broches,
Monograph II.

[5] Letters from Rivera to the great Providence merchant Nicholas Brown (John
Carter Brown Library, Brown University, Providence, R. I.) indicate that as late
as 1773 he was still indefatigable in keeping the oil and candle manufacturers united
under trade agreements. Newcomers were invited to join and amongst them were
the Jews: Moses Isaacs, Manuel Myers, Solo'n Myers Cohen, Solomon Simson &
Co. (N. Y.), and a Mr. Polock of Newport.

BIBLIOGRAPHY

A. STARBUCK, History of the American Whale Fishery from Its Earliest Inception
to the Year 1876, Waltham, 1878.

J. T. JENKINS, A History of the Whale Fisheries, London, 1921.

GEO. F. DOW, Whale Ships and Whaling, Salem, 1925.

W. S. TOWER, A History of the American Whale Fishery, Phila., 1907.

Commerce of Rhode Island, *Mass. Hist. Soc.*, Boston, 1914 and 1915.

Hakluyt's Voyages, Glasgow, 1904, volume VIII, p. 10.

M. J. Kohler, "The Jews in Newport," in *A. J. H. S.*, VI, pp. 61–80.
Samuel E. Morison, Maritime History of Massachusetts 1783–1860, Boston, 1921.
George C. Mason, "The United Company of Spermaceti Candlers, 1761," in
   Magazine of New England History, vol. 2, p. 165.

NOTES TO CHAPTER 27

UNIFORMS

[1] No record is found of formal and official action by the Red Cross adopting such
a costume. The uniform was the result of gradual evolution. As early as 1913 the
National Committee appears to have busied itself with the question of a nurse's
uniform for the Red Cross nursing service, but it appears as still undecided as late
as 1916. It is said that "the grey uniform for ward duty and the white uniform for
dress wear both worn with Red Cross cape" were still in use when the organization
of base hospitals and units for the army was undertaken in connection with the
American Expeditionary forces. At the 20th annual convention of the Red Cross
at Philadelphia in the spring of 1917 the question of official Red Cross uniform was
still under discussion. Levinia L. Dock and Others, *History of American Red
Cross Nursing*, pp. 359–362, New York, 1922.

BIBLIOGRAPHY

New York Times, December 28, 1922; January 7, 1923; June 21, 1933.
M. H. Dix, An American Business Adventure, The Story of Henry A. Dix, N. Y.,
   1928.

NOTES TO CHAPTER 28

CLOTHING

[1] "Human dignity owes much to the Hebrew organizers of the garment trades,
who wiped out class distinctions in dress." (S. E. Morison, *Oxford History of the
United States*, vol. II, p. 375).

[1a] Rudolph Glanz, "Jews in Early German-American Literature," *Jewish Social
Studies*, vol. IV (April 1942), p. 99.

[2] By 1820: "The street dress of gentlemen consisted of a blue coat with gilt buttons, white or buff waistcoat with gold buttons (I retain a set), knee breeches of
buckskin, buckles and top boots. Spencers, or cloth jackets, in cold weather were
often worn over coats, as they were termed, that is great-coats with one to seven or
more capes buttoned on." Charles H. Haswell, *Reminiscences of an Octogenarian*,
N. Y., 1896, p. 75.

[3] *The Boston News-Letter*, March 1–8, 1713 #516, also #517, 519, 520, 521, 524.

[4] *Boston Gazette*, May 28, 1764 #478; March 4, 1765 #518.

[5] In New Bedford, where one-third of all whalers were fitted out, a sailor's outfit usually consisted of one or two jackets, a Guernsey frock, oil suit, an assortment of trousers (thick, duck and denim), shirt and underwear supplied by an outfitter at an average cost of $70.49 per man. The outfitter purchased the cloth and had it made up under the "putting out system." The women of the town did the sewing in their homes. The pay was 12½¢ to 15¢ for trousers made of denim, plaid and duck, and 15¢ to 20¢ for thick trousers, 12½¢ for denim frocks, and 35¢ to 58¢ for reefing jackets and monkey jackets. The outfitters were also prepared to furnish "long togs" or shore clothes (Elmo P. Hohman, *The American Whaleman*, New York, 1928). By 1841 ready-made clothing was being advertised in New Bedford:

Gentlemen's Furnishing Store
S. Dale
No. 5 South Water Street
Keeps constantly on hand a general and First Rate
Assortment of
Ready-made Clothing of
every description
Suitable for all Seasons
Garments Warranted Well Made.

[6] "There were at this time but two 'slop' tailors, as they were termed, and they in Cherry Street (New York City); that is, stores where one could purchase an outfit of garments designed for the convenience of seamen, boatmen, and longshoremen." Charles H. Haswell, *Reminiscences of an Octogenarian*, N. Y., 1896, p. 76.

[7] In 1841 not one of these 25 exclusively second-hand clothing establishments was run by a Jew. Of the clothing stores, 8 were in Jewish hands: A. Bronstein, M. Ehrenreich, J. S. Leftowich & Co., Lewis Bornstein, S. Reinstein, George Wolf, A. Raphel & Co., N. Jacobs.

[8] In 1737 James Murray in New York, describing to the Minister of the Parish of Anghelow, County Tyronne, Ireland, the opportunities for the Irish in America, wrote: "a Tailor gets 20 shillings for making a suit." *New York Gazette*, no. 627.

[9] *Eighty Years Progress of the U. S.*, New York, 1861, vol. II, p. 390.

[10] Freedley says that Boston sends goods out, "cut and trimmed," to parts of New Hampshire and Maine, as well as of Massachusetts, to be made up. In these cases agents receive the goods in large quantities, convey them to country places, where they are made, and return them to the manufacturer. He reports that this method was not favored by the Philadelphia and New York manufacturers.

[11] *Eighty Years Progress of the U. S.*, vol. II, p. 310.

[11a] The second annual report of the Boston Board of Trade (1856) says of the city's wholesale clothing business: "Few persons among us are aware of the magnitude of the clothing business of Boston, or its rapid development and increasing importance.

"In 1840 there were only two houses which made any pretensions to selling goods at wholesale and their united business did not probably exceed $200,000. per annum.

"We have now in our midst thirty wholesale ready made clothing establishments, giving employment to near 50,000 persons and having an annual production which will not fall short of $12,000,000.

"The garments are made in great measure in the families of our farmers and mechanics throughout New England, which accounts for the great number of persons employed.

"A market is found for the products readily, and they are distributed all over the United States, north, east, south and west."

[12] Strictly speaking there were sewing machines invented before Howe. By reversing the ancient methods, threading a needle through the point instead of at the blunt end, and constructing a machine to drive it through the cloth instead of pulling it through, as had been done in sewing, Howe made mechanical sewing practical.

[13] Edwin T. Freedley, ed., *Leading Pursuits and Leading Men*, Philadelphia, 1856.

[14] For example: "What the Balls are to Muncie, Ind., the Meier and Frank families are to Portland. The first Meier was named Aaron, a German-Jewish immigrant who followed homesteaders to the Northwest, set up a store for prospectors in the clearing called Portland where the Willamette River runs into the mighty Columbia. The first Frank, Sigmund, joined Meier in partnership and married his daughter. By 1883, when the Northern Pacific came through, they were prosperous. After that, as Portland's deep draft harbor thrived and the cool city grew around it, the Meiers and Franks became rich and powerful. For years their 15 story building has been the financial fulcrum of the city, its advertising the lifeblood of Portland's three newspapers. And the store has won the final tribute of a nickname — 'Murphy & Finnegan'.

"So potent in Portland were these families of cousins that in 1930 the first member of either to take a flyer in politics, President Julius L. Meier, was promptly and overwhelmingly elected Governor of Oregon." (*Time*, April 19, 1937).

"In the once-great trading post of Vincennes, Ind., there is no longer a Gimbel Brothers-owned store; but four Gimbels went there last week to honor their tribe and business, founded there just 100 years ago. At table's head sat grandson Bernard, president of Gimbel Brothers, Inc. and present family hetman.

"When 20-year old Adam, immigrant Bavarian peddler, opened his 'Palace of Trade' in Vincennes in 1842, his policies looked mighty suspicious to the 1,700 townspeople; no haggling, one price to all. But it worked. His seven sons, banding together as the Gimbel Brothers, mushroomed the business into a chain of nine great stores, whose sales in 1941 were probably about $115,000,000, profits (before taxes) $6,000,000." (*Time*, January 26, 1942).

[15] Edwin T. Freedley, ed., *Leading Pursuits and Leading Men*.

[16] Wilson's *New York Business Directory* for 1848 makes no listing under "Clothing" but gives 59 concerns as "wholesale tailors." Of these, five are Jewish; Bern-

heimer, Newhouse & Co., Seligman & Samuel, Morrison & Levy, Jacob L. Bach and George Levie.

[16a] The report of the Quartermaster General of the United States for the year 1862 shows that the difficulty in obtaining soldiers' clothing in America was so great that "a purchase was made of a considerable stock of clothing and equipage from France. It was purchased from the contractors who supply the French Army, at the price of their contracts with the French Government, and was made of the material used in the French Army."

[17] "In Rochester the clothing industry started when Meyer Greentree moved there from Canadaigua and started to make clothing on Front Street in the year 1850." Harvey F. Morris, *The Story of Men's Clothes*, Rochester, 1926. (See also *Rochester 1906*, p. 35, Rochester Chamber of Commerce).

"Rochester stands third in the United States as a manufacturer of clothing. There were, at the last record, 39 wholesale dealers therein with an annual output of goods to the amount of $18,000,000. The Jews, to whose excellent quality as citizens reference has been made already, control, if they do not monopolize, this branch of trade." Charles E. Fitch, *A History of Buffalo*, (J. N. Larned, *The City of Rochester*, N. Y., 1911).

[18] Cincinnati, which had been a large and growing center of German-Jewish immigrants during the period of 1840–1860, by 1857 claimed to have become as large a clothing center as New York. In the seventeen years from 1840, its clothing manufacturing had increased from $1,223,800 to $7,569,600, and the number of hands employed had grown from 813 to 8,750. (Annual Report of the Commissioner of Statistics, Columbus, Ohio, 1858). In a description of the city in 1851 (Charles Eliot, *Cincinnati in 1851*, Cincinnati, 1857), it was pointed out that clothing manufacturing was "a very extensive business here, which is principally engrossed by the Israelites in Cincinnati."

[19] In 1845–6, for a population of approximately 10,000, Cleveland numbered 21 "Drapers and Tailors," of which one was designated a clothing store. These stores did an annual business of $111,800, employed 246 and had an invested capital of $28,000.

[20] By 1864 four of Chicago's thirteen largest wholesale and manufacturing clothing companies were Jewish: Forman Brothers, Kohn & Brothers, Kuhn & Leopold, and Clayburgh & Einstein (A. T. Andreas, *History of Chicago*, Chicago, 1886).

[20a] The census of 1880, in a national production of $79,861,696 men's clothing and $8,207,273 of women's, indicates the following relative ranking of the ten leading clothing cities:

CITY	FACTORIES		OUTPUT	
	MEN'S	WOMEN'S	MEN'S CLOTHING	WOMEN'S GARMENTS
New York.........	736	230	$22,396,893	4,805,665
Philadelphia.......	426	49	8,726,276	792,950
Chicago..........	102	19	6,439,650	353,500
Cincinnati........	237	19	6,279,783	194,802

| CITY | FACTORIES | | OUTPUT | |
	MEN'S	WOMEN'S	MEN'S CLOTHING	WOMEN'S GARMENTS
Boston............	328	25	4,200,193	319,900
Baltimore.........	188	27	3,848,851	136,750
Milwaukee........	52	—	1,895,128	—
St. Louis..........	100	13	1,351,335	140,800
San Francisco......	11	27	1,126,164	424,250
Cleveland.........	73	4	1,086,600	138,000

[21] An example of the number of Jews in the retailing of clothing is indicated in the history of the Jewish pioneers in early Iowa as it began to be settled in the eighteen–fifties. In a list of 68 of Iowa's earliest Jewish residents, including two described as tailors, 41 kept clothing shops. Jack Wolfe, *A Century with Iowa Jewry*, Des Moines, 1941, pp. 30–35.

[22] Isaac Markens, *The Hebrews in America*, New York, 1888, pp. 151–7.

[23] Describing New York conditions just previous to 1830, *Valentine's Manual* for 1864 records: "Cherry Street from James to Market was the great center of the clothing trade, and here some of the first wholesale houses were established. Conspicuous among them were Henry Robinson (with whom was at one time associated Joseph Hoxie), George Opdyke, our late mayor, John J. Cisco, present sub-treasurer of the United States in New York, Robert T. Haws, late Comptroller of the City, were all at one time in the clothing business in Cherry Street; . . . . ."

[24] "Potent I. L. G. W. U.'s Dress Joint Board (86,000 members) has been a closed shop, industry-wide agreement since 1933 with Manhattan's 2,100-odd dress manufacturing shops, who make nearly 75% of U. S. dresses . . . . . . A shop can be started on a corset string; given a loft and a few cheap machines, anybody can try it. Although dressmaking is Manhattan's biggest manufacturing industry ($349,482,204 in 1939), its units are pygmies; only 60 firms gross as much as $1,000,000 annually." (*Time*, vol. 37, no. 8, February 24, 1941, p. 84).

[24a] Only the other day (*Time*, June 7, 1943, p. 81) another new "Garment Workers First" was announced in the ready-made ladies' garment trade. The International Ladies Garment Workers' Union signed a new contract with their employers by which the latter established an old age insurance fund. An employers' contribution of $2,000,000 a year was to provide each cloakmaker at 65 with an old age benefit of $600 a year. At the same time, the article called attention that two years previously another trade innovation had been established when Manhattan dress manufacturers agreed to penalize themselves for inefficiency as defined by the union.

[25] This had its start in the "Boston system," where first a team made a garment by subdividing the work so that each workman devoted himself to one particular item. Thus one made coat-collars, another bottonholes, a third pockets, and so on until the combined team produced the finished coat.

²⁶ An article in the magazine *Time* (April 19, 1937), on the occasion of the fiftieth anniversary of the Chicago firm of Hart, Schaffner & Marx, incisively exemplifies, in a tribute to this firm, the story of Jews in the clothing trade, an epic which could be repeated for many such another concern in other cities. The following excerpt is reprinted here with the kind permission of the publishers:

The old clothing company is credited with having been the first in the trade to go in for national advertising (1897), first to adopt an 'all-wool' policy (1900), first to abolish contract homework (1910), first to sign a collective bargaining agreement (1911), first with the camel's hair coat (1912), first to guarantee color-fastness (1915) . . . . .

The Brothers Hart, Max and Harry, were German Jews from Eppelsheim who had been taken by their parents to the U. S. with eight other children before the Civil War. Vice President Hart recounted last week how the twelve big and little Harts, upon debarking in Manhattan after a 60-day crossing in a sailing vessel which caught fire twice, marched into the first restaurant they spotted. Finding the only meat available was ham, they all marched out again.

Max and Harry Hart throve on the strenuous Chicago pace, opening a small clothing store in Chicago in 1872. When an out-of-town merchant admired their stocks, the Hart boys offered to supply him with a few suits, a move which soon led to the establishment of a wholesale house, one of their backers being a relative named Marcus Marx, who had run a general store in Hastings, Minn. Aside from drawing down profits, that was all that Marx ever had to do with Hart, Schaffner & Marx.

For anniversary purposes the company dates from 1887, when Joseph Schaffner threw in his lot with his distant cousins, the Hart boys. After 17 years as a bookkeeper and credit man in a Chicago drygoods house, Joseph Schaffner decided that the opportunities were limited and, at 40, was about to start afresh in the mortgage business in St. Paul. Joseph Schaffner always said the Hart boys were 'wizards,' but the rise of Hart, Schaffner & Marx to its present status as a national institution is generally credited to wise, scholarly Mr. Schaffner.

He it was who began to spend money for advertising, a move which had made Hart, Schaffner & Marx a household name and a music hall gag for the last third of a century. Hart, Schaffner & Marx copy forms a faithful record of what the U. S. dandy has believed were the styles of the times. Best advertising stunt in the company's history was to plaster France with $50,000 worth of banners right after the Armistice, announcing to the A. E. F.: 'Stylish clothes are ready for you in the good old U. S. A.— All-wool guaranteed — Hart, Schaffner & Marx.' . . . . . .

In its time Joseph Schaffner's recognition of the Amalgamated Clothing Workers was no less spectacular. Any dealings with unions were regarded, particularly in Chicago, as little short of treason. In 1910 the whole clothing trade was in the midst of bloody strikes, the Hart, Schaffner & Marx workers being led by Sidney Hillman. With a sharp sense of the value of goodwill and a social conscience so precocious that even before the War he was speaking of the employer as the workers' trustee, Joseph Schaffner decided to experiment in industrial democracy . . . . . . The Amalgamated Clothing Workers of America and Hart, Schaffner & Marx cooperated in a labor-management relationship that was not only steady, unbroken and progressive, but also mutually beneficial.

BIBLIOGRAPHY

JESSE E. POPE, The Clothing Industry in New York, Columbia, Mo., 1905.

J. L. BISHOP, A History of American Manufacturers, 1608–1860, Philadelphia, 1861.

"Immigrants in Industry," Senate Document 633, 61st Congress (2nd Session), Washington, 1911.

SYLVIA KOPALD & BEN SELEKMAN, "The Epic of the Needle Trades," in *Menorah Journal*, XV, 293, 414, 526; XVIII, 303.

VICTOR S. CLARK, History of Manufacturing in the United States, 2 vols., Washington, 1916 and 1928.

EDWIN T. FREEDLEY, ed., Leading Pursuits and Leading Men — a Treatise on the Principal Trades and Manufactures of the United States, Philadelphia, 1854.

A. A. IMBERMAN, State of Maryland — State Planning Commission #14, Men's Clothing Industry, Maryland, 1936.

PAUL H. MYSTROM, Economics of Fashion, New York, 1928.

The Men's Factory-made Clothing Industry, Department of Commerce, Miscellaneous Series No. 34, Washington, 1916.

CHAUNCEY M. DEPEW, One Hundred Years of American Commerce, New York, 1895.

ELMO P. HOHMAN, The American Whaleman, New York, 1928.

NOTES TO CHAPTER 29

ASHER POLLOCK, PRIVATE

[1] K. W. Porter, The Jacksons and Lees, Cambridge, 1937, vol. I, p. 218.

[2] *Tax Book, 1772*, Newport Historical Society.

[3] From the original document in the possession of the American Jewish Historical Society.

[4] According to the Regimental Book of the Rhode Island Regiment, Asher Pollock was furloughed as a result of the General Order of June 2, 1783, under which men enlisted for the duration of the war were so furloughed. The regiment was then at Saratoga. (*Regimental Book, Rhode Island Regiment*, p. 95, Rhode Island State Archives.)

BIBLIOGRAPHY

S. G. ARNOLD, History of the State of Rhode Island, 2 vols., New York, 1778.

MORRIS A. GUTSTEIN, The Jews of Newport, New York, 1936.

Memoir of Samuel Smith, New York, 1860.

SIDNEY S. RIDER, An Historical Inquiry Concerning the Attempt to Raise a Regiment of Slaves by Rhode Island During the War of the Revolution, Providence, 1880.

Rhode Island State Archives.

American Jewish Historical Society Publications.
MRS. (CATHERINE R.) WILLIAMS, Biography of Revolutionary Heroes, Providence, 1839.
THOMAS C. AMORY, The Military Services & Public Life of Major-General John Sullivan, Boston, 1868.
The Diary of Colonel Israel Angell, 1778–1781, Providence, 1899.
LOUIS L. LOVELL, Israel Angell, New York, 1921.
The Parliamentary History of England, vol. XXII, page 226 (Hansard), London, 1814.

NOTES TO CHAPTER 30

GENERAL AND GOVERNOR

[1] The communication announcing the appointment is given here on p. 361. It is dated June 15, 1865. Since, however, the appointment was to date from March 13, it is fair to assume that it had been made by President Lincoln.

BIBLIOGRAPHY

The War of the Rebellion — Official Records of the Union and Confederate Armies, Washington, D. C., 1880–1900.
The Builders of San Francisco, Past and Present.
EDMOND S. MEANY, Governors of Washington, Territorial and State, Seattle, 1915.
SIMON WOLF, The American Jew as Patriot, Soldier and Citizen, Philadelphia, 1895.
H. K. HINES, An Illustrated History of the State of Washington, Chicago, 1893.
PAST COMMANDER EDWARD S. SALOMON, "Gettysburg," San Francisco, 1913.
The Reminiscences of Carl Schurz, New York, 1907.
Biographical Sketches of the Leading Men of Chicago, Chicago, 1868.
The National Archives, Washington, D. C.

NOTES TO CHAPTER 31

THE WARRIOR

[1] Mary Antin, *The Promised Land*, Boston, 1912, p. 225.

BIBLIOGRAPHY

RABBI MARTIN ZIELONKA, "The Fighting Jew," in *A. J. H. S.*, vol. XXXI, p. 211.
"A Soldier of Fortune's Story," in *Liberty*, 1925.
Army and Navy Journal, March 28, 1925.
New York Times, March 15, 1925.
American Hebrew, March 20, 1925.
SYDNEY G. GUMPERTZ, The Jewish Legion of Honor, N. Y. 1941, pp. 211-223.

INDEX

INDEX

The abbreviations f. and ff. indicate that the reference is to the page designated and to that next following or to the two next following.

Isle à Vaches, 82
Isles du Vent, 81
Italian Jews, 92
Italy, 372
Ivanhoe, 162; quoted, 393, n. 5

JACKSON, ANDREW, 53, 107
Jackson, Brigadier-General, 358
Jackson, George, 311
Jacobite rebellion, the, 288, 292
Jacobs, B. E., 129
Jamaica, 246, 285, 297, 299, 300, 306, 307
Jefferson, Thomas, 19, 31–42, 141, 186, 203
Jenkins, Robert, 305
Jepson, Samuel, 125
Jerusalem, 70 f., 252
Jeshuat Israel Congregation, 247
Jessurum, Reuel, 282
Jessurum, Sarah, 282
Jesuits, 84, 86 ff.
Jew, The, 161, 163
Jews' Naturalization Act of 1753, 289
Jew Street, 284
John, the Apostle, 189
Johnson, George Pigot, 227, 242
Johnson, Sir Henry, 227–244
Johnson, Sir Henry Allen, 227, 242
Johnson, Lady Rebecca (Franks), 227–244
Jonathan's Coffee-house, 288
Josephson, Manuel, 29
Josephus, proposed American edition of, 176 f.
Joshua, 28
Juan II, 76
Juarez, 371
Judah, Naphtali, 191
Judaism, 34
Judas Maccabeus, oratorio by Handel, 111
Jump, Edward E., 262

KABALA, 164
Karigal, Rabbi Isaac, 183
Kayserling, Meyer, quoted, 73
Keach, Benjamin, 191
Kempenfelt, Richard, 173 f.
Kempton, Edward, 177
Killingworth, Connecticut, 182
Kingston, Jamaica, 292
Knights of Malta, 43
Knights Templars, 43
Köln, 6, n.
Krohngold, Jacob, 380, n. 4
Ku Klux Klan, 269

LADIES' HEBREW BENEVOLENT SO-CIETY, 124
Ladon, Barnado, 299
La Fargue, Jacques, pseudonym of Esther Brandeau, 217 ff.
Lafayette, Marquis de, 249
Lafergue, Sieur, 225
Lafosse, Cotrel, 294–297
Lancaster, Pennsylvania, 271
Land speculation, 108
Langdon, Edward, 312
Languillet, Captain, 85
La Rochelle, 217, 222
Las Casas, 63
Latin America, 369
Laval, François de Montmorency, 219
Lawrence, Amos, 251
Lawton, Henry Ware, 367
Lazarus, dog, 261
Lee, Robert Edward, 355, 356, 357
Lee, Samuel, 181
Leghorn, 114, 281
Leicester, Massachusetts, 173
Leo, Ansel, 127, 128
Lessing, Gotthold Ephraim, 160
L'Estrange, Sir Hamon, 158
Levi, Aron, 155–159
Levi, David, 34 f., 190 f.
Levi, Higham (Haim), 147
Levi, Simeon, 147
Levinger, Lee J., 380, n. 4